FROM IDEA TO APP

STEVEN HØJLUND, CHRISTIAN NIELSEN AND MICHAEL THING

FROM IDEA TO APP
Here's how you do it!

idetilappbogen.dk

SAMFUNDSLITTERATUR

Steven Højlund, Christian Nielsen and Michael Thing

From idea to app

Here's how you do it!

1st edition 2019

This book is a translation of the Danish book *Fra idé til app*, 2018.

© Samfundslitteratur 2019

Publishing Editor: Henrik Schjerning

Copy Editor: Anders Juhl Gajhede

Translation: Clem Luxford (CML Translation Ltd.)

Cover: Danny Lund / dannyvirke.dk

Type and figures: Danny Lund / dannyvirke.dk

The book is set with Playfair Display and A Grotesk

Print: Latgales Druka

ISBN: 978-87-593-3222-1

Samfundslitteratur

info@samfundslitteratur.dk

samfundslitteratur.dk

All rights reserved.

No part of this publication may be reproduced by institutions or companies without prior agreement with Copydan Writing, and then only within the provisions of the agreement. Brief extracts for review are excepted.

CONTENTS

PREFACE 13

INTRODUCTION 15

HOW TO GET STARTED 17

1. The first step 18

    The first step is the hardest part 18

    Get off to a good start 19

    First one, then the second, then the third … 20

    You will become wiser along the way 21

    Make a decision 22

        Motivation 23

        Trigger 24

        Ability 26

2. Is an app the right solution? 27

    The state of things 28

    You have to define the use-case 30

    App versus a mobile website 32

    You're not Batman … 33

    The smartphone as the focal point 34

3. App stores – your marketplace 37

    App market anno 2018 38

    The value of an Apple user versus an Android user 40

    The spoilt users 43

4. How do you make money from your app? 45

    Revenue models 46

        1. Premium 47

        2. Adverts. 49

        3. Freemium 51

        4. Ecommerce 55

        5. Ecommerce platform 56

        6. Subscription 59

        7. In-app purchases. 60

        8. None to start with 62

5. What does it cost to make an app? 66

    What does an app cost then? 68

        The small package: DKK 200,000 + VAT 68

        Medium package: DKK 600,000 + VAT 69

        The big package: DKK 1,000,000 + VAT 69

        XXX-large: DKK 5,000,000 + VAT 70

        Reservations 70

        Wow! 71

        Beware!. 71

    What does it cost to maintain an app? 72

        How much are we talking about? 74

    What does an app cost with your own team? 74

        Full-time and full salary 75

        Ownership share 76

        A middle ground 77

    Outsourcing. 77

        Involve a friend 79

        Where? 79

        Who? 79

WORKING WITH THE IDEA 81

6. What is the need and the problem? 82

    What is the problem? 82

    App idea 84

    What's the difference between an idea and a business opportunity for an app? 85

    Follow the trends 86

    The correlation between a problem and a need 87

    The five whys method 89

7. Who is your primary user? 92

    The crucial early users 92

    "First movers" 93

    The early adopters 96

    Persona 98

8. What is your app's business model? 100

    The value of BMC 100

    How to use BMC 104

        1. Customer and user segments 104

        2. Value propositions 105

        3. The way to the customers 106

        4. Customer relationships 107

        5. Revenue streams 107

        6. Key resources 107

        7. Key activities 107

        8. Key partners 108

        9. Cost structure 108

9. Validation of your idea 112

    How do I get knowledge of an area? 113

    Examine problems and the need 114

    Observation 114

    The 50 unstructured interviews 115

        Themes in the interview 117

        Interview guide. 120

    Focus group interviews 121

    Expert interviews. 122

FROM IDEA TO CONCEPT. 123

10. Mapping and selecting features 124

    Mapping and analogues 125

    Antiloggers 128

    Prioritise your features 128

    Think viral from the start 131

11. Find your MVP features 133

    MVP – Minimum Viable Product 133

    Categorisation of features 137

        Value to the user 137

        Your users' motivation and ability to use the feature 138

        Development time for the feature 140

        Significance for the business 140

        The feature's relation to other features. 140

    Planning app versions 141

12. Create a complete user experience 144

    The user journey 144

        User journeys based on interviews 145

        User journeys based on workshops with various stakeholders 146

    The Hooked Model 149

        Use of the Hooked Model. 152

        Variable reward 154

13. Is it still a good idea? 158

    Explore "knowledge gaps" 160

    Test your hypotheses 162

        Make a mockup 163

        Use DKK 1,000 on AdWords or Facebook ads 163

        Make a Facebook page or landing page 163

        Make a website 164

        Use a competitor's service 164

        Create a Facebook group 165

        Check out Google search words 165

        Create a blog 165

        Teach and hold presentations 166

        Meet the users where they are 166

        Why is it so important to establish early relationships with users? 168

THE DESIGN PHASE 171

14. Design your app 172

    Design in layers 172

        The app's architecture and navigation 174

        User interface design 178

15. Test your prototype 187

    Quantitative tests with professional testers 188

    Qualitative tests 189

    Expert tests 190

FROM TESTING TO APP 193

16. Choice of technology 194

    Native apps 195

    Web apps 197

Hybrid apps 198

What type of app should you choose? 200

What is best practice? 202

The critical thing that nobody is talking about — the backend 203

    Where does the data come from? 206

17. The development process 208

When development starts 210

Development phase 212

Development never stops 214

18. Skills you will need 216

The product manager with many hats 217

    What does the product manager do? 217

    If you aren't the product manager 218

    A judge of character — focus on the product 219

    The business person — focus on business 220

The software developer 221

    Your app has a house, and it must have a proper foundation 221

    What should you look for? 223

The designer 225

The app design, branding and everything in between 226

What is a good designer? 226

    Experience with the app format 226

    Knowledge of the target group's psychology and sociology 229

    Brand design 230

Who is going to be your designer? 231

19. Develop an app with a mobile agency 232

Collaboration 232

    Start small 236

    Fixed price versus hourly rates 237

    Might they develop in return for a share of ownership? 240

20. Investment – how do I finance my app? 242

    How much is your app worth? 243

    Bootstrapping 248

    Friends and family 248

    Crowdfunding 249

    Loan 250

    Business angels 250

    Venture capital 251

    Public-private equity 253

    Pitching your concept 254

        1. Tell a story 254

        2. What value do you provide for your customers? 255

        3. Your successes 255

        4. Customise the length of the presentation 255

        5. Focus on customer needs, rather than what the app can do 255

        6. Remember competitors 256

        7. Be realistic regarding market potential 257

    The structure of the presentation 257

LAUNCH 259

21. How do you get users? 260

    The acquisition path 260

    Attribution and conversion 261

    Downloads and users 263

    Acquisition – how? 264

  Marketing channels: "Owned, earned and paid" 265

  Your marketing mix 266

 Activation 268

  Signup 270

  Information for the user 270

22. Retention and referrals 273

 Retention – what do I do? 276

  Don't promise more than you can deliver 277

  Control of the activation 277

  Push notifications 277

  The counter on the app icon 278

  Text and e-mail 279

  Re-targeting with advertising 279

  In-app notifications 279

  Other factors 280

 Referrals 280

EPILOGUE 287

RECOMMENDED LITERATURE 289

 About the entrepreneurial process and planning 289

 About funding 289

 About habits and motivation 289

 About launching on the market 290

 About methods 290

INDEX 291

REFERENCES 294

PREFACE

In 2008, Apple and Google introduced their respective app stores and gave developers the opportunity to develop and release applications (apps) for smartphones worldwide. Since then, more than 5 million apps have been released, and apps have never been more popular. However, despite the popularity of apps continuing to increase around the world, there is still plenty of mystery surrounding the whole process from the idea to the finished app. This is a shame because each of us has learned that many aspiring entrepreneurs dive into app projects every year without possessing the necessary fundamental knowledge.

In the spring of 2017, we put our heads together to discuss whether there was a basis for writing a practical book on the subject. We researched the market and found no books that specifically and practically guided the reader from their idea to a finished app project. We have a lot of experience in this field ourselves, and we believed that we had an excellent basis to write the book with Steven's background as an app entrepreneur, Christian's experience as an adviser in leading mobile agencies and Michael's knowledge as a teacher in entrepreneurship.

It was just over a year from when we had our first thoughts about writing the book until the original Danish version was published, and we are immensely proud of the finished result which can hopefully take some of the mystery out of the "from idea to app" process and answer the questions you may have before starting your app.

This book can be read in its entirety or be used as a handbook to dip in and out of if you need help with a specific area in the app process. The premise of the book is practical, so you as a reader are motivated and able to take the first step.

Therefore, the book can be used as a sort of roadmap that you can follow on your journey from idea to finished app.

In addition to a huge thank you to our family, friends and colleges, who have both supported and shown great understanding for the project, we are also incredibly grateful to Jonas Gottfredsen, Nicoline Hvidt, Thomas Rathje, Mikkel Sonnenschein, Frederik Lysgaard, Sara Green Brodersen, Emil Kjer and Morten Resen for reviewing and providing critical feedback on our manuscripts for the book. Thank you so much for your help!

We must also say a big thank you to Samfundslitteratur for sharing our motivation and for the valuable help from Henrik Schjerning, Inger Lomholdt Vange, Anders Juhl Gajhede, Danny Lund and Clem Luxford.

If you have any feedback on the book, enquiries about lectures, advice or similar, you are more than welcome to write to us.

You can find everything you need at www.idetilappbogen.dk, where you can contact us directly.

We hope you enjoy the book and good luck with your idea!

INTRODUCTION

"You can just make an app!" is perhaps the first thing you hear when you tell others about your app idea. Surely it can't be that hard to get an app on the market. Or is it? What's actually involved? How do you do it? Where do you start? What's important? What can go wrong? And how much does it cost? The questions are piling up, but the app idea lives on. So, what do you do?

This book aims to give you the answers to the questions above and hopefully give you the courage to get started on your app. We would also like to offer a helping hand to those who are stuck, and perhaps help someone to avoid the mistakes that we have made or seen others make. We want to equip you as best we can before you head out on the often very long journey towards a successful app.

At the same time, we hope that the book can be used as a practical and useful aid in teaching digital concept development and innovation. We've written the book in a language that everyone can understand, but at the same time, we've gone to great lengths with the examples and practical application of models that are used in the innovative work at most app companies.

Even though there are millions of apps on the market, there are still only relatively few people who have experience in making apps and succeeding with an app idea. To bring a highly specialised product to the market requires a high degree of multidisciplinary collaboration between, amongst others, programmers, designers, and business developers. The multidisciplinary collaboration, users and product development are the focus areas of this book. Not the actual coding of the app.

A great many apps end up having a quiet, idle life in app stores that means a vast amount of time and money has been wasted. Part of the explanation is that competition in the app market has become increasingly fiercer, and the demands of users have become greater, but also that the needs of target users have not been studied thoroughly enough. We argue that many more apps can be successful with more focus on users and appropriate adjustments made along the way in the development process.

We've divided the book into six main sections, and in the first section, "How to get started", we touch upon the preliminary considerations you always need to take before diving into an app. The section also gives an overview of how to make money with an app and what an app can cost. The second section, "Working with the idea", contains suggestions on how to get an overview of your business model, as well as to validate and test your app idea. The third section "From idea to concept", gives some suggestions of how to select and prioritise the features you must have in your app.

In the fourth section, "Design phase", we give suggestions on how to approach the app's design and how to test the design with users. In the fifth section, "From testing to app", we talk about our thinking behind the choice of technology, as well as suggesting which essential skills to have in a team. In the sixth and last section, "Launch", we give our experience of, amongst other things, marketing, acquisition and retention of users.

Many of the examples in the book are taken from a Danish context but they are likely to apply also in a different context. The book came out first in Danish and was later translated into English.

HOW TO GET STARTED

1. THE FIRST STEP

All great journeys start with a first step. It's a trivial and yet such a vital point that we have chosen to write a whole chapter on the first step on your journey from idea to app. The fact is that far too many great ideas get forgotten and tucked away in a drawer because the person behind the idea never took the first step. A crucial characteristic of entrepreneurs is that they – unlike others – did more than just talk, they seized the opportunity and took the plunge – he who dares wins!

Life is made up of numerous choices that shape our lives. The only person who is responsible for the fact that your dreams don't end up in a drawer, but are realised, is you. Nobody else. The most important thing for you is to find out which dreams and goals you need to prioritise if you want to realise them. If you dream of making an app, it might be necessary to drop other projects to achieve it. This chapter is about prioritising, taking the first step, making a choice and getting started.

THE FIRST STEP IS THE HARDEST PART

The first step is often the hardest part because you are venturing out into the unknown, and because your choice will usually result in rejection and perhaps economic or career uncertainty. Therefore, you owe it to yourself, and probably your loved ones, to get clarification as soon as possible as it will likely require much of your strength to go from idea to app. And keep in mind that it can be annoying for others to hear about your app idea for years, without anything happening, so you must choose: either make the app or stop talking about it.

Actions speak louder than words

We hope that by reading this book, you can get greater clarity as to whether you should take your app idea from the idea stage by taking the first step, or whether you need to shelve it and find a new idea.

GET OFF TO A GOOD START

What is the first step? When can you say that now you have taken the first step from the stage where you just dreamed about your app, to the train leaving the station and you are on board? It's not easy to answer, but try to reflect over it a little, not least because you may already be in the process of persuading others to take the first step with you. Can and will they, or are they quite content just dreaming about the success of the app without actually doing anything about it?

Make a choice and move on

The first step is not necessarily as dramatic as quitting your job, but it must, however, be a significant step that takes you further in your process. It must have an element of no turning back, and it should feel as if you are standing on a ship that has just left the quay and sailed out of the harbour, and your family and friends are standing and waving on land.

That's why the first step is so crucial. Once you have taken it, you are committed, but all the other steps will also follow naturally because you are already in motion and forced to set a direction.

An example of the first step for many entrepreneurs is when they create a company together with one or more partners. An ownership agreement must be signed, and suddenly you are committed to each other to move forward with the process. Perhaps you have invested money in the company, and you have both corporate responsibility and the risk of losing money. Legal and financial commitments are excellent litmus tests to check any partners' willingness to take the first step and share the risk. The legal or financial risk brings reality to your project, and suddenly, it's serious and not just chit-chat and idle talk.

FIRST ONE, THEN THE SECOND, THEN THE THIRD ...

When you have taken your first step, then the next step is much easier. Think about what it's like to walk. You take one step, and if you don't quickly take the next step with the other leg, you fall. In other words, it's both necessary and natural to take the next step.

You are now in motion, and you have made a decision that commits you and which encourages others to act. Maybe you have found a partner, and you have entered into a binding agreement. You have set meetings each week where you brainstorm, and you are well on the way to taking the next step together. It may also be that you have set up a private limited company and invested, say, DKK 50,000, which is quite a significant amount for most people. It can also be incredibly motivating to get started.

Commit yourself to others and yourself

We would recommend that you find one or two partners where your skills complement each other, and where at least one of you is a programmer. It's crucial that you formalise your collaboration in a company and an ownership agreement, and that you are as equal as possible regarding performance, ownership, etc. A lawyer can help, but there are also ownership agreements available on the Internet. You must not just shake hands and make a gentleman's agreement on it, because many unforeseen things may happen over time, and then it's invaluable that there are clear lines for who owns what, and how you do things in practice.

You must also specify that ownership of the company is subject to working for two years on the project, and you should consider and discuss with each other that it takes time to start something new. For example, it's our experience that it takes many months to get used to life as an entrepreneur. There are unfortunately plenty of examples of working as a team for many months until one partner suddenly decides to throw in the towel but still believes that they should own 50% of the company. It's a regrettable situation for not only is the remaining partner left with the entire workload but often such an experience can eat away at one's motivation to drive the company forward. So, a matching of expectations is vital in this first phase.

YOU WILL BECOME WISER ALONG THE WAY

You have now set off on a long and winding road. People think in straight lines, but the world is far too complicated for our plans from A to B and all the way to the final goal to unfold in a straight and predictable line. Each time you take a step, you will become wiser, and you can compare it to mountaineering. Once you have reached one summit, then you move on to the next and the next and so on. However, the view from each of the peaks is different.

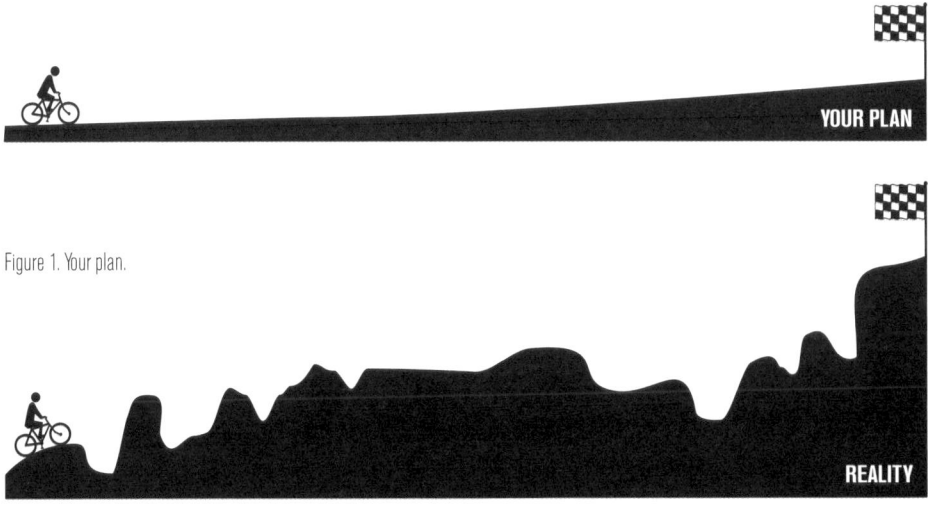

Figure 1. Your plan.

Opportunities arise when you act

When you have taken one step and have learned something new, then you suddenly see new opportunities. Maybe you have met someone who can put you in contact with investors. Perhaps you have a programmer on the team who knows a designer who can take your "wireframes" and turn them into a real design.

The point is that if you stand still, the opportunities won't arise. If you don't bring yourself to the attention of people, then there is nobody to contact. It's also for this reason that you should never just put your app idea in a draw and wait for things to happen by itself. You must get out and talk about it with others. Don't worry – no one will steal it.

Solve one problem at a time

The road from idea to app can be seen as one long learning journey, and you will travel furthest by focusing on solving one problem at a time. Once you have taken the first step, then the "challenges" will very quickly present themselves, and sometimes many more than you want to think about. And here it's crucial that you and your team focus on tackling one challenge at a time so you can move forward from there.

MAKE A DECISION

According to B. J. Fogg from Stanford Persuasive Tech Lab, we humans don't act on the basis of motivation alone. We must also have an *incentive* to act and the ability to do so.[1] Before you begin, it might help to reflect on whether you have the 3 elements and whether your business partners have them. You can use Fogg's model to consider what it takes for you to take the first step and begin working on your app idea. Is it motivation, incentive or ability that is lacking?

Motivation

It's healthy to consider what motivates you to realise your idea. Do you have the same motivation? Do you want to save the world, become filthy rich or just make an app that people love? Are you seeking social status or fancy job titles? It doesn't really matter, as long as you know what motivates you and whether you are motivated enough to take the first step.

Motivation fundamentally stems from either the expectation of a reward or the hope of avoiding a penalty – a dynamic we know as "the carrot or the stick". It works for specific tasks, such as going to work, where the penalty is clear if you don't, and you may lose your job. However, it's not quite as simple in relation to you and your app idea, because there is no penalty if you *don't* start the project.

On the contrary, it saves a lot of blood, sweat and tears. The prospect of reward is usually far in the future and is so uncertain that it probably shouldn't be your biggest motivation to start the project. In other words: Why spend time on an uncertain app idea, when you can work and earn money like everyone else? In most cases, it will be a better investment if you compare it with the slim chances of having commercial success with your app.

What motivates you?

Your motivation to take the first step most likely stems from a mixture of the hope of great success (despite the slim chance), curiosity, the ambition to create something big, a vision to do something better and a desire to learn or gain social status. We live in an affluent society, and as long as our survival is not directly or indirectly dependent on our app idea becoming a reality, then there are other things to motivate us.

In his book *Drive: The surprising truth about what motivates us*, Daniel H.

Pink describes how we are motivated by autonomy, mastery and purpose rather than by the classic carrot and stick. Money only motivates people to work harder if there is uncertainty about whether you can satisfy your basic needs, or if the work you perform is very monotonous. The freedom to do anything that creates meaning for others, and to learn something at the same time will often be far better motivating factors for you and your business partners.

Entrepreneurship has become a trend, but we believe that your chances of success are highest if you choose to become an entrepreneur because you are passionate about your app and your customers. So, even though in principle it doesn't matter what motivates you, we would advise you to know your motivation and ask yourself whether you are motivated enough to spend several years on your project.

Trigger

According to B.J. Fogg, you must also be motivated or have a trigger to take the first step. Try to consider situations in which you think about your app idea. Is it at family reunions, where you always talk with cousin Colin, who has already found success with his app company? Or maybe every day you encounter a problem that your app idea could solve?

Find a partner

You need a trigger that forces you to take the first step, and it can be extremely difficult to say what the trigger is, but it's something that can get you moving. Often other people are the best trigger because you can be committed to other people and lose face if you aren't consistent in your actions. Therefore, you can look for opportunities at entrepreneurial trade fairs and for presentations, where you can be motivated, but where you also can meet a potential partner who can hold you to your promises. It's tough to take the first step alone, when it may involve unforeseeable changes in one's life. So, excuses tend to sneak in, and with the excuses comes the postponement of the project.

> **The step towards the WHAT app**
>
> In 2003, Steven Højlund got the idea for the WHAT app midway in his PhD project at Stanford University. In 2014, he hummed and harred about the idea, and then he met a trigger and then another, both of whom ran away when the idea was formalised legally in a company with an ownership agreement, etc. It was not until Steven met Christian Thode Larsen (CTO at WHAT) that the company became a reality and in December 2014, he completed his PhD and quit his job as a consultant.
>
> Let's take a closer look at what triggered Steven to make this decision and take the first step. It was a scorching summer day in 2014, and Steven worked for a major Danish consulting firm. He had been given a tedious task, but he couldn't help but think about the app idea. As he sat there on the 5th floor of the consulting firm in the middle of the summer holiday period, he felt an almost physical loathing and lack of motivation, while the idea of WHAT filled more and more of his thoughts. The decision was taken right there to quit his good job and dive into an uncertain future without pay.

Ability

The final point of Fogg's model is the ability to take the first step. It goes without saying that you must have some relevant skills, a good network, financial room for manoeuvre, sufficient time, and so on, and that you will have to decide for yourself whether the entrepreneurial life is, in fact, an option, if you have five children, live for your hobbies and/or work a lot.

What is the extent of your app project?

We believe that your ability depends a lot on the extent of your app project. If you want to start the new Facebook, then it's more than a full-time project. However, if your app idea is straightforward, and you can get it developed and designed by others, it's affordable to get started even though you have a busy schedule, or you can't program the app yourself. Therefore, an essential point that this book explores in many chapters is when you need the help of others and to what extent. It's mainly determined by the complexity of your app. Therefore, it's far from certain that you need to quit your job, drop your studies or get an au pair to look after your children to get off to a good start with your app idea.

2. IS AN APP THE RIGHT SOLUTION?

It might seem like a silly question as the book is all about apps, but we ask it because we have learned that many take it for granted that an app is a right choice for them. For the most part, it's due to the significant popularity that apps have experienced. And apps are as popular as never before.

There's no doubt – apps are extremely popular

The latest report from the Agency for Culture and Palaces[2] shows that 83% of all Danish families owned a smartphone in 2016, whereas 5 years earlier it was 50%. Since it's quite common that people don't distinguish between a mobile phone and smartphone when they refer to their device, then there is a significant likelihood that the spread of smartphones in Denmark is, in fact, even higher. Therefore, the Agency for Culture and Palaces concluded that 96% of Danish families owned a mobile phone in 2016.

The Agency for Culture and Palaces[3] also concluded that almost three quarters (73%) of people in Denmark between the ages of 16 and 89 accessed the Internet via their smartphone in 2016, which is more than a twofold increase since 2011.

If you look outside of Denmark's borders, where it's legal to collect more detailed usage data, Mary Meeker's annual report on Internet trends[4] points to the average American spending more than 3 hours every day on their smartphone in 2016. The US analysis firm Flurry claims that it, in fact, is about 5 hours every day.[5] American Phunware[6] says 4 hours. And according to Google, we check our mobile 150 times a day.[7] In other words, smartphones have made their entry and are here to stay.

If we look at app usage, then the figures speak for themselves in that many sources point unequivocally to consumers prefer mobile apps rather than surfing the Internet. So, comScore[8], eMarketer[9] and Flurry[10] conclude that over 80% of the time we spend on our smartphone is used on apps rather than surfing the Internet. In countries such as Germany, Spain and Italy, almost 90% of mobile time is spent on apps.

THE STATE OF THINGS

However, even though apps dominate, we, unfortunately, can't avoid the fact that the overall popularity of apps shouldn't be the only argument for why you should develop an app. Times have changed significantly since that day in July 2008, where Steve Jobs launched the App Store with only 500 apps. After only a few months, Google followed suit and introduced their Android Market, which was later renamed Google Play.

The number of apps has risen so dramatically that according to Statista[11] in January 2017, you could download 2.2 million apps in the App Store and 2.8 million apps in Google Play. Statista stated in a subsequent report[12] that the number of apps in Google Play in December 2017 had increased to 3.5 million apps.

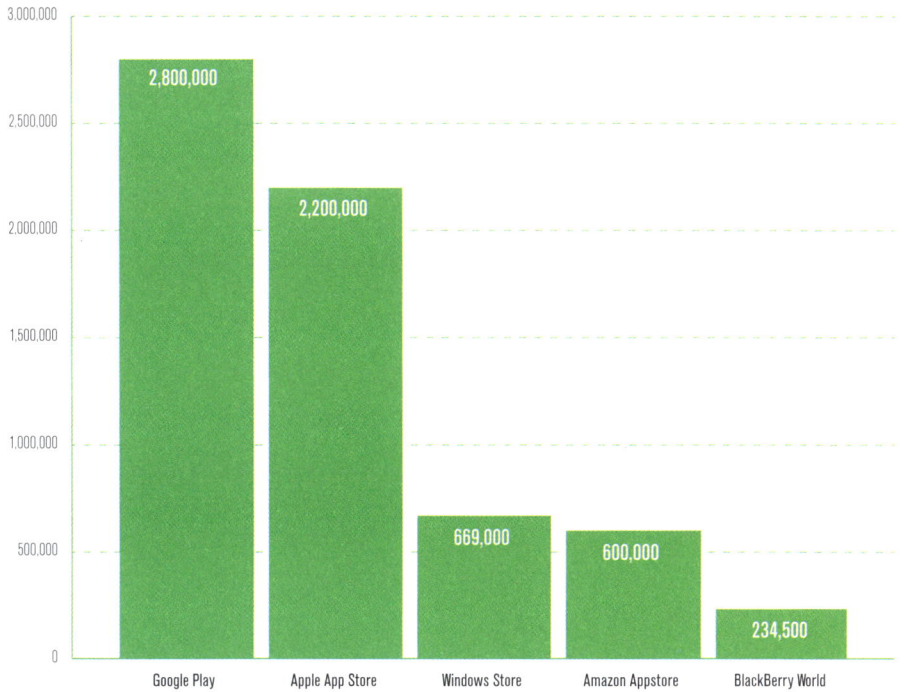

Figure 2. The number of apps in the various app stores.

However, it's worth noting that according to Google[13], 60% of the apps on offer are never downloaded, and if an app is downloaded, then 80% of users have disappeared within 90 days.[14] In short, there's an app for every need, but by no means a need for every app.

There's no doubt that part of the reason is that users can easily download free apps to test them and quickly delete them again if they fail to live up to their expectations. The experienced adviser and investor Andrew Chen concluded in a blog post[15] based on a comprehensive study of Android users that 77% of users had already disappeared within 3 days, and over 95% of users no longer used the app 90 days after the download. In other words, app publishers only have a very few days to catch the users' attention. Chen, in turn, also concluded that users who are still there after 7 days, often stick around for much longer.

You only have a few days to catch the user's attention

Therefore, the issue is quite apparent. In your "why will I develop an app?" considerations, you are forced to bear in mind that competition for user's attention is fierce, and that the market is a buyer's market rather than a *user's* market.

Where previously a success was "merely" to develop and release a relevant app, the increasing number of apps has led to success only being celebrated once you have managed to stand out from the crowd and then capture the user's attention within a few days.

YOU HAVE TO DEFINE THE USE-CASE

When we encourage you to challenge your focus on wanting to develop an app, it's because, by its very nature, there's a chance that you can get just as good a start, maybe even better, with more than an app. As we will explain later in the book, app projects are often a lot more extensive than you think. To reduce the risk of wasting unnecessary time and money, the aim is to get as far as possible for as little as possible.

It takes more than just popularity

Don't misunderstand us – we completely understand that your dream is to develop an app, but keep in mind that an app is a technological means to achieve a goal, but not the goal in itself. Therefore, you owe it to yourself to investigate what other technological resources can enable you to obtain the same goal. You wouldn't choose a means of transport without first assessing what the best solution for the journey you have to take is.

Apps are the means to a goal and not a goal itself

Rather than focusing on wanting to develop an app at all costs, then instead start by defining the use-case (a list with some actions that define the interaction between a person and a system to achieve a goal) you want to offer. This means that you need to make a list or a chart, which, from the user's point of view, you describe the actions that the user can do with the system to achieve a specific goal. Here is an example of a very simple use-case for social media:

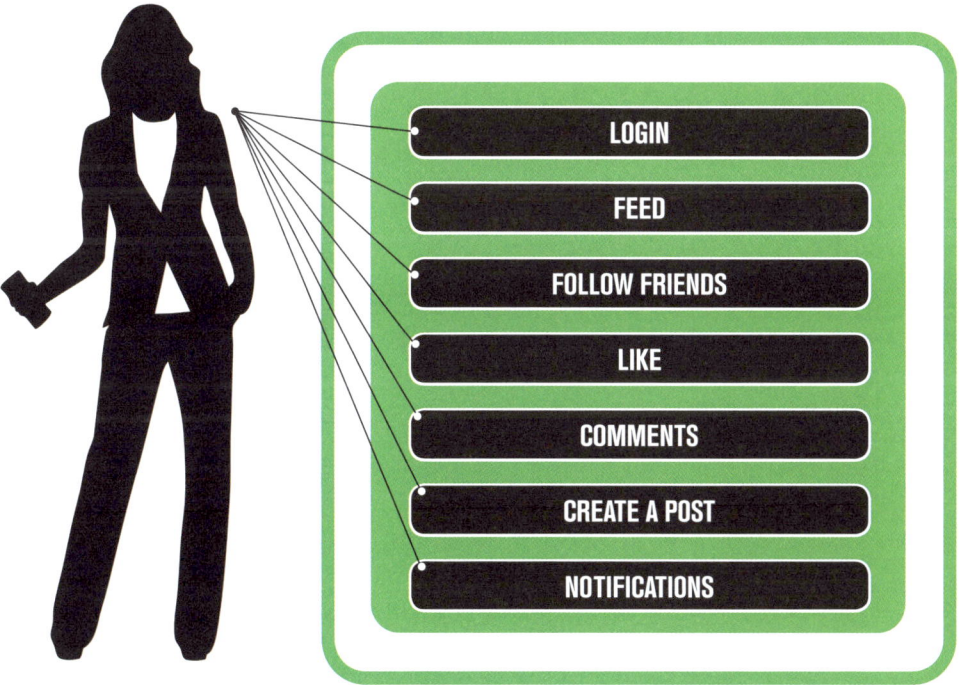

Figure 3. A simple use-case for social media.

You must expect that your use-case is going to change many times, so there is no need to go into too much detail. The most important thing is that you can easily communicate to others with your use-case what it is that your solution can do.

It's vital because it puts you – and any partners that are more technically savvy – in a better position to assess whether an app is the best technological solution, or, for instance, a mobile website will suffice.

APP VERSUS A MOBILE WEBSITE

Make no mistake, apps have many advantages over mobile-optimised websites, even though they are not downloaded like apps. If an app is designed and developed well, then it's usually faster and more stable than mobile websites that depend on a constant Internet connection. Unfortunately, in many cases, apps are significantly more expensive to design and develop, and as we looked at earlier, it's a significant challenge to get users to discover, download and use apps. Therefore, it can be an excellent idea to start with a mobile website and then develop an app.

According to Google[16], you must look at what it is you want to solve for users when you are assessing what technology is best suited:

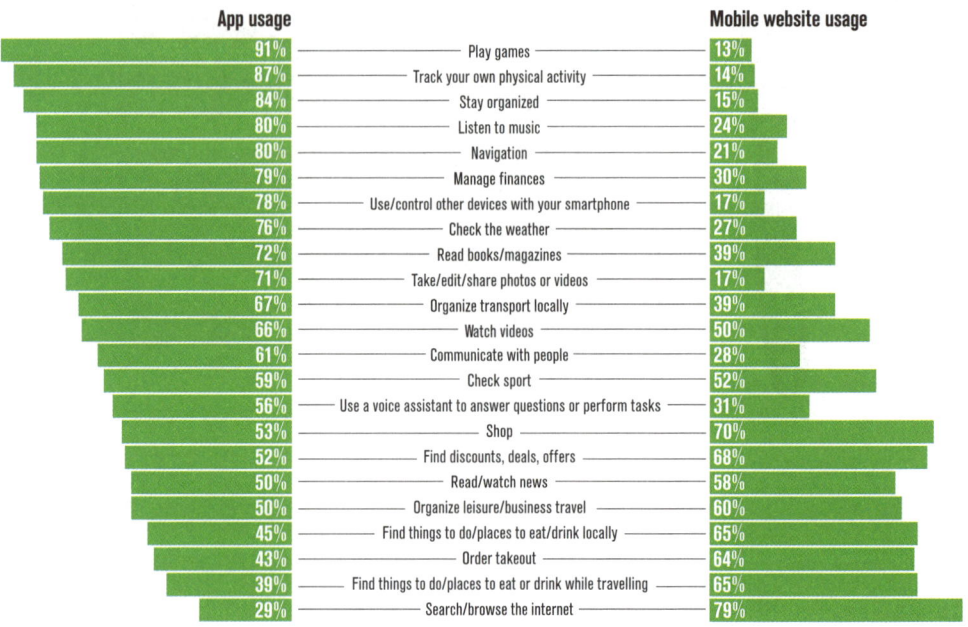

Figure 4. Comparison of the use of apps and mobile websites for users who have used them in the past 30 days.

Google[17] has also studied what features users prefer in apps:

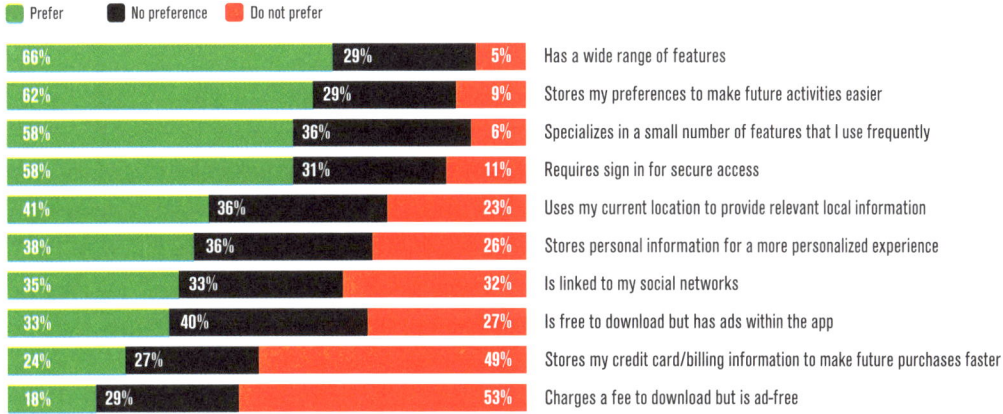

Figure 5. Favourite features of apps according to Google.

YOU'RE NOT BATMAN …

In his book on success, Eric Barker shares his inspiring vision of how entrepreneurs can benefit from considering their situation. Barker writes that Batman is the superhero who we can most relate to because he has no superpowers. Of course, it helps him having billions in the bank and having cool gadgets, but it doesn't change Batman's over-riding problem: He can't lose a single fight! If he loses, then his identity is revealed, and then he's lost because he has no superpowers that can save him. In other words, Batman can't make any mistakes in any of his fights against Gotham's villains.

But you're not Batman! So, quite specifically, that means you can easily cope with making mistakes. The only problem is that the vast majority of us act as though we are Batman. We are terrified of doing something wrong, even though it's from a rational point of view, it's the best way to learn something new. If you can reconcile yourself to that and dare to try new initiatives, then you will quickly learn that you *can't* lose when it comes to the crunch. Either you fail, but learn something important, or you succeed with the initiative.

According to Chris Barker[18], the former venture capitalist Peter Sims says in his book *Little Bets* from 2013: "The most successful entrepreneurs don't begin with brilliant ideas – they discover them ... They are doing something to find out what is the right thing to do" (p. 107). He recommends that you should focus less on your idea and more on the concrete action if you want to discover and succeed with unique opportunities.

Proceed slowly to reduce the pain of possible failure

It's also a good idea to proceed as slowly as possible, because the more time and the more money you have invested, the harder it becomes to shrug your shoulders and flatly admit that you were wrong and failed.

THE SMARTPHONE AS THE FOCAL POINT

Let us return to your use-case. In the vast majority of cases, you will learn that it's the smartphone and not the app that is the central focal point in your use-case.

Mobile first is the way forward

Times have changed since the Internet's inception, where users accessed the Internet via their computers to today, where the total Internet traffic from smartphones far exceeds traffic from computers. This has forced designers and developers to think "mobile first" when they need to create the best user experiences. However, it's significantly harder to give a great user experience on the tiny screen of your smartphone because there is less space to play around with than on a computer. And since it's much easier to adjust a design from a small screen, so it also can be used on a large screen, while the reverse is almost impossible, so mobile first is the right way forward in most cases.

Where for a while mobile first was synonymous with apps, web technology has developed in line with the popularity of smartphones. This means, depending on the need for functionality and use scenario, that you can often get off to a great start by merely developing a website optimised for smartphones as development costs are significantly lower. Our point is not that mobile-optimised websites can replace the user experience of an app completely. Our point is instead that you should look at it as a staged journey where you, if the functionality and use scenario allow it, can usefully start with a mobile-optimised website and later build an app. In Chapter 16, we will go into more detail about the choice of technology, including so-called "hybrid apps".

Apps are developed to be used by users

It's also worth noting that many successful IT companies started as websites, even though today they also have an app. For example, Mark Zuckerberg admitted[19] that Facebook only very late in the day adapted to the screen sizes on smartphones, because he underestimated the amount of Facebook's traffic that would come from smartphones. However, in 2011 when he finally realised it, Facebook pulled out all the stops and spent two years of development to turn the entire company around to think "mobile first" and build both an excellent mobile website and a fantastic app. Facebook has since developed all their designs and features for mobile first and only then did they design for the big screen sizes. Instagram is another service that is also mobile first, which is quite apparent from their website that only has minimal functionality.

Usage patterns on websites are different and they depend on the purpose of the website. Facebook and Instagram are social networks that people use often and briefly. The same applies to JustEat, for example. Other platforms such as GoMore and Airbnb are used for transactions and booking, which are situations characterised by users spending more time creating ads and juggling a lot of complex information. Therefore, these websites are typically not mobile first, as they develop their service for computers before smartphones.

Usage patterns depend on the purpose

As apps on smartphones take up so much of our daily lives, it may be tempting to choose an app as the solution to the problem that you have identified. However, it's crucial that the *problem* determines whether you choose to start by building an app or a mobile website and that you are 100% focused on proving that your idea can succeed in the market as quickly and cheaply as possible.

3. APP STORES – YOUR MARKETPLACE

If you want to develop an app, then you can't avoid having to release it on Apple's App Store and/or Google's Google Play, but there are some pros and cons that an app publisher needs to be aware of.

ADVANTAGES:
- With just a few clicks they give you the opportunity to release your app for free on a global level, which compared to other kinds of software and physical products is a fantastic opportunity.

- Apple and Google deal with the direct contact with users through their app stores. Users can't contact you directly, which is a big advantage, especially when angry users aren't happy about something. However, it's also a great advantage that they handle users' payments, saving you the hassle of dealing with credit and debit cards.

- App stores make it easier for users to search for and find apps. They also handle updates so that your users are automatically notified.

DISADVANTAGES:
- Apple review all new apps and updates before they can be released in the App Store. It usually takes a few days, but Apple is very strict about apps complying with their guidelines, which you can find by searching for "App Store Review Guidelines" on Google. Google also has an approval process, but they are nowhere near as strict.

- Apple and Google take a percentage of the revenue you create through their app stores.

- Apple owns and has a monopoly on the App Store, so has Google on Google Play, which means that you are 100% in their power, even if it's your app they release. The source code of your app will always be yours, but they may, for instance, change their terms and conditions which is beyond your control.

- The global spread has led to extremely fierce competition.

Apps are a billion-dollar business, but you're not alone in the market

APP MARKET ANNO 2018

It can be difficult to imagine just how big the entire app industry has become on the industry's 10th anniversary. Therefore, we have compiled a few statistics that illustrate the development of the total number of active smartphones, the total number of app downloads and how much Apple and Google turn over annually through their app stores.

If we start by looking at how many smartphones are in use worldwide, according to Statista[20], it's just over 3 billion (2017), which means that over 40% of the world's population has a smartphone. If you look closely at the bar chart, you will see that the annual growth rate is slowing.

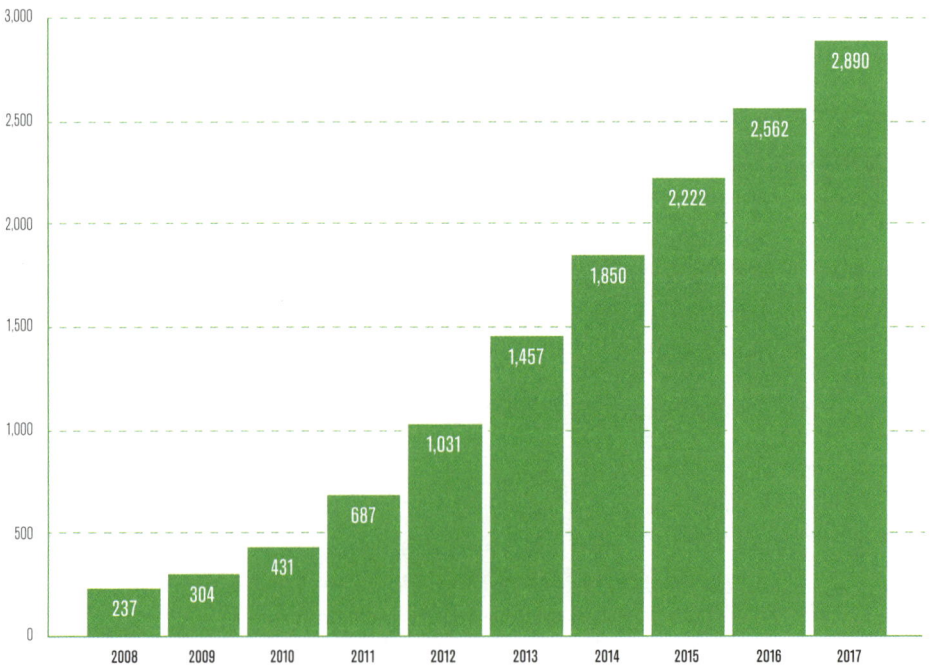

Figure 6. The number (shown in millions) of active smartphones worldwide – from 2008 to 2017.

According to the American company App Annie,[21] who is one the world's largest app market data companies, the figures for app downloads are as follows:

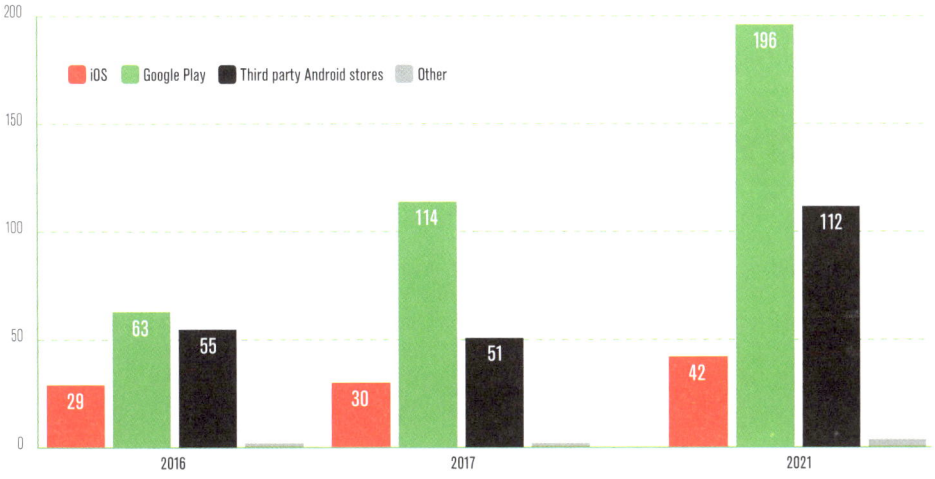

Figure 7. The number (shown in billions) of annual app downloads worldwide.

Also take note of the levels that App Annie predicts for the App Store and Google Play in 2021, where Google races ahead with nearly five times as many app downloads as Apple. If we look at how Apple's and Google's turnover is distributed across their respective app stores in the same year, it looks like this:

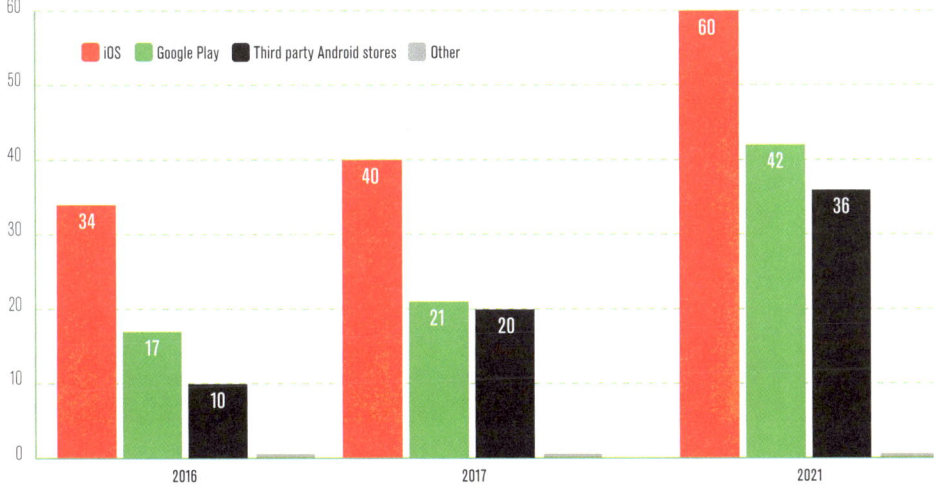

Figure 8. App stores' annual worldwide turnover (shown in billion dollars).

It's worth noting two things in particular here: Firstly, their turnover continues to increase. Secondly, Apple's turnover is significantly higher, even though we have just seen that many more apps are downloaded from Google Play. We will now delve a little deeper into the numbers and see why.

THE VALUE OF AN APPLE USER VERSUS AN ANDROID USER

If in the startup phase, you need to decide which platform your app must be developed for first, for instance, because you initially want to limit yourself to only one platform and so save on development costs, then it's crucial for you to look at which users are the most valuable. We will now look at some numbers that can shed some light on this.

There are many ways to calculate it, but a useful method is to compare the annual number of users per platform with the annual turnover on the same platform.

According to Statista[22], users are distributed per platform as follows from September 2015 to November 2017:

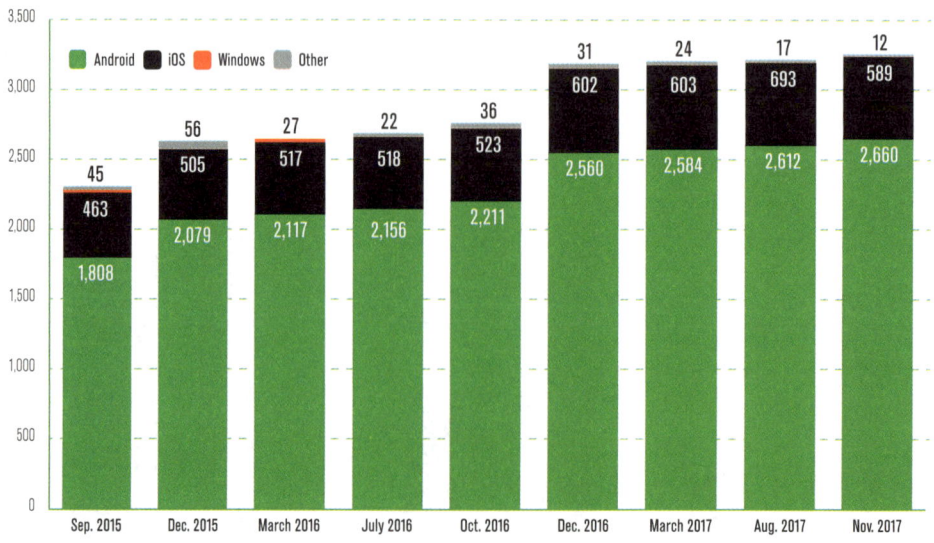

Figure 9. The number of smartphones (shown in millions) broken down by platform.

There are four times more Android smartphones than iPhones, but Apple turns over twice as much on apps

If we combine these figures with those from App Annie at the beginning of the chapter, we know that as of December 2016, Apple had 602 million users, and they generated a total of USD 34 billion from their App Store. This means that we can roughly conclude that in 2016, Apple generated USD 56.5 per user.

For comparison, in the same period, we know that Google had 2.56 billion users worldwide and that generated a total of USD 17 billion from Google Play. This means that Google generated USD 6.64 dollars per user.

Based on the above rough analysis, we can conclude that the average Apple user is 8.5 times more valuable than the average Android user.

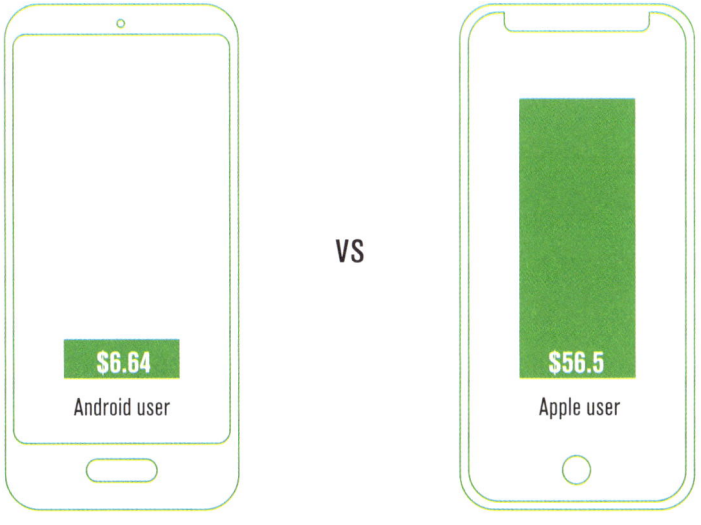

Figure 10. The value of an Android user versus an Apple user.

If instead, we look at the app downloads and again use App Annie's figures from 2016, then Apple had 29 billion app downloads worldwide, which generated USD 34 billion. This means that Apple generated more than USD 1.2 per app.

In comparison, Google had 63 billion app downloads worldwide, which generated USD 17 billion. This means that Google generated USD 0.27 per app.

Based on the above rough analysis, we can conclude that an App Store app earns on average 4.4 times as much as an average Google Play app.

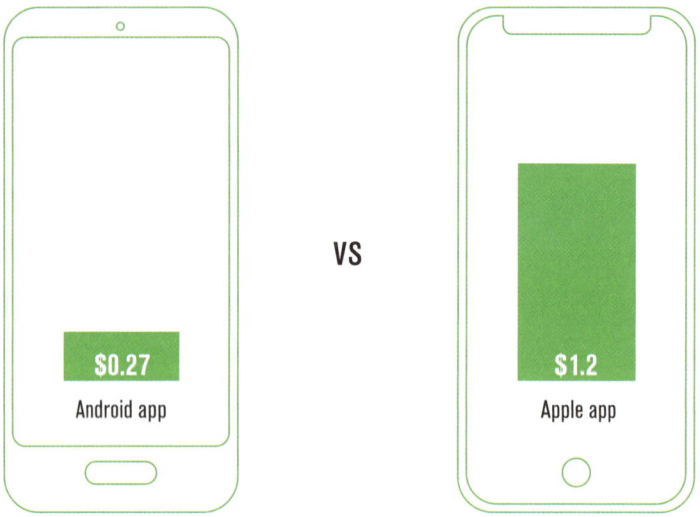

Figure 11. The value of an Android app versus an Apple app.

If you've wondered why most choose to develop for iPhone first, here is the explanation. Apple users are simply the most valuable. Some app publishers decide never to release their app for Android for the same reason. However, before you decide that you will only develop for Apple users, it's worth remembering that we have looked at figures from around the world. According to DeviceAtlas[23], Denmark has the second highest market share for Apple products (65%) and the UK has 59%. The report also gives an insight into the market share of Apple and

Google when you look at the number of smartphones. Here it's apparent that Android has its primary markets in developing and low-income countries.

You can read more about the choice of platform in Chapter 16.

Worldwide, Apple is most popular in Japan, Denmark and Australia

THE SPOILT USERS

Before we delve into the revenue models available for apps, it's worth emphasising how spoilt we've become as users as the industry has evolved.

There are primarily three factors that have led to our high expectations for apps:

1. Competition for users has become tougher as the number of app publishers and the number of apps has increased. This is because it's limited how many apps people bother to use. And as popular apps are getting better and better, so the level of what users expect from apps has also generally risen.

The limitation of the number of apps per user has, according to comScore[24], come so far that worldwide we spend 40% of our total time on apps using the same 30 apps. They also conclude that an average American spends as much as 95% of their total time on apps on the same top-10 apps.

2. Social media like Twitter, Facebook, Instagram, Snapchat and LinkedIn have had enormous success, and it's led to users being able to benefit from the social media's eagerness to reach a so-called critical mass, i.e. enough users to maintain their business. The vast majority of social media is offered for free because the value attributed by the individual user depends directly on the total number of active users. The phenomenon is called a *network effect*. To attract and retain as many users as possible, social media makes sure to give users a fantastic experience for free.

Apps are a buyer's market

3. Habits naturally influence people because we save energy when we don't need to make new choices all the time. We quickly get used to having access to powerful features on the go with apps that, for example, save us time, entertain us and keeps us in close contact with friends and family. Over time, the effect is that we, as app users, automatically raise our expectations of what apps should do as a minimum. If apps can't live up to this, it creates emotional discomfort such as irritability, frustration or anger, because our brain reacts negatively to spending extra energy to break the habit.

It may sound slightly abstract, but you surely know yourself, for instance, when you try a new app that can't do the same as Google Maps. Imagine how annoying it would be if an app with a map didn't start by showing you where you are, so you must navigate around the map yourself.

As app users, we have ended up as spoilt individuals who only want the best. But not only that, we also see no reason to pay for good apps when there are so many great free solutions. Unfortunately, this is the reality that challenges your ability to create both revenue and profit through your app.

4. HOW DO YOU MAKE MONEY FROM YOUR APP?

People often use the term *make money* indiscriminately without thinking about the difference between revenue and profit. If you intend to make a good business from your app, or at least cover the development costs, it's vital that you know the difference.

Is your app idea profitable?

The concept of *revenue* is used to describe the money that you receive when people buy your service – In this case, your app or in-app purchases and advertising. The term *profit* is used to describe the money that you actually earn when the accounts are made, and you deduct your expenses from your revenue. Expenses include things like app development and maintenance costs. If the number is positive, you've made a profit. If it's negative, you've made a loss. In other words, profit is the money that you have freely at your disposal. For the same reason, we sometimes hear about companies that have a huge turnover, i.e. revenue, but they still run at a loss.

For those who may be in doubt: It's possible to generate both revenue and profit on apps. That said, it's essential to remember our description of the app market anno 2018 in Chapter 2, as it may take a long time to make a living from releasing an app. Therefore, you should, among other things, consider whether you need one or more investors. More on this in Chapter 20.

Fortunately, both Apple and Google have a financial interest to both make it easy for app publishers to charge and users to buy. This has led to many different revenue models that we will now take a closer look at.

Before we go any further, here's a sobering thought: According to Google[25], only 50% of users have ever paid for an app:

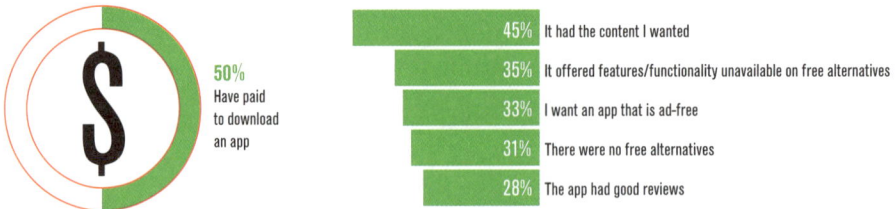

Figure 12. The most common reasons for paying for apps, according to Google.

REVENUE MODELS

You probably already know that you can generate revenue through apps in many ways. However, it can be problematic to get an overview of what the options actually are, not to mention the pros and cons of each model.

Therefore, we have made a list of the most common revenue models.

Know your revenue model

If your app is still only at the idea stage, it's difficult to know what revenue model best suits your idea. Hopefully, the list can give you some idea of what options are available for each model. Even though you must test out which model works best on the market, it's worth knowing that most revenue models must be built into the app's logic.

The eight models we will look at are:

1. Premium: pay before downloading.
2. Advertising: in-app advertising.
3. Freemium: locked features that require payment.
4. Ecommerce: the marketplace.
5. Ecommerce platform.
6. Subscription.
7. In-app purchases: virtual goods.
8. None to start with.

1. Premium

Premium means that users must pay for the app through the App Store before they can download it. The price is up to you, but it's important to be realistic because users are very price sensitive, even when it comes to minimal amounts such as DKK 9, 25 or 55. Fortunately, by simple trial and error, you can change the price on an ongoing basis.

ADVANTAGES:
- It forces your users to think beforehand about what value the app has for them.
- It's a simple revenue model, which means that your revenue will follow the number of downloads proportionally.
- The model makes it relatively straightforward to make marketing budgets because you know that you don't have to pay more for one download than you earn on one download.
- Apple and Google handle all the administration of payments and revenue, which – minus their fee – is paid directly into your bank account.
- It's reasonable to assume that your users are more loyal and will use your app more often than if it was free because they paid for it.

DISADVANTAGES:
- Premium apps must have an extra high added value to justify the price in relation to any free alternatives.
- You must pay a 30% fee to Apple and Google of the price you sell your app at.
- Users are frugal because they have become accustomed to having access to great apps that are free.
- Even though Apple and Google transfer payments directly to your bank account, you can never be sure exactly when they will do it. Therefore, it can be challenging to set reliable budgets.
- Users who pay for an app are often more demanding and less forgiving. Also, most users don't realise that you pay a high fee to Apple and Google, so they think that you receive the entire amount.
- The proportion of premium apps in app stores is declining.

TYPICAL APPS THAT USE THIS MODEL:
- Apps that cater specifically for niche markets with a need for customised and unique solutions.
- Business to business apps, because companies are less price sensitive than private individuals.
- Particularly complex and unique games.

EXAMPLES OF PREMIUM APPS:
- 1Password – Password Manager and Secure Wallet
- Things
- Monument Valley 1 + 2
- Camera+
- Airmail – Your Mail With You.

2. Adverts

A revenue model can also rely on advertising revenue, and in most cases, the app will be free but contain advertising. This means that advertisers pay you to expose their content to your users in the app. Depending on how the model is precisely implemented in an app, it's often possible to tailor the adverts that users see based on their profile in the app on the basis of, for instance, demographics, preferences, location, friends' interests, etc.

The big question is how to get ads into your app. Although it's possible to enter into agreements with advertisers directly, most people choose to partner with an advertising network because they already have good partnerships with small and large advertisers with quality content. You must first spend some time familiarising yourself with the various revenue models, such as "Cost Per Click" (CPC), "Cost Per Action" (CPA), "Cost Per Install" (CPI), "Pay Per Click" (PPC), to understand how you can best take advantage of them.

The largest advertising networks are AdMob (Google), Millennial Media, Flurry, StartApp, InMobi and Tapjoy, just to name a few.

ADVANTAGES:
- Makes it possible to get users faster because the app is free.
- Makes it possible to generate revenue, even though the app is free.
- You don't have to pay fees to Apple and Google.
- The use of advertising in apps is booming, and growth looks set to continue.
- It can potentially generate a stable source of revenue if you have many returning users.
- Many advertising networks have solutions that can easily be implemented in your app.

ADVANTAGES:
- Advertising is currently available in formats that are easier to implement without compromising too much on the user experience.
- Over time you will be able to show more and more relevant ads to users.

DISADVANTAGES:
- Most users consider adverts as a nuisance, which means that the model will have a negative impact on your retention of users.
- Ads can make it difficult to create a good user experience because the smartphone's relatively small screen already limits the screen space.
- Advertising revenues are 100% dependent on the number of returning users, i.e. no users, no revenue. It can be a major obstacle for startups that often have no users in the beginning.
- For some app publishers, it's a controversial model because they don't like to annoy their users with ads.
- It's complicated to obtain an understanding of what works and what doesn't so your business can benefit from it.
- It requires an active effort to enter into a good agreement with one of the advertising networks.

TYPICAL APPS THAT USE THIS MODEL:
- Since the generation of revenue is dependent on the number of users, the model is best suited for apps that are likely to have more and more users over time, i.e. social media, social networking and games with social elements.
- Apps where advertising can be implemented without ruining the user experience.

EXAMPLES OF ADVERTISING APPS:
- Facebook
- Instagram
- Twitter
- LinkedIn
- Flipboard
- Snapchat

3. Freemium

In 2017, freemium was among the most popular revenue models according to App Annie:[26]

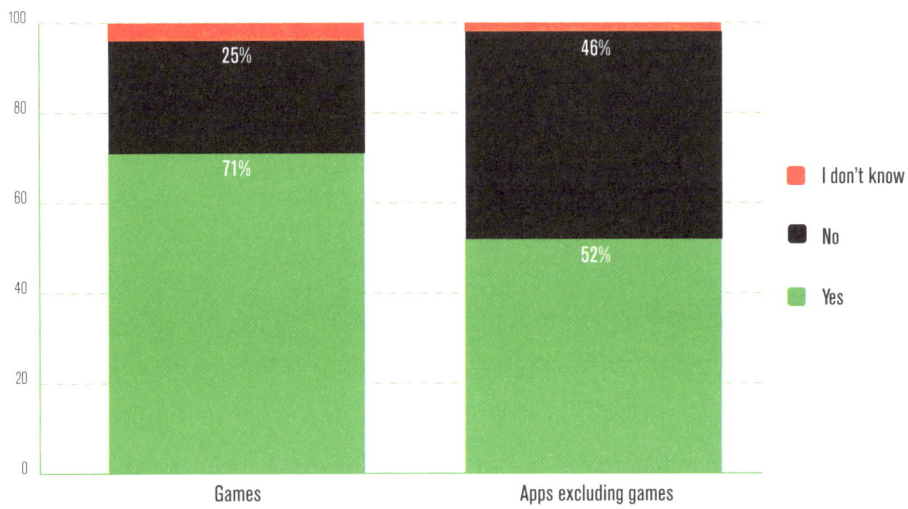

Figure 13. The proportion of apps that use the freemium model.

In 2013, Statista[27] pointed to the popularity being due to freemium is the revenue model that generates most revenue across most app categories:

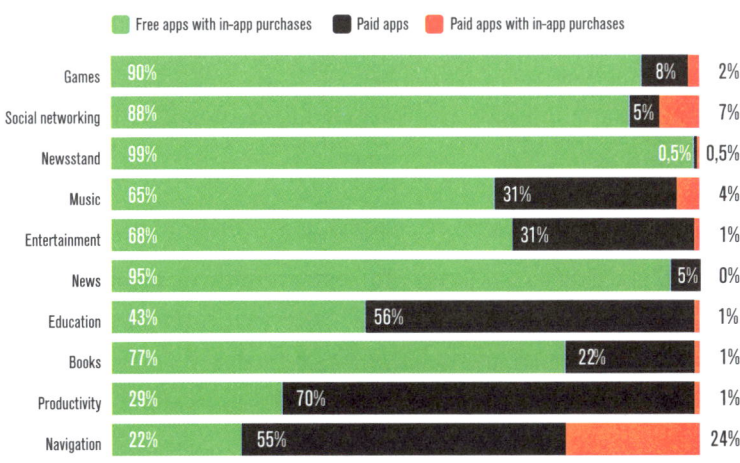

Figure 14. The proportion of freemium apps across all app categories.

Freemium apps can be downloaded for free, but they have one or more features or content that is locked. It's one of the most efficient models, as it allows users to get a good feel for the app, its content and performance before they decide whether they want to pay for it.

It also means that app publishers utilise the model to create new habits among users, so they can't do without the app after using it over a long period. You will also find examples of apps that give you full functionality for a limited time, after which you must purchase it.

More successful apps are designed so that users start experiencing the full value, but through prolonged use, it automatically develops a need for new features in the app, which users have to pay for. This may be an offline feature, more storage, synchronisation across multiple devices or better sound quality. It's a delicate balance between avoiding irritating users so much that they ditch the app and giving them sufficient value to stay long enough to get the need for new features and then pay for them.

Dropbox limited the amount of free storage space so that at some point their users are forced to either delete content or buy an upgrade with more space. They combined this with users could expand the amount of storage space for free if they recommended new users who created a profile. A so-called *reference model*.

Other apps have combined the advertising model with freemium so that users can pay to stop having ads in the app. Some have even made adverts so annoying that users had to upgrade. The popular word game Wordfeud did this, for instance, by starting a full-screen ad in the middle of a game, so users often ended up accidentally pressing the ad to then be sent to a website. A major irritant that often destroyed the otherwise good gaming experience. Had it not been for the social dimension, where players could play against each other online, then most users would probably just delete the app.

The combination of advertising and freemium has the advantage that the app publisher creates revenue in both scenarios. You either generate app advertising revenue, or users pay to get rid of the adverts.

Figure 15. Screenshot of the Wordfeud app.

ADVANTAGES:
- Makes it possible to get users faster because the app is free.
- Experience indicates that users who can try an app before they pay, have the potential to become more active and loyal users of the app.
- The model is easy to communicate and easy for users to understand.
- The upgrade can be both charged as "pay once" or "repeated subscriptions", i.e. both "non-renewing" and "auto-renewing".
- It's a flexible model that can easily be adapted to many kinds of apps.

DISADVANTAGES:
- You still need to build and maintain a basic app that doesn't generate revenue. The basic model serves as marketing for the paid part, so it's vital that the fundamental component works well and gives users a good impression.
- It's challenging to find the balance between how much the basic version should offer users for free – "too little" may mean that they aren't interested, while "too much" prevents them from upgrading.
- You must pay a 30% fee to Apple and Google of your revenue on in-app purchases.
- Paying users place even greater demands on the app.

TYPICAL APPS THAT USE THIS MODEL:
- Apps that offer enough value to be split into both a free and paid version.
- Apps that meet a need that can reasonably be expected to exist among users in the long-term.
- Many games, but also utility apps make use of this model.

EXAMPLES OF FREEMIUM APPS:
- Tinder
- Vivino
- Endomondo
- Evernote
- Dropbox
- Angry Birds

4. Ecommerce

In all its simplicity, this model is based on providing users with access to an online marketplace through an app. In most cases, the app will be free to download, because the publisher doesn't want to limit potential customers' options to shop in their business. These apps are available in many forms, but the focal point is usually to allow users to search and purchase goods and/or services.

In some cases, the marketplaces also allow users to sell and buy goods from other users, such as Den Blå Avis (DBA). Here users can both buy and sell goods without paying the fee to DBA because DBA earns money by showing adverts and offers. Users have the option to purchase various advert packages for more views and so sell faster. If the app publisher doesn't sell the goods themselves, it's called an ecommerce platform, and we will review them in the next section.

ADVANTAGES:

- You don't have to pay fees to Apple and Google because it's either a case of physical goods or because the transaction is made independently of app stores.

- The profit margin is often higher than in traditional physical shops because you can reach everyone without having to open shops everywhere.

- The business case is simple both to relate to and budget for on an ongoing basis.

- It's often less risky than starting a physical business because it requires less capital.

- App design allows you to create a superior buying experience in relation to the Internet.

- Studies show that good ecommerce apps not only convince more users to buy, but also to buy more than online shops.

DISADVANTAGES:
- Ecommerce apps require continuous testing and optimisation to function optimally.
- Ecommerce apps only generate revenue if there is a high demand for products in advance.
- The known brands dominate, typically because they find it easier to get people to discover, download and use the app in relation to unknown startups.
- It requires a warehouse, logistics and a payment agreement to sell physical goods.

TYPICAL APPS THAT USE THIS MODEL:
- Ecommerce platforms that sell physical goods and have already mastered the handling of storage, delivery and payment.
- In particular, commercial companies with an established brand, for example, H&M and Amazon.

EXAMPLES OF ECOMMERCE APPS:
- Zalando – Fashion and Shopping
- nemlig.com
- Amazon
- ASOS
- H&M
- Apple Store
- EasyJet

5. Ecommerce platform

Another kind of marketplace that has gained considerable ground over the world are the so-called ecommerce platforms such as JustEat, GoMore and Airbnb. Here a company creates a new market by building a bridge between two parties who would like to do business with each other, but basically have no place to meet or do business directly. In economics, such a market is called a two-sided market because it creates a network effect among at least two specific groups of users, such as tenants and landlords of apartments. Platforms with a two-sided market existed long before apps made their breakthrough, but the proliferation of smartphones has had a massive positive impact on their success because it gave users access to the ecommerce platform anywhere and anytime.

Apps have given ecommerce platforms new opportunities to provide users with a more personal, but also superior user experience compared with the Internet on a computer. Ecommerce platforms typically generate revenue by taking a percentage fee of the transaction between the two user groups, but it may also be in the form of a subscription (see the next section).

Although it might sound like the perfect model, three particular challenges mean it's difficult to succeed with an ecommerce platform.

Firstly, it requires a lot of resources to get a platform off the ground that can attract, serve and satisfy two different user groups simultaneously.

Secondly, the interdependence of the two user groups makes it difficult to attract one group without already having the other. Why should you, for example, put an ad on Airbnb if they have nobody to rent? And why would people go there if there are no apartments to rent? If often happens secretly that the ecommerce platform will either pay for the most important of the two user groups to create content or offer to create content themselves. If you ask the platforms, they will most likely deny it, but we know from experience that this is often how a snowball gets rolling.

Last but not least, it's vital that the user groups are growing at roughly the same rate so that the balance between supply and demand is maintained. Otherwise, you risk that one group loses interest because the platform's value disappears. It's always important to remember that the platform's value for one user group is created by the other and vice versa, and the ecommerce platform in itself has very little value to users.

ADVANTAGES:
- You don't have to pay fees to Apple and Google because the transaction doesn't take place directly in the app but through the ecommerce platform's backend.
- The value of the ecommerce platform increases with the number of users.
- The model provides excellent opportunities to enter into strategic partnerships with others who have an interest in the user groups.
- The model is highly scalable because the value created between the user groups means that the majority will serve themselves.

DISADVANTAGES:
- It's challenging to succeed with an ecommerce platform because it must both attract and serve both user groups at the same time.
- The ecommerce platform's backend is often a substantial part of the solution.
- The publisher must often get the ecommerce platform up and running, for example, to make it free at the start for both user groups, which often requires large amounts of capital.

TYPICAL APPS THAT USE THIS MODEL:
- Two-sided ecommerce platforms that bridge the gap between two or more user groups.
- In markets where demand is mainly constant, such as travel, accommodation, transport and food.

EXAMPLES OF MARKET PLATFORM APPS:
- GoMore
- Airbnb
- JustEat
- TooGoodToGo
- DBA/ebay
- Etsy
- Reshopper
- Autobutler
- Booking.com
- Hotels.com

6. Subscription

With this model, users can purchase access to content and specific services through a subscription. The subscription can either be *auto-renewing*, which means that it runs until it's cancelled, or *non-renewing*, which means that it's only valid for a limited period. The subscription model is often combined with the freemium model because it allows users to try the app for free for say 30 or 60 days before they must decide whether to pay to continue using the app or purchase access to additional features with a subscription.

To succeed with a subscription model, it's necessary to update the app with improvements, new content and features.

ADVANTAGES:
- Subscriptions are fantastic for generating repeat revenue.
- Subscribers are often more loyal and engaged users.
- The model can easily be combined with other models.
- Apple and Google handle the auto-renewing and non-renewing subscription logic.
- Users are accustomed to paying for value on an ongoing basis.
- If the subscription is based on innovative content, such as Netflix, the same content could be sold many times and so create profit.

DISADVANTAGES:
- The subscription model must be built into the app and the backend logic.
- If the subscription is sold in the app, a 30% fee must be paid to Apple and Google for the first 12 months and then a 15% fee.

DISADVANTAGES:
- It may take several attempts to learn when users have used the app enough to be willing to take out a subscription to continue.
- It requires more than just regular maintenance to keep the app updated and users happy.
- Subscriptions create high expectations for the quality of the app's content.

TYPICAL APPS THAT USE THIS MODEL:
- Service-based apps where content changes automatically over time, for instance, news, lifestyle and entertainment.
- App concepts with enough content to both give something away for free and still have something left to pay for.

EXAMPLES OF SUBSCRIPTION APPS:
- Tinder
- Spotify
- Dropbox
- Headspace
- Mofibo
- Netflix
- HBO Nordic
- Audible

7. In-app purchases

This model is based on a principle that makes it possible for users to buy virtual goods in the app. In most cases, the app is offered for free, but it offers users the option to buy virtual "consumables" directly in the app, such as game currency, lives and points. Virtual goods differ from physical goods and subscriptions in that they can be used in the app, and only in the app. They can also only be used once.

ADVANTAGES:
- Makes it possible to get users faster because the app is free.
- The ability to generate good profit margins, because it doesn't incur extra costs for the app publisher when more virtual goods are sold.
- Virtual goods can be offered precisely when users need them in the app, such as extra lives to continue their game.
- Sales of virtual goods can be combined with other revenue models.

DISADVANTAGES:
- A 30-40% fee must be paid to Apple and Google of your revenue on sales of virtual goods.
- Revenue per user is often quite small.
- The model has received some negative publicity, especially with apps for children because some users have ended up spending vast amounts of money on virtual goods.
- It may prevent some users from downloading your app because they fear they will enjoy the app and then they must pay for it.

TYPICAL APPS THAT USE THIS MODEL:
- Apps where it's natural to implement and offer virtual goods, such as games.

EXAMPLES OF APPS THAT STARTED WITH IN-APP PURCHASES:
- Pokémon Go (PokéCoins)
- Candy Crush Saga (life, moves etc.)
- Clash of Clans (gems and packs)
- Happn (coins)
- Tinder (super-likes)

8. None to start with

This model is much debated because for many it's controversial to start a business without a source of revenue. For the same reason, it can be extremely challenging to convince potential investors that they should invest because there is a high financial risk. We have chosen to include the model in the overview to explain how it's been possible for many great apps, including Facebook, Instagram, Tinder and Endomondo, to start out using this model.

Many of the apps that start with the no revenue model are known as *community apps*. The app's primary purpose is to create and grow a community among users, who have a common interest in a topic or entertainment. Looking at Facebook's beginning, it was the users' common interest that they were all American college students who, like all other students, wanted to know more about their fellow students. In Instagram's case, users were interested in sharing their photos with each other on the go.

The idea of community apps is to create a critical mass of users, which means achieving an amount that automatically spreads among the target group and so has automatic growth. The app must create a mutual dependency between users. Then it's "just" about increasing the number of new users and retaining them. This means that it's primarily about optimising how much time each person uses the solution, and how much information can be collected on each user. It may seem slightly unrealistic, but the trick is to build an app that can grow by itself because users want their friends to use it as well. If you want to achieve this *network effect*, it's crucial that users are sincerely motivated to introduce the app to others without them asking. Also, the app needs to be free to maximise the number of new users. So, it's the number of users and the time they spend using the app that counts, and not the revenue from the users.

Take for example the world-famous dating app Tinder (first launched in 2012), as one of the first to use the swipe feature on smartphones to create matches between users, which opens a direct chat between them. Tinder started as a 100% free app, and their focus was to achieve critical mass to create a powerful network effect. They were aware that the value of the individual user increased in line with more users and so more potential matches. Therefore, Tinder didn't want to limit the number of new users by charging for the app, subscriptions, or the like.

Although along the way Tinder was beginning to show ads within their app, it took three years until in 2015 they decided to introduce their revenue model called Tinder Plus. The subscription allows users to have unlimited likes of other peoples' profiles, i.e. a yes-swipe, but to also get rid of advertising, undo likes and change location. They have since also introduced "Super Likes" as an in-app purchase that allows the user in advance to make someone else aware that they have liked him or her.

However, Tinder has also been forced to continue to offer value for free to maximise the number of new users and to ensure that those who do pay have access to a large number of other active users. You can still download and use Tinder for free, but it's limited how many likes you can make every day as a free user.

ADVANTAGES:
- Makes it possible to get users faster because the app is free.
- The ability to maximise spread because users can recommend a free app to others.
- No fees to Apple and Google.
- Freedom to focus on the app and user satisfaction.

ADVANTAGES:
- Ample opportunity to experiment with what works and what doesn't work.
- Gives you time to understand exactly what value the app gives users so that the revenue model can be subsequently based on this value.

DISADVANTAGES:
- Success is 100% dependent on the ability to build a solution that manages to thrive and achieve critical mass.
- It requires deep pockets and patient investors.
- It's hard to find investors.
- Users are demanding, even when the app is free.
- The cost of serving increases as there are more and more users, although there is no revenue to cover costs.

TYPICAL APPS THAT USE THIS MODEL:
- Community apps whose success depends on their ability to achieve critical mass and powerful network effects, i.e. especially social media and networks.
- Two-sided platforms that rely on a balance between supply and demand between the two user groups.
- Startups who can afford to experiment with their revenue model.

EXAMPLES OF APPS THAT STARTED WITH THE NO REVENUE MODEL:
- Facebook
- Instagram
- Snapchat
- Tinder
- Endomondo
- Vivino

The models we have reviewed in this chapter will no doubt evolve as the app landscape changes. It should again be emphasised that the models can be combined in different ways to adapt to the users in the best possible way. In principle, the only limitation is your imagination, and here it's necessary to experiment your way to what works best. It's very common for an app to start with one revenue model, which changes to gain a better understanding of user behaviour – until this behaviour changes again.

However, the crucial factor is that you always stick to models that are easy for users to understand. It's natural for people to only buy goods and services that they understand. And for users to use your revenue model it is, of course, a prerequisite that you can make money from your app, i.e. generate revenue and so see a profit on the horizon.

5. WHAT DOES IT COST TO MAKE AN APP?

This question is among the most searched question on Google when it comes to apps, and with good reason, because we can't deny it's quite an important factor since most people can't design and program the app themselves. Development costs are the first major obstacle to overcome on the journey from idea to app.

Price depends on the functionality, which depends on the problem you want to solve

You can't look up the cost of an app anywhere – it's like asking "How long is a piece of string?" The cost of an app is dependent on many factors, including the following:

- App complexity and size, i.e. how heavy and extensive the project is measured in the number of development hours.
- What kind of app it concerns, i.e. Internet, hybrid or native (see Chapter 16).
- Which platform(s)[28] the app is to be released on, i.e. iOS and Android.
- Where the data comes from and in what format.
- Who is responsible for developing the app.
- The pay level in the country where it will be developed.

In principle, the question is the same as asking: What does it cost to build a house? Again, the answer depends on how big it's going to be, what kind of house it is, what materials are preferred, and so on.

Therefore, it's not meant in a bad way if you hear a sigh down the phone or get a brief reply to an e-mail when you ask a mobile agency. In short, a mobile agency is a consultancy firm that develops various solutions for smartphones, including apps. They hear the question several times a week, and the answer is almost always the same: It all depends on what you want. Therefore, it helps to be well prepared before you contact a mobile agency. If you use the checklist in Figure 46 in Chapter 16 and provide some prepared answers to the questions, then there is a much higher chance that they can give you a realistic cost estimate.

Talk to as many people as possible about your app idea

Unfortunately, there is still a tendency that people are afraid to openly share their app idea because they fear others will steal it and make the app themselves. Let's make it clear from the start that you can only proceed with your idea if you dare to share it with others. In principle, it's true that people can steal your idea, but as you will learn through the book, the idea is only the beginning of a very long and challenging journey that very few people bother to embark on. Also, the likelihood that they will share your motivation, see the same reasons and have the skills to do it is very small.

You may think that mobile agencies are particularly dangerous, because with both designers and developers on hand, they could easily turn your idea into reality, but their business doesn't work like that. The vast majority of agencies work as consultants, which means that you hire them to make your app and pay them for the time it takes. Their business can only operate if they always have clients on their books, so they can pay their employees' salaries, cover the rent and so on. Their business is to develop apps for other people, not to drive them to success. As the book will hopefully give you an impression of, it requires much more than just developing an app to succeed as an app entrepreneur. Mobile agencies also rely heavily on their reputation and client satisfaction, as well as recommendations. This means that they will very quickly destroy their own business if they steal clients' ideas, so they have absolutely no interest in doing so.

The best thing you can do is to be well prepared and take the time to meet with the agency to openly share your idea. Then you also get a feel for whether it's someone you want to work with, which is also a critical parameter.

WHAT DOES AN APP COST THEN?

As you might have noticed, we have elegantly avoided answering the question until now. The point is now fair enough – cost always depends on what you must have built and who will build it.

Having said that, we can give you an idea of the price level you can expect in three complexity categories for an app developed in Denmark or in countries with many socio-economical similarities to Denmark.

The small package: DKK 200,000 + VAT

This level assumes that you need a very simple app designed and programmed with a maximum of 20 screens for only one platform without an associated backend. The level doesn't account for how much time you must spend on it yourself.

There will be about 200 hours of work at an hourly rate of DKK 1,000 per hour plus VAT. The working hours will typically be distributed as follows:

> Design: 40 hours ~ 1 week
>
> App programming: 160 hours ~ 4 weeks

This is a typical level for what it will cost to develop a Minimum Viable Product (MVP), i.e. the first version of your app with basic functionality (see Chapter 11).

Medium package: DKK 600,000 + VAT

This level assumes that you will design and program a standard app with a maximum of 40 screens for only one platform with an associated simple backend. This level also fails to take into account how much time you spend on it yourself.

There will be about 600 hours of work at an hourly rate of DKK 1,000 per hour plus VAT. The working hours will typically be distributed as follows:

> Design: 50 hours ~ 1.5 weeks
> Backend programming: 250 hours ~ 6 weeks
> App programming: 300 hours ~ 8 weeks

The big package: DKK 1,000,000 + VAT

This level assumes that you will design and program a complex app with a maximum of 40 screens for two platforms with a corresponding semi-simple backend. This level also fails to take into account how much time you spend on it yourself.

There will be about 1,000 working hours at an hourly rate of DKK 1,000 per hour plus VAT. The working hours will typically be distributed as follows:

> Design: 100 hours ~ 2.5 weeks
> Backend programming: 400 hours ~ 10 weeks
> App programming: 500 hours ~ 13 weeks

XXX-large: DKK 5,000,000 + VAT

This is a trick category to remind you of our recommendation that you always start as small as possible. If you insist on building a complex app from the start that all markets could use, then you should be prepared to have access to large amounts of capital, and that you run a very high risk of losing all or a lot of the money. You will most certainly find that one or several of your assumptions about the market is wrong so you will need to modify large parts of the app to deliver what users really appreciate. And why take the risk when you can start small and still move in the same direction? Start small, it's easier, more fun and cheaper.

> *The truth is that apps are expensive to develop and maintain. End of story!*

Reservations

Do yourself a favour, take the ranges for the categories with a large pinch of salt. The development cost of your app can't be predicted. It's as simple as that. If you ask a mobile agency, then they will only confirm that the price depends on what you want to have developed.

Even though you don't develop your app with a mobile agency, then we would still advise you to contact them to get their feedback on your app idea. They have many years of experience and have seen most things, so there is a good chance that even a one-hour coffee meeting may make you much wiser. And they are usually open to this.

Keep in mind that prices don't include the maintenance of the app. However, that's a crucial element that we will go into later.

Wow!

If the numbers in the various "packages" made you fall off your chair, you're not alone. The level of what it typically costs to develop an app in Denmark or similar countries is a surprise to many because they have no idea where this level is.

However, even if this reaction is widespread, you need to realise that you can only conclude whether something is expensive or not if you compare the cost with something comparable. This means that you must get more than one quote to assess whether the price is reasonable compared to the rest of the market. And we certainly recommend that you always get a minimum of two quotes because it gives you a better basis.

Beware!

You must take heed because in Denmark you can get quotes for apps for DKK 25,000-50,000 + VAT. We would strongly advise you to remember the good old saying "If something sounds too good to be true, then it probably is!" In other words, you must assume that the price will rise in the end, for example, because something has been omitted, or because the person who made the quote is too inexperienced. You can, at worst, end up never getting your app made, so be wary.

getQueried

getQueried was an iOS app that was launched in haste to find out if there was interest in the concept of questions and answers. When getQueried was to be released as an Android app, Steven Højlund got a quote. They ranged from DKK 250,000 for a junior external consultant and up to DKK 500,000 from the best mobile agencies in Denmark. A new IT company quoted to do the job for DKK

50,000 plus VAT, and after that, the consultants' skills were tested and a contract was signed. Time passed, and despite good project management from getQueried's experienced programmer team, it soon became clear that the IT company had utterly underestimated the scale of the job. They had also only been able to offer the low price because they forwarded the job to a team in India who couldn't cope with the job technically. After six months, 90% of the job was done, but the IT company now threw in the towel and had to give the entire code base to getQueried without payment as the contract stipulated. However, that was minor, because half a year had been wasted, and getQueried still couldn't finish the app themselves, and it would cost DKK 100,000-200,000 to resume the work or start from scratch with a new team of developers.

WHAT DOES IT COST TO MAINTAIN AN APP?

When talking to agencies about what it costs to develop an app, then you should be aware that it also costs money to maintain the app over time. Our experience shows that this is, unfortunately, an element that many forget when they are considering developing an app. In most cases, it's because they don't know that apps require maintenance if they are to continue to operate as intended. Another reason is that some are scared of how much money it costs just to develop the app and can't relate to what it costs to maintain it afterwards. However, if you fail to maintain it, you will be shooting yourself in the foot. If the app is worth developing, then it's also worth maintaining.

30% of your development budget should be allocated to maintenance

Your app must be maintained, both to ensure that everything works as it should, and also to keep it up-to-date with the latest standards, so it doesn't become obsolete and lose its function and value. Think of your app like a house that must be maintained to ensure that it retains its function, but also to be updated with extensions to increase its value. However, if the app is made correctly and with excellent workmanship, why should it not work as intended? In short, apps are incorporated into a complex ecosystem composed of other services. These services evolve independently of your app, which is therefore forced to follow suit. The best example is the operating system on your smartphone, which on an iPhone is called iOS. Once a year, Apple releases a new main version of the operating system, such as switching from iOS 10 to iOS 11, and more often than not this leads to some fundamental changes. Since neither Apple nor Google release their exact plans for the next operating system in advance, developers have no chance in advance to ensure that your app will work 100% smoothly with future operating systems. When the new OS is released, the app must therefore likely be tested and adjusted to ensure that everything works as it should.

Another example of external factors that are vital for your app are third parties – an example is Facebook. You may have a login feature in your app, so users can use their Facebook login to create a new profile. However, Facebook continually changes, and often without warning, the service that makes this feature possible. In principle, this means that the feature in your app may stop working from one day to the next because Facebook makes a change in its system. And the same principle is repeated for virtually all such third-party services that your app uses. In other words, your app is dependent on other services and therefore needs to be continually adapted to the ecosystem it's part of.

How much are we talking about?

Just as the price of an app depends on what the app should do, which platforms it must be released on, etc., maintenance costs are dependent on the same parameters. Therefore, there is no clear answer to the question.

That said, there is a rough rule of thumb that says you can at least expect that the annual maintenance cost of an app to represent 20-30% of the app's total development cost. If the app costs DKK 500,000 to develop, then you should assume that it will cost between DKK 100,000-150,000 a year to maintain it and ensure it is kept updated to the latest standards.

WHAT DOES AN APP COST WITH YOUR OWN TEAM?

The alternative to getting an agency to develop your app is to put together your own team and develop the app yourself. This can make good sense because, in addition to employees' hourly rate being significantly lower than agencies, it ensures that their experience and knowledge lies in your business rather than an agency.

However, there are some critical factors you should take into account when considering assembling your own team. We have divided it into three scenarios, giving you a concrete idea of the options and the corresponding costs.

Full-time and full salary

In this scenario, we assume that the app project you are considering falls into the category of a medium package with a requirement of 600 hours. We must also add 20% for maintenance, so we land at 720 hours. The outline need is more or less one mobile developer (iOS or Android), and one backend developer, i.e., a total of three people, including yourself, as a handyman to take care of everything from strategy and project management to sales. The designer, we will assume you hire as a freelancer since there will not be a need for six months of full-time work, even though you will also make the marketing materials. Let us assume that a freelance designer is DKK 100,000.

Your team must be lean and mean, but it should still be fun

If all three work full-time on the project, you all quit your jobs and need a salary, so you can continue to live. So, we are talking about a cost for three full-time salaries + a freelance designer at DKK 100,000. If we then assume that the three of you agree to work hard over six months, and we also assume that each of you has a salary of DKK 35,000 a month, then we are talking about a total cost of DKK 730,000. To this you need to add costs for holiday pay (12.5%), office space, various equipment, administration, insurance, legal and accounting help, etc. You will, in other words, quickly go over DKK 1 million. In such a scenario, it's more money than you probably imagined.

You can reasonably argue that it's not realistic that all three work full-time on the project because it's "only" a matter of 600 hours. In a very rough comparison, three people working 37.5 hours a week for six months is approximately 2,900 hours, which quickly puts the job into perspective in relation to the roughly outlined 720 hours with an agency.

Although an hour with a mobile agency is not directly comparable to an hour with your own team, because the mobile agency is likely to be far more efficient with their time, we can still easily conclude that it's far from profitable to put together your own team for an app project of this magnitude when we only look at the time needed for the first version of the app.

Ownership share

However, what impact would it have if you offer employees shares instead of pay? If we continue with the example and assumptions from before, then let's assume that you start the company yourself, which means that you own 100% of the company. You still need three people (of which you are one), but because you have no money you offer them a 33.33% stake each instead of pay.

Give ownership – get an app

So far so good, but how will you continue to pay your own living expenses when you have no income? In most cases, you will need to remain in your current job to pay your regular expenses. The compromise is that you must prioritise your job over your startup because the job is still your livelihood. In other words, your startup is a leisure time project. It can often be an excellent way to start, but you will likely soon come to see that progress is too slow.

In some cases, people have saved up enough that they can do without a fixed salary and can dedicate themselves 100% to their startup for a certain period. It can be a great blessing to have one or more individuals with this option in a startup, as long as you make sure it doesn't create discord among the team members of how much time each one spends on the project.

A share of ownership can create an excellent financial base for your startup because you can get going without startup capital, but unfortunately very few have saved up enough to survive long without income. This means that you can quickly end up in a situation where the fate of your startup depends on how the team prioritise their leisure time. It can also be the cause of high anxiety to enter into such a partnership unless you already know your partners very well.

A middle ground

A realistic alternative to getting your app developed with a mobile agency is probably somewhere between the above two scenarios, where the team members are compensated with both pay and a share of ownership. Exactly how much the team members must be compensated depends on many factors, but it could be, for example, DKK 15,000-20,000 a month and 10-15% stake with an expectation that they work full-time in your startup. You will still need to raise startup capital, but you get the opportunity to show how dedicated you are in relation to the team and the project.

OUTSOURCING

The standard of living and level of education in Denmark is high, and so is the tax burden. This means that the pay level in Denmark is among the highest in Europe, which is reflected directly in the hourly rates of Danish mobile agencies and freelancers. Therefore, it's only natural to consider outsourcing to countries where the level of education is good, but the pay level and tax burden are lower, so it's possible to reduce development costs.

You get what you pay for

However, as you have probably already figured out, you won't gain any extra sleep with the savings, as it takes work to succeed with outsourcing. To help you along, we have listed some of the factors that you should be aware of when researching a potential outsourcing partner's company:

- The hourly rate and VAT terms.
- Any language barriers.
- Experience level.
- Portfolio, i.e. previous projects.
    - References, i.e. names of previous clients (perhaps ask them to be allowed to contact a few of their clients).
- Reputation.
- The development process.
- Exchange rate fluctuations in its currency in relation to the Danish kroner.
- Contract terms and conditions, notably:
    - Rights to the finished code.
    - Non-disclosure.
    - Payment terms.
- Travel expenses.

It's entirely possible to succeed with outsourcing the development of an app project, but it's vital to be realistic: It's going to require more work from you since you must both make a preliminary investigation and handle the ongoing project management to ensure that you receive what you expect. Unfortunately, it's often extremely difficult to match your expectations and clarify the details of the project, which often leads to wasted development hours.

Involve a friend

It may seem silly, but if you don't have a technical background, then you can do yourself an enormous favour by getting a friend with a technical background to help you before, during and after the development of your outsourced project. The fact is that you are buying software, but if you don't have the right technical skills, how do you know whether the quality of what you are buying is in order and that you get what you pay for? If you don't know anyone with the right technical background, then we strongly recommend you either completely abandon outsourcing or hire a consultant with technical insight.

Where?

If you take your starting point in consulting firm A.T. Kearney, which annually publishes a list called the Global Services Location Index (GSLI), then you can quickly get an overview of the 55 most attractive outsourcing countries in the world. A.T. Kearney compares financial attractiveness, ability and availability, as well as the business environment.

In addition to the global top-3, which is made up of India, China and Malaysia, the top-5 European countries are Poland, Bulgaria, Czech Republic, Germany and Romania.

Who?

It can be tough to know where to start when you must find outsourcing partners, but thankfully American company Clutch (www.clutch.co) offers a free and extensive database of names, descriptions and customer reviews of more than 7,000 agencies worldwide sorted by industry. Here you can get a quick summary of what outsourcing partners exist in the countries you have decided to look at.

You can easily succeed with outsourcing, but you often hear stories to the contrary. Therefore, we recommend that you choose another option unless you have a lot of project management experience and in-depth technical knowledge. Otherwise, the project may flounder and fail, or you will find that the price increases, so it ends up being just as expensive or more expensive than a Danish mobile agency or your own team.

WORKING WITH THE IDEA

6. WHAT IS THE NEED AND THE PROBLEM?

An app makes sense if it meets a need in a satisfying way for a group of people. Your target group must at least see the problem or the need as big enough, and then your app will solve the problem or meet the need satisfactory and typically better than other apps. Great app ideas may help to create new needs, and a new app can add a value that we didn't immediately know was missing. But after being introduced to it, we can't do without it – Snapchat is an example of this. Before the app was launched, you could send photos and messages in numerous ways, but Snapchat's setup and changed features have given a new dynamic and value.

WHAT IS THE PROBLEM?

It's a good exercise to find out what problem your app solves or what needs it meets for those who require it. Often, what you think is a problem, either proves not to be a problem, or the problem is not big enough that anyone bothers to download an app to fix it.

Do you create a new habit with your app?

Therefore, before embarking on your app, you must ask yourself:

1. *Has the problem been correctly identified? How big is the problem perceived to be by those who experience it?*
   In 1992 MD Foods (now Arla) launched Cowey, which was a mixture of juice and milk. Despite a massive marketing campaign, including

sponsorship of the national football team, the product failed entirely and turned into a joke, as most Danes aged over 30 still remember. The need for juice-milk simply wasn't there.

2. *How many people are experiencing the problem? Do some people experience the problem in different ways than others?*

   Segway is an excellent example of the manufacturer not having the same view of the problem as users. In this case, the manufacturer had overestimated how much people perceived the problem of walking. Segway was mega-hyped as an invention in line with the Internet.

3. *What is the quality of the problem – is it a problem with a potential or could a slightly different problem perhaps be more relevant to focus on?*

   Tinder is an example of a target group that "rotates" as users find a boy/girlfriend on Tinder and so stop using it. However, Tinder is also used differently in different countries. Tinder is, for instance, a "hook-up app" in the US, where it's primarily about finding a sex partner and not a long-term relationship. In Denmark, Tinder is used to the same extent as a dating app if you need to find a boy/girlfriend. The solution can carry both, but it creates some confusion at times.

4. *Will users be able to understand your solution?*

   Twitter is an app that many have never understood how to use – especially here in Europe. Twitter grew in the US because there was a need for one type of messaging service since the US had three standards. In Europe, we use text messaging, and so there wasn't the same problem in Europe.

5. *Will users pay for your solution?*

   90% of all apps are free, so an app must be unique if you have to pay to download it.

6. *Will your solution solve the problem better than other existing solutions?*

   There are plenty of examples of Tinder clones, but it doesn't seem that they solve users' problem as effectively as Tinder. Bumble is an example of a successful app, which has a twist on Tinder's swipe feature and had great success with it.

7. *How difficult it is for users to switch from an existing app to yours?*

It's straightforward for users to switch from Tinder to another dating app, but to switch from Facebook or Instagram is another story. It's hard to build a social media as a competitor to Facebook, because people over time post photos, create groups, add friends, etc., have made a significant "investment" in time and contacts. They would have to walk away from that if they started using another service.

8. *Should users form a new habit with your product?*

Habits are hard to form with users. Exercise, meal plans and weight loss apps face these challenges. When you are part of a family that has set habits and perhaps don't do much exercise, it can take a surprisingly long time to change this pattern.

APP IDEA

Often, it's by observing over time that we notice there is a problem and an unfulfilled need. Once we have had the idea, we can begin to validate it with structured interviews that we will talk more about in Chapter 9.

It's vital to emphasise that the initial idea you get may prove not to solve the problem because:

1. The "problem" is not identified correctly. Feedback from users later in the process perhaps points towards an entirely different problem that turns out to be more relevant to focus on.

2. Users won't use the solution:
    a. They don't understand it.
    b. It's too expensive compared to the alternatives.
    c. It's not significantly better than the existing one.
    d. It's "too difficult" to switch from the current one.
    e. Users must change habits, which is often very difficult to get them to do.

For an idea to become a reality, it must do something better, faster, smarter or cheaper than existing solutions

Therefore, you should initially realise that the identified problem and the corresponding idea and solution is a preliminary exercise that must be tested again and again. Often, a good idea is built upon something that already exists that you change some points or combine in a new way. In many cases, you don't just get a good idea because you work at it, but it subsequently suddenly comes to you, perhaps because you have previously worked with the area.

WHAT'S THE DIFFERENCE BETWEEN AN IDEA AND A BUSINESS OPPORTUNITY FOR AN APP?

An idea that doesn't fulfil a need is not a business opportunity. For an idea to become a reality, it must do something better, faster, smarter or cheaper than existing solutions. The EasyPark app is an example of this: You can extend your parking via the app and stop it, so you only pay for the time you park. MobilePay is also an example of an app where you can transfer payments faster and easier than before.

FOLLOW THE TRENDS

One way to find business opportunities is to follow current trends. There can be various factors that influence trends, such as financial factors, social factors, technological development or political and regulatory changes. Within these trends, you can identify changes, problems and needs. Some entrepreneurs are better at spotting opportunities in trends than others, depending on experience, knowledge of the area concerned and the person's tenacity. You often see that entrepreneurs who have been employed within an area can spot a trend or see a need clearer. This may be, for example, in mobile telephony or tourism. A current trend is a peer-to-peer economy. Many ideas and companies have emerged in the wake of this trend: Airbnb, GoMore, Uber and MinBilDinBil.

Here are some trends that can help to identify opportunities:

Trend	App	Feature
Peer-to-peer economy	GoMore	Private car hire and car-pooling
An increasing number of people live as singles	Single.dk	Finding a partner
The health wave	MyFitnessPal	Following your weight, your exercise and other health factors
Global trade over the Internet	Alibaba.com	Trade with Asian countries
New initiatives in the experience economy	TripAdvisor	Suggestions and reviews of attractions, entertainment and restaurants
Processes are automated	Penneo	Digital signature of legal documents
An increasing proportion of the population is older	Medisafe	You can keep track of medications

Figure 16. Examples of trends.

The world's largest search engine, Google, has a tool called "Google Trends" that can help you to spot the online trends that may arise and disappear within a very short time. With Google Trends you can see current searches and so monitor the trends that come and go on the search engine.

Generally, you should think about this: You don't need to reinvent the wheel. Find something similar that already exists and change it slightly, and occasionally, it's possible to redefine an existing solution using new technology. Addressing an established problem saves a lot of resources compared to having to find and build your market. Be inspired by competitors. Start by finding out how they have overcome those challenges and reuse what you can.

When you start to develop a solution to the problem, most people tend to forget the users

THE CORRELATION BETWEEN A PROBLEM AND A NEED

When you get an idea and begin to develop a solution to the problem, then most people tend to focus on the solution and forget the users. It's easy to measure and observe the actions of users of the app, but it's much more difficult to know with certainty why users are using your app.

People's use of products is related to a need and that is why it's essential to have a good understanding of the needs that ultimately make people begin to use your app and keep using it.

Figure 17 shows how we often focus on what we can control when we make solutions.

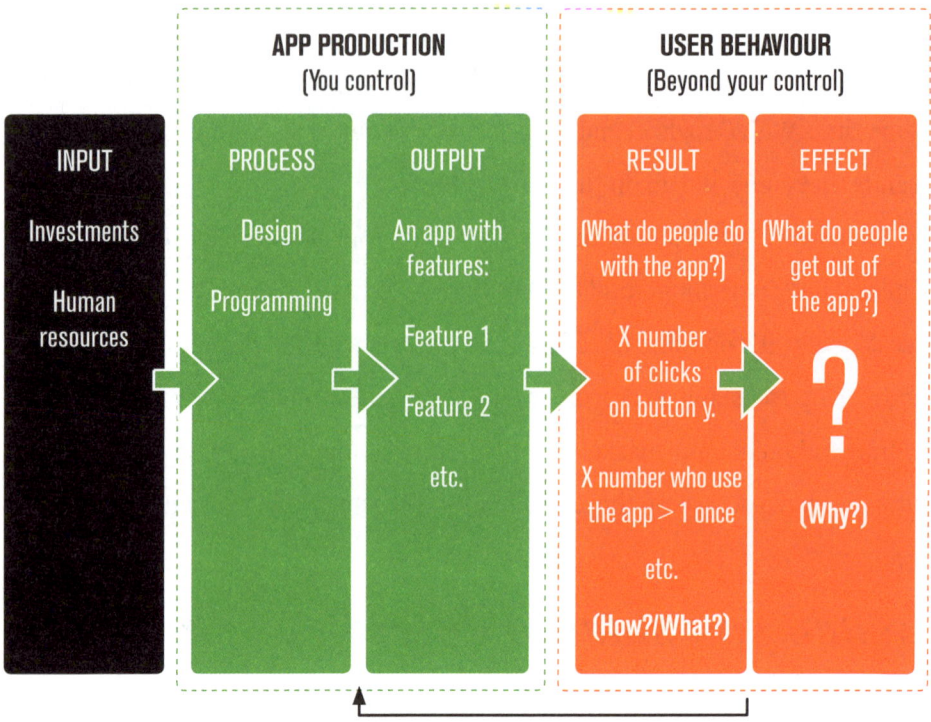

Figure 17. The difference between a problem and a need.

The model illustrates that you have some resources concerning capital and human resources (input) that you use to design and program the app. Your app with its features is your output, but your result is created based on how your users behave in the app. How do they use the app? What do they click on? You can measure this and make sure to improve the app continuously.

From your perspective, you have made an app for people to use it (the result) and fulfil their need (the effect). You have a good sense of what people's needs are and how your app will solve the problems that lead to the fulfilment of needs. However, if you don't communicate with your users, it's difficult to find out *why* users behave as they do in your app. And that's the key question to answer.

But how do you answer it when you have neither an app nor users yet, and if you haven't conducted interviews with potential users?

THE FIVE WHYS METHOD

You can use the "five whys" method, which helps app developers to understand the underlying problem that is related to a user's needs and hence motivations to use your app. The method is simple and developed by Taiichi Ohno, who designed Toyota's famous production system.

To illustrate the power of this method, we can use the Arono app as an example. Arono is a meal plan app that was developed to provide vegans, families with children and people who want to lose weight with an alternative to a dietician. The table below shows how to schematically analyse the current idea about the target group's need – i.e. "the effect" of the app.

Ideally, you ask some potential users "why?" five times. Why do you need a meal plan app? The answer is: "So I can vary my recipes and get inspiration." It's followed by another "Why?" and so on. With just a little knowledge of the area, you can ask yourself and fill out a form like the one below.

Output and result	To whom?	Why? (1)	Why? (2)	Why? (3)	Why? (4)	Why? (5)
App with a meal planner	Vegans	Varied recipes/ inspiration	More certainty of getting vitamin B12	Avoid getting sick	Not to die	Get as much out of life as possible
	Families with children	Easier everyday life	Have more time	Get a better overview	Become a better parent	Children feel better
	Weight losers	Lose weight	1) Live healthier 2) Look better	1) Live longer 2) Get a boy/ girlfriend	1) Not to die 2) Have children	1) Get as much out of life as possible 2) The meaning of life

Figure 18. An example of applying the Five Whys method.

If we follow the logic of Figure 18, then we plan to make a meal plan app (Arono), where users can see meal plans and recipes. Weight losers, families with children and vegans should be able to click and use the recipes in the app (result) and pay a subscription to do so.

But why would the three target groups do this? Which group is most likely to pay for a subscription? How much will they pay? There are already some questions at this stage. By asking yourself Why five times, you can answer for the user groups, and so the first hypotheses about the needs of the target groups appear. At this stage, these hypotheses are enough to give a sense of a need out in the market.

It's important to emphasise that this method is particularly effective at the very beginning when the idea must be tested before you start to conduct market studies, analyses of competing apps and user interviews and so on. However, you can always return to the model when you have conducted user analyses and confirmed or disproved the hypotheses.

The important point is that there is always an underlying feeling behind a need and a problem

In the example, the starting point was to plan meals better because the team behind Arono had seen that it was hard to find good customised meal plans in the Danish market. The example clearly shows that the three target groups have very different needs and so reasons to use Arono. Therefore, one consideration was whether Arono should focus on one target group rather than three. It's a very crucial consideration because any marketing of the app should be based on the emotions and the underlying needs of the specific target group.

The crucial point is that there is *always* an underlying feeling behind a need and a problem. For example, fear, love, joy or excitement. Emotions are usually linked to a basic need as defined by Maslow in his famous hierarchy of needs where self-actualisation, esteem, loving/belonging, safety and physiological is the underlying motivation for human action. When these needs are satisfied, the overriding human needs such as social affiliation, recognition and personal development become more important. We return to what motivates people to use and return to your app in Chapter 11.

7. WHO IS YOUR PRIMARY USER?

It's vital that you identify your primary target as soon as possible as many people make the mistake of starting with an overly large target group. When Mark Zuckerberg launched Facebook, it was initially other students at Harvard University who tested the social media. This gave Zuckerberg a lot of useful feedback while also being close to his users. He was a student himself, and so he knew his target group incredibly well.

THE CRUCIAL EARLY USERS

Venyo is a dating app where users date in discos and nightclubs, and it was launched by Andreas Porsborg Gatten in 2016, but it didn't take off with users. We use Venyo as an example here because the app has gone through a process that many apps experience. When Venyo was launched, it tried to get numerous clubs in Copenhagen to use it. One year after, one of the founders, Andreas said that in retrospect, they should have started with one club. It would have created more value for the club and given the opportunity to test the app and get direct feedback from users.

Let's take a closer look at the app. Venyo is a two-sided platform which, on the one hand, has some users and on the other hand, some nightclubs and discos. In the middle is the app developer who must ensure that there are both enough users, so the clubs are happy, and also enough clubs so that users will use the app. As a two-sided platform, Venyo needs a critical mass of users and clubs to function.

A critical mass is the minimum number of persons required for the app to work and have value. The more clubs associated with Venyo, the greater their critical mass of users must be. If they had started with one club, it would have meant that their critical mass would be about 100 people. With 10 clubs, the critical mass of people increases to about 1,000 people. So, it's both a matter of finding the primary target group and not involving too many of them at once – because it's easier to reach 100 people than 1,000.

You must find the group of people who are eager to try your app

You must find the group of people who are eager to try your app, and getting relevant and useful feedback is essential. The group also needs to be manageable, and when you've tested your app, it will be easier to spread it to a larger target group. If you start with too broad a target group, you'll often find it more difficult to test. Moreover, you'll spend unnecessary time and money on a group that only might be interested.

"FIRST MOVERS"

The former serial entrepreneur Steven Blank wrote the book *The Four Steps to the Epiphany*, and he deals with how important it is for startups to find the first enthusiastic users of a product, the so-called "first movers". These first movers can and will provide quick feedback, and they can also be used as ambassadors. First movers are characterised by:[29]

1. They have a problem.
2. They have seen and understood that they have a problem.
3. They actively try to solve the problem.
4. The problem bothers them so much that they have made a temporary solution.
5. They have allocated a budget to solve the problem.

(Points 4 and 5 are probably only relevant when we are talking about companies who have a problem and a budget to pay for a solution to the problem).

It's not always easy to find these first movers, and sometimes we assume that the target group is different than what it actually is.

As mentioned earlier, many entrepreneurs made the mistake that they started with one of the overly large target groups. Therefore, entrepreneurial literature has dealt with this first target group a lot. Everett Rogers wrote the book *Diffusion of Innovations* on how users usually adopt new technology and begin to use it.[30] Rogers uses a curve of what he calls "technology adoption". It shows how different groups of people typically use a product. We have taken the model because it illustrates user adoption/market penetration based on research.

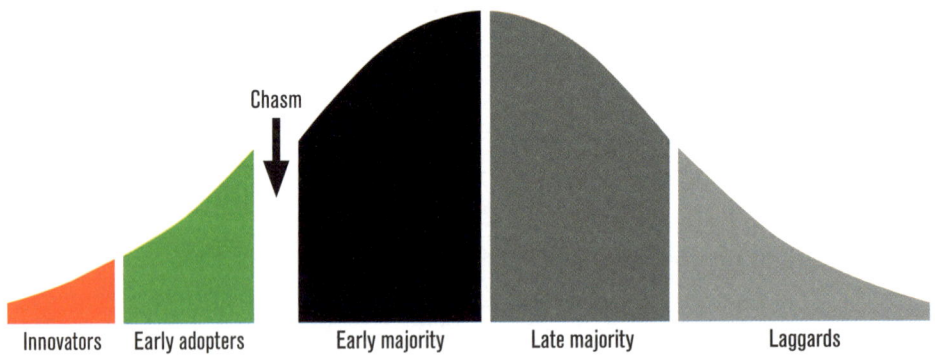

Figure 19. Rogers' model for technology adoption.

In the graph, the first users are characterised as innovators, who are the ones we call the first movers. They may also be users who are just wildly excited about your app idea, and it's usually the group that your app meets the need for, and who are aware of the need themselves. If your app entertains (e.g. a game), then it's the group of players who are captivated by just that type of game.

Once the app has become known among the early users and enthusiasts, the app will spread to the "early majority" and "laggards". We all know the types who sigh about the family reunion: "What use is it to me?" Or "Oh yes, there are so many new things that you have to familiarise yourself with". Once you've got these kinds of users on your app, then it's become mainstream (read more about this in Chapter 6). For the early majority, it's often the case that the "pressure" to get the app has increased, and the risk is decreased by that person being repeatedly exposed to the app's brand and seeing how people enjoy using it.

The development from being an app for a few enthusiasts to becoming mainstream is very complicated and takes time. As Geoffrey Moore describes it in his book *Crossing the Chasm*, it's a kind of "chasm" that technology must cross. This is illustrated in Figure 19, where the chasm is between the innovators/early adopters on the one hand and the early majority/late majority/laggards on the other. You often see that it's relatively easy to get the first two groups to use an app, while it's very difficult to cross the chasm and go mainstream. In Denmark, it took almost 10 years before Facebook became mainstream.

People are generally conservative, and psychological studies by, among others, Nobel laureate Daniel Kahneman, shows how our brains try to avoid strenuous tasks, such as learning new technology. If a lot of time and thought must be invested in using a new app, it becomes harder to reach mainstream users.

Only the first movers accept imperfect features

The chasm that Geoffrey Moore speaks of (see Figure 19) is often referred to as the "Valley of Death". The reason is that a lot of apps only ever manage to attract the most enthusiastic users. If these users don't recommend the app to a large circle, it becomes the "death" of the app because they don't manage to generate revenue among mainstream users. Moore argues that the fundamental problem entrepreneurs face when trying to cross the chasm is the fact that only first movers accept imperfect features and early technologies. The pragmatists only accept the app when it's solved an actual problem they are facing. For them, the app is a practical improvement on what they already do.

THE EARLY ADOPTERS

The group of early adopters of technology products are curious and accustomed to using technology. They find it easier to switch technology, and, therefore, they are perhaps also more disloyal than the pragmatic and conservative users who, once convinced, don't just turn their back on an app.

Everett Rogers estimates that the first group of enthusiasts constitutes about 2.5% of the market you aim to reach. If the first users don't return and use the app again, nor recommend it to others, it's inconceivable that the app will be successful. Rogers has made a number of studies about how fast innovation is accepted and used by users. How quickly an app is used partly depends on how big a problem it solves for users, or how great the need is. If the app is something new and groundbreaking, it will take longer to convince users. Likewise, it will take longer if the app provides a service or product where users have very ingrained habits.

An example of this was a group of students at Copenhagen Business School (CBS), who wanted to make an app that would be a two-sided platform for hairdressers and their clients. After talking with some hairdressers, the students discovered that there was no basis for making the app. Almost all hairdressers said that people are very conservative when it comes to changing hairdresser. The hairdressers had their regular clients, and it was relatively rare that people changed hairdresser. This example shows why it's so important to find out whether the area the app is aimed at is associated with ingrained habits and fixed traditions.

One challenge can also be to find first movers, and of these, who is the most enthusiastic? In some cases, it will almost be obvious who the first movers are, and in other cases, you must use trial and error.

The first 500 users are the most important

One way of using trial and error is to make a landing page, which is a simple website with only one page. Here you briefly tell about your app and ask, for example, people to click one of three buttons: "I am interested", "I am not interested" or "I may be interested". You can also offer part of your service free of charge if people send their e-mail address. In that way, you can get an indication of who might engage in your particular app.

Another method is to create a Facebook ad to your landing page. If people click on the ad, it's an indication that they see a value in what you promised in the ad.

Everett Rogers' model emphasises the importance of being focused on defining and satisfying even a tiny target group's needs, so this group can become ambassadors for your app and spread the message. A product reference from someone you trust is significantly more effective than most other marketing. According to Statista, who compile comprehensive statistics on Internet and app searches, 31% of all downloads in the US in 2016 were based on friend's recommendations (see Figure 20).[31] Therefore, word of mouth marketing can't be underestimated.

A rule of thumb is that 500 users of an app is a reasonable initial target because then you have reached beyond the 50-100 friends and acquaintances who are just doing you a favour. If you have 500 weekly active users on your app, then that's a good start.

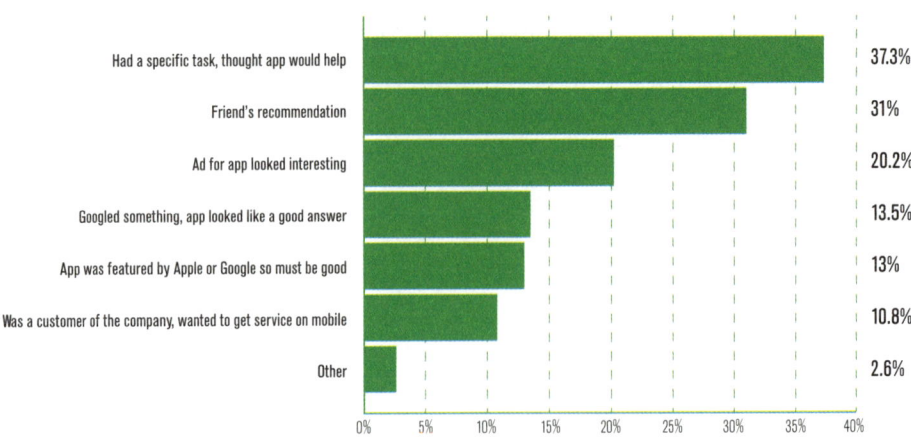

Figure 20. Reasons why users download apps.

PERSONA

You never finish getting to know your target group – it's a continuous process. A good exercise is to create personas, which is are A4 pages with photos of your typical user, as well as some demographic information: Sofie Nielsen, female, 21-years-old, studying at Copenhagen Business Academy, rents a room in Frederiksberg, etc. You also briefly explain why "Sofie" uses your app. You may want to take this description from a genuine user interview. You can also draw a persona or make a collage containing all the relevant information.

To create personas as accurate and precise as possible, you can ask these questions along the way:

- What is the gender, age and level of education of your users?
- Where are they located geographically?

Once you have answers to the questions, you can find out how big your target group is. You can go to Statistics Denmark and find general figures on the size of the population. You can also use Facebook (you need to create a marketing account) and then make an ad and ask Facebook to assess how many Facebook users there are in the target group you specify for your ad.

Then, find out how you can best get in touch with your target group. Often, it's through institutions, work or events where there are many people gathered that it's most worthwhile to contact your target group. However, it must be aimed at the target group correctly. If you turn up at a festival full of hope, you will probably be disappointed when you discover that people have paid for their ticket to listen to music and drink beer and not to download a "new and exciting app".

8. WHAT IS YOUR APP'S BUSINESS MODEL?

Now you've found your primary target group, understood their needs and made some preliminary thoughts about whether your idea meets these needs. Then you need to try to get an overview of what work you need to do on your app in the future. You've made some assumptions about your idea that you must now test, and an excellent way to get an overview is to use Business Model Canvas (BMC), which was developed by the Swiss entrepreneur Alexander Osterwalder.

As the name suggests, it's a method of creating a systematic overview of the business model. We often use the word "business model" as a synonym for how to make money, but in fact, there are many components of a business model. BMC is a matrix with nine building blocks that together show you how your app creates value for your users and your company. BMC allows you to not only get an overview of how your business should be put together, but it also gives you the easy option to assess how alternative models might look.

THE VALUE OF BMC

What can BMC as a "normal" business model not do? A traditional business plan consists of perhaps 40 closely typed pages, and for comparison, BMC is a very concise and useful tool that is simple to adjust as you become wiser and gain more knowledge of your potential users. It's an excellent exercise to force yourself to "reduce your business" to one page. If you can do that, you will find it easier to convey your idea to others – investors, users, potential partners, etc.

Start with BMC rather than a traditional business plan

BMC allows you to get a quick visual overview and an excellent guideline for the principal considerations that may affect the structure of an app, and it also makes it apparent what direction the startup must go in. If BMC is set up in poster size, you can use Post-its to assess actual and potential changes in the business model and their impact.

BMC makes the content transparent and allows you to share quickly. When the canvas hangs in a central location, it becomes a very manageable communication of the app's business model. In the busy life of a startup, it can sometimes be difficult to spend the time thinking of something new, because there are so many practical things that must be done. BMC is very flexible. It's easy to adjust and update. You don't have to plough through and correct 15 pages of three-year-old budgets, which can be the case with traditional business plans.

With BMC you start by filling in all the boxes you can. Your first idea will almost always be an untested hypothesis, and so the first things you type into BMC are only assumptions since you haven't tested anything in the initial phase. As you gain more insight into your users and your app, you can adjust BMC. You will typically adjust the plan once a month.

During this initial phase, BMC can give you a clue as to whether there is business potential with your app. You can see at a relatively early stage with some apps whether there is potential, whereas in other cases it will take a while before you can determine whether the potential is there. It's because some assumptions are harder to test than others. However, what is quite clear is that you must have evidence of your assumptions in BMC. This means that you need to test each area and then update the contents of BMC.

Start by putting Post-its in each box, and here you write what you *assume* will work for your app. Later you can update each box when you can validate that your assumption was correct. Your work with each box continues on an on-going basis until you have validated everything, and then you move forward. In principle, the process is never quite finished because the environment is continuously changing. In this way, BMC is a kind of conversation paper in your team, where you regularly discuss the progress you have made. You can also use BMC to compare it with possible competitors to see if you have long-term competitive advantages.

KEY PARTNERS

Who are our key partners?

Who are our main suppliers?

What resources do we need from our partners?

Venyo:
Nightclubs
- Promotion
- Special deals
- Collaboration on events
Festivals
- Event organisers
- Promotion.

KEY ACTIVITIES

What are the key activities we must do to create value?

Venyo:
Match people who go to the same nightclub or festival.

KEY RESOURCES

Who is going to code our app?

Who is going to design our app?

Venyo:
A great app
Solid network in the club and music scene
Social media marketing expertise
Product/customer development expertise.

VALUE PROPOSITIONS

What value do we provide to our customers?

Which of our customers' problems do we solve?

Which of our customers' needs do we fulfil?

(If the app is a two-sided platform, there may be a different value on each side, for example, customers and users).

Venyo:
We match people who go to the same club/event at the same time, they can meet faster in reality and save time — instead of messaging each other for weeks before meeting like a "regular" dating app. People save money by us offering free admission and drinks if you show the app at the door at selected clubs that we collaborate with.

COST STRUCTURE

What are the most important costs?
What key resources are the most expensive?
What key activities are the most expensive?

Venyo:
Marketing — main/highest cost
Development and maintenance of the app
Facebook ads, social influencers and promo events clearly represent the highest cost.

Figure 21. Business Model Canvas with Venyo as an example. The nine building blocks cover the four main areas of a business: customers (red), product (green), infrastructure (blue) and finance (black).

BMC is an excellent tool for creating structure in this initial "unstructured" phase

Many entrepreneurs work quite unstructured at the beginning, which in some cases can lead to a waste of time and money. When it comes to apps, "structure" can often be guided by when and how quickly the programming of the app is finished. However, before you get there, you must have a handle on your app's business potential. BMC is a great tool to structure your thoughts about the business potential in the initial "unstructured" phase.

CUSTOMER RELATIONSHIPS BEYOND THE APP

What relationships can we create for our future customers before the app is launched?

What relationships do we already have?

What does it cost to have these relationships?

Venyo:
It's crucial that the app is local and "the new thing in Copenhagen" rather than just a new international dating app. It has a significant impact on an app's reputation whether young people find it cool or not.

CUSTOMER SEGMENTS/USER SEGMENTS

Who do we create value for?

Who are our primary customers?

Who are the first movers?

Venyo:
Anyone who already uses Tinder or other dating apps.
Everyone who wants to save money when they are out on the town.
The main customer segment is the 18-24-year-olds.
First movers are people who are fed up of existing dating apps.

THE WAY TO THE CUSTOMERS

How will we create a relationship with our future users?
What kind of PR will we use?

Venyo:
Facebook and Instagram ads (targeted at 18-24-year-olds).
Promo-parties at trendy clubs where you must download the app to get in.
Social media influencers who write about us.
Clubs, events and online magazines that write about us.

REVENUE STREAMS

Which value are customers willing to pay for?
How will customers pay?
How will revenue be generated?

Venyo:
Premium features
Advertising space.

HOW TO USE BMC

1. Customer and user segments

Start by completing the box with customer segments. When you start with a new idea, it's important to find a specific customer segment. What characterises the customers that you want to please with your app? It must be a group that is very eager to try your app, and it's crucial because you can get excellent feedback from them. If they like your app, they will be terrific ambassadors for you. Many renowned companies started with small groups of customers. Endomondo began by going to running events in Denmark to get runners to download their app. Larry Page did the same when he started Google. As mentioned, in the beginning, many new entrepreneurs choose a customer segment that is too big. If you think that your customer segment is too big, then you're probably right. If instead, you can quietly build a network of interested potential customers, you are well on your way.

There can also be multiple customer segments, for example, if it's a two-sided platform.

As stated in Chapter 7, you can create personas to characterise your typical customer. Your assumptions about the "typical customer" can often change when you start the initial testing. For some apps, it may take a long time before there is any revenue from customers. This may be because the app publisher must validate the app and the idea before it can be launched, and this takes time. In the case of Venyo, they had to change the target group along the way, and they would then validate the app with users who are nightclub guests.

Figure 22. Business Model Canvas in use.

Why is your app so much better than an existing one?

2. Value propositions

After the customer segment, you must formulate what value your app creates for customers. When the words "value proposition" are used here, it's because the focus should be on what it is you do for the customer, and not on what features you have built into your app. That's precisely the difference between an idea and a business idea. Why is your app so much better than an existing one, so customers choose to buy it? How do you solve the customer's problem or meet their needs? (Read more about this in Chapter 6). Our experience is that it can be difficult to be precise and concise when you have to talk about the value of your app. If you find it hard to say what the value is, then your customers will certainly also find it difficult to see the value. Therefore, it's good training to formulate the value of your app in one sentence.

The following factors may have a significant impact on the customers' perception of value:

1. It's cheaper than other solutions.
2. The problem is solved quickly, so the customer saves time.
3. Risk is reduced in comparison to other solutions.
4. Some are easier to access.
5. It makes it easier to implement.
6. Attractive and tasteful design.

If your app is aimed at a two-sided market, the user group and customer group each have their own value propositions. The user group is defined here as those who don't pay (in this case the nightclub guests), and the customer group are those who pay (in this case the nightclubs). The value for the nightclubs was that the app could attract more guests and for the nightclub's guests, the value was that it was easier to make a date.

Once you have completed the first two boxes in BMC, you may feel you are on thin ice. If you are at a very early stage, you may want to wait to fill in the remaining seven boxes until you have more knowledge.

3. The way to the customers

How will you reach your customers? No or very few start-ups can afford to pay for marketing. Therefore, you must consider how you can do free marketing for your app. Is it via Facebook? Is it via publicity from bloggers? Is it by word of mouth? Have you created a kind of social network of potential customers via a website? Write down how you can do free and paid marketing. Perhaps look at Chapter 21 for ideas.

4. Customer relationships

How do you meet customers? Is it face-to-face or online? Can they communicate with you or others from your company via chat or e-mail? How have you established relationships with your customers? If it's a two-sided business, there may be differences in how the relationship is created for the two segments.

5. Revenue streams

What is your revenue model? Is it a two-sided platform where you earn a percentage on the sale between the customer and the user? Is there a freemium and premium version? Do you charge users to download the app? How often do your customers expect to return and purchase? Read more about this in Chapter 4.

6. Key resources

Is your app dependent on certain people being constantly present? In that case, those specific people are key resources – it may be a programmer. If the activity only takes place via the app, the key resource is the persons who optimise the app. Likewise, people who create free viral marketing are key resources. Choose people who are good at what you can't do yourself. It's a vital acknowledgement for an entrepreneur. Key resources are all the resources you need to deliver value to customers. A good robust network is often a key resource. At Venyo it was, for example, crucial to create a good network to all clubs.

7. Key activities

What activities are most important for your app? What kind of tasks do you need to solve for your business to work? What process does it take for customers to get the most value? Is it a continuous optimisation of the app? Are there activities to supplement what the app offers? At Venyo the key activity was to match people at a nightclub or festival.

8. Key partners

Your key partners are the partners that really add value to your app or product – they may be important suppliers, designers or programmers. It may also be partnerships where you add mutual value in addition to doing business with each other. As we'll see later, the founders of the Venyo app discovered that it would simply be too difficult to make money if they entered into a very close partnership with nightclubs who would determine what the app should contain. This partnership should have value for the nightclub owners (customers), app publishers and nightclub visitors (users).

> *Strong partnerships can easily mean the difference between success and failure*

9. Cost structure

What are your costs? How much are your fixed costs? Are they primarily variable or fixed? And are there high development or start-up costs (see Chapter 5)? The last point gives an overview of what it will cost to start and run the app, and also whether it's a good business or not.

When it comes to an app, development costs will take a huge chunk out of the budget. Does a salary have to be paid to a developer? Is a company going to be paid for developing the app? What will it cost to update the app continuously? Is there to be paid marketing? Most entrepreneurs work without pay for a year or two and must look closely at every penny used. So, it would be great if there isn't a fixed rent, or at least only a small one. Of course, you could work at home in the bedroom, but it's a motivator to get out in an inspiring environment that is the "workplace". Fundamentally, all new startups need to keep costs down (read more about this in Chapter 5).

Fundamentally, all new startups need to keep costs down

It's essential to point out that BMC doesn't deal with market size or business potential, so it's necessary to supplement your canvas with considerations of these.

Does it even make sense to talk about the business potential of your app so early in the process? Yes, it does. It's not sure that the business potential will be triggered and it's not certain that you are aiming for an enormous business potential. Business potential is always linked to the market size. But it's important that you relate to it. If your app is a service for takeaway in a small Danish town, then there isn't a huge business potential. Many apps will have the possibility to get out in a global market if they are translated into other languages. GoLittle is an app that caters to families with children with the same concept as TripAdvisor. It recommends places that will be especially attractive to families with children. Morten Resen from GoLittle has found out that there are 70 million families with children in Europe. If GoLittle can manage to create sufficient value for its users, there will be a potential of 70 million users – what is called the "total available market".

Venyo's first objective was to cover all the nightclubs in Copenhagen. In this case, the "total available market" equals the number of clubs in Copenhagen. The number of guests at the clubs was more difficult to estimate since the clubs probably wouldn't say how many guests they had. Therefore, the number of users has to be an estimate. Then Venyo had to estimate how many of these guests were singles, and finally, how many of these singles wanted to date. To assess this, they used Statistics Denmark to establish how many singles there are in Denmark in the 18-24 age group. This could be combined with their own survey at a nightclub, with the approval of the owner, where guests are asked if they were single and whether they were interested in a date.

In some cases, there is no existing market to study. This applies, for instance, if your app is very innovative and something similar hasn't been seen before. In such cases, you must test whether it's something users would use. It doesn't make sense here to analyse a market when it doesn't exist. It may take a while to get potential users to accept something new. For example, it took a few years for ecommerce to break through in Denmark.

Entrepreneurs typically commit these three errors when filling out BMC:

1. You fill it in just once and think you're done.
BMC must, like any other canvas in a Lean Startup, be a living document. Lean Startup is a term that Eric Ries launched in his book of the same name. In short, the point is that in a startup you should try to work with as few detours and unnecessary processes as possible. This means that you fill it out based on what you know today, with the understanding that you possess right now. You will be wiser later on once you have tested your hypotheses.

2. You fill in everything at once.

New entrepreneurs often download the template, print it and then spend several weeks discussing what each building block should contain. It's only natural that you are very unsure about what each building block must contain at an early stage. The best advice is to instead focus on the interaction between the customer segment and value prepositions because the two building blocks are central to the remaining building blocks of BMC.

3. You formulate everything too generally when you fill in the boxes.

This is often seen with startups. If you are too general in your value propositions, it will be impossible to explain what you do for your customers. A generic customer will block the creation of value for your specific customers and make it difficult to get anything from your tests since you don't have a clear target to analyse the data against. If you aren't specific regarding marketing, the result will probably be that it will be more expensive than it should, and you will waste time and money with lower conversion rates than if you had a clearer picture of who your customer is, what language they speak and what their habits are. The same goes for the rest of the boxes, which specificity means you can work with a greater customer focus.

9. VALIDATION OF YOUR IDEA

You are now at a stage where it should be clear to you what problem your app must solve and for whom. It's now the right time to talk to potential users of your app to find out if your idea is any good. The idea must be specified using some hypotheses that you can test. In other words, you must start the process of validating your idea.

> When the idea of the WHAT app was developed, Steven Højlund spoke with as many people as possible. The most useful was people's associations with other apps, radio programmes and services that had something to do with questions and answers. In this way, other people helped him to map his competitors and other apps that Steven could then analyse afterwards. Among other things, he was aware that people associate opinions with facts and that there were conceptual challenges in relation to understanding what the app could do. Then he started working with some user examples, which he had since taken as his basis when he had to describe the app to people. For instance, young girls understood the app's purpose through a user example of a girl who needs feedback on a dress or a boyfriend problem. Older people understood the app's purpose best through the opportunity to ask about a dilemma just like the radio programme *Mads & Monopolet*.

HOW DO I GET KNOWLEDGE OF AN AREA?

The most obvious place to find knowledge is from potential users. However, initially, you can save some time by finding existing knowledge in the area you want to work with. Start by asking people you know: Do you know something yourself, do you know somebody who knows something, or do you have some friends who can help me? You can ask on Facebook if there's someone who can help with networking. You also need to look at more professional knowledge, such as scientific articles within the given area (logistics, elderly care, social interactions, etc.).

Start by asking people you know

You can get in touch with people with knowledge in almost any area through educational institutes. Find an expert on the school's or university's website, then send them an e-mail asking if you can call them or stop by for 10 minutes and ask a few questions. They are almost always ready to help or even more than happy to talk to anyone who is sincerely interested in what they are researching.

For some, this may seem like an imposition to contact experts directly, but this is often how entrepreneurs start to form a network. The Indian-American scientist Saras D. Sarasvathy has shown that successful entrepreneurs mainly use their network to gain knowledge.[32] The entrepreneur's resources, networks and knowledge are the basic building blocks when the idea has to be translated into practice. The entrepreneur focuses on what help it's possible to get from colleagues, friends, family, etc., rather than from some pre-defined goals they must achieve.

EXAMINE PROBLEMS AND THE NEED

Unfortunately, too many entrepreneurs base their process on assumptions rather than evidence or knowledge of customers. You can use the following methods to learn more about your potential customers, and perhaps more importantly, knowledge that can help you to make a decision on whether to abandon the idea before you've spent a fortune and wasted years on it or put 100% of your efforts into it.

OBSERVATION

Making an observation of potential customers means that you observe the given situations with these customers that are relevant to your app idea. The purpose of the observation is to gain an understanding of a person's or a group of persons' behaviours by looking at their lives and daily routines. You merely have to try and understand how the potential customers think and what matters to them. The observation must, of course, be made in situations related to the problem you want to solve. An entrepreneur wants, for example, to make a learning game for children in 3rd-4th grade. Therefore, he spent one week observing a 3rd-grade class in a state school to take note of how the children behave during a school day.

> *Observational studies allow you to see how people actually act*

The strength of observational studies is that you can see how people actually *act*, and not just hear them talk about how *they think they would act*. People are biased, generalised and overly positive in their belief in their own abilities. There is often a tendency in interviews and focus groups that interviewees will gladly meet with you and talk positively about your idea. If instead, you observe a specific situation, such as whether people buy something or click on something specific on a website, you can get a much more accurate conclusion of what people will do under other circumstances, for instance, in an app.

Observational studies can be difficult to conduct in practice because you can't see users engage with your app yet. You can only see them use competing services (see more in Chapter 10). It means there are some obvious limitations.

A good rule of thumb is that you need to talk to 50 potential users of the app to see if they can recognise the need

An alternative to observations is questionnaire surveys, but we would advise you not to do this unless you keep your questions open. It will generally be far too early to make these types of surveys, since you will both get too little data, and your data will not be sufficiently detailed because people usually have limited time to answer questionnaires. Your data may very well prove to be useless after a short time as you had simply asked the wrong questions because you didn't know the area well enough when you designed the questionnaire.

THE 50 UNSTRUCTURED INTERVIEWS

Hopefully, you've already gone out and talked to everyone who bothers to listen to you and your idea. However, if you haven't and are maybe a little nervous to talk too much about your fantastic app idea, then thorough preparation can, fortunately, help your nervousness. Now is the time to be slightly more specific and set a target of how many potential users to talk to.

The aim of an early conversation with a potential customer is to give you practical knowledge about what the customer's everyday life and worldview look like. You must be aware that the purpose of the interviews is to get people to say whether your idea is good or bad. The interview will give an understanding of the potential customer's habits and behaviour. Therefore: 1) Talk about the customer's everyday life rather than your idea. 2) Ask for details of their experience instead of views on future scenarios. 3) Talk less and listen more.

The purpose of the interview is to understand the world from the user's perspective. It's essential that you don't ask questions that are too technical or theoretical but leave room for everyday descriptions and everyday language. It's important in the interview to keep trying to move away from attitude chit-chat and "you do" and "others say". You must be on the same wavelength as your user. Only interview one person at a time, making sure that the user isn't disturbed, for instance, by their phone. Use a voice recorder or camera, so you record all the details. Allow enough time for the interview – you shouldn't expect to get anything useful from a 10-minute interview. Create trust and a calm atmosphere, so they feel at ease. Perhaps find a quiet room, take a walk, or get close to the actual situation you are interviewing about.

A good rule of thumb is that you need to talk to 50 potential users of the app to see if they can recognise the need, and for you to be more focused on your target group. The number is no coincidence, because researchers who work with interviews as a method, know all about the phenomenon that the last interviewees don't say anything that you haven't already heard. This is called "saturation", and it often happens between the 30th and 50th interview, depending on the complexity of what you are studying. When you feel that you aren't getting anything new, then it means with reasonable certainty that you have covered most associations that your interviewees have to the app idea you've presented.

Be careful not to structure the interview too tightly with too many questions at this early stage. You still need the people you meet to associate freely based on a few ideas that you give them. In this way, they help you map your field, and you also learn about them and how your potential target group thinks.

Themes in the interview

The trick is to have an easy method that you can use to introduce your app idea to potential users while getting feedback from the person. If you follow the checklist below, in a few minutes you can both validate and get excellent feedback from every person that you randomly get into a conversation with:

1. The elevator pitch aimed at the potential user: X is a Y-app, which helps Z do A.
2. An application situation aimed at each user group that you can follow up the elevator pitch with: "Imagine that you have problem X. Then you can use the Y-app to do A in such and such a way."
3. 3-4 questions about the features that would make the interviewee use the app.
4. General questions such as: Would you use the app yourself? How often would you use the app?

For example, imagine that you have been invited to dinner with the in-laws. Your father-in-law is in your share trading app's target group, so you give him the pitch and a relevant use-case: The busy man on the move can now trade his shares on the app and get alerts about market fluctuations and chat online with experts.

It turns out that the father-in-law has never traded with shares and generally doesn't think highly of market speculators as they – according to him – were responsible for him losing a lot of money during the financial crisis. While he speaks, he puts an older model of an Android phone in a leather case on the table – a phone that you know can't use any modern apps. You don't get the chance to ask about features or ask general questions before dessert is served, and the conversation turns to *Strictly Come Dancing*.

The example here should illustrate that you can get something out of talking to everyone. Although the father-in-law obviously doesn't belong to your primary target group, you've gained new knowledge: That money spent on advertising in his direction will be wasted. Therefore, the target group must be re-focused, and another more specific common denominator may exist or be tested in the next interviews. Maybe you should merely aim for younger men who are just starting to trade securities, and who are also more IT-literate.

Overall, it's vital to focus on the need because even people without the need may, for the most part, be well acquainted with the needs of others. For example, the father-in-law would able to point out that the busy financial men who are always on the go, may not have time to get alerts and expert advice. Maybe what they really need is to make rules for how their shares are to be traded in advance if certain things happen in the market. It's also generally extremely difficult for people to understand the features that you explain to them if they can't see them. Functional design prototypes may seem too clumsy and flawed for people to really appreciate the app. In Chapter 11, we explain how you can develop a prototype that people can relate to better than just words and text.

> **Don't give up too early – it may be that only some parts of your idea must be changed before you get potential customers "on board"**

Your starting point should always be that people as a minimum have an opinion, which is probably shared by some others too. And at best, they can help to describe the needs, features, existing solutions and feelings and so on. For example, it's important to note how people react emotionally to your idea. Emotions can move people to action much more than rational arguments. At the same time, negative emotions may also be warning signs that you should be aware of when you need to create a brand. Or you can see the negative emotions as opportunities to put a humorous and positive spin on something that people see as a negative.

Unstructured interviews are easy to conduct because you can do it in a normal conversation without recording people or taking notes, and the conversation takes place naturally. However, it's a good idea to get things down on paper. After 50 unstructured interviews, you should have reasonably good answers to the following questions: Does the target group have the need? Is the target group aware of the problem? Who experiences the problem most? Which features could remedy the problem? Which emotions do people have about the app idea?

In Chapter 7 we wrote about a group of students, who wanted to make an app that would be a two-sided platform for hairdressers and hairdresser customers. After a series of interviews with hairdressers, they had to conclude that people are very conservative when it comes to changing their hairdresser. The hairdressers had their regular customers, and it was relatively rare that people changed hairdresser. This insight led to the group dropping the idea. But you shouldn't give up too early. It may be that only some parts of your idea must be changed before you get potential customers "on board".

Talk about the user's daily life rather than the idea

Interview guide

Prepare an interview guide in advance with the questions that are about up to, in, before, during and after the situation you'd like to interview about. Use open questions – if you can you answer yes or no to your questions, they aren't open and need to be reworded. Begin the interview with "please describe ..." or "please tell about ...". Remember, it's the user who is the expert and it's you who has to learn. The shorter the questions and the longer the answer, the better the interview. Start with the overall topic instead of the specific app or specific situation. You're looking to understand how users behave, their habits and what their every day life is like. Ask WH-questions: who, what, why, where and when. Constantly use the answers to delve deeper. Take breaks. Allow time for the user to think about things along the way. It will increase the chance of interesting reflections. If the user says something that you find interesting, get them to elaborate: "Can you say more about ...". You can also choose to use tools during the interview. For example, let the user write or draw the main points. It gives you an insight into what users think is important. It's not necessarily the same as what you hear. As the interviewer, you must dare to be thorough without being afraid of seeming naive and ignorant. Ask about the experience and be responsive both to what is said and what is not said. Be clear, attentive, gentle, confidence-building and recollective.

Remember in an interview:
1. Talk about the user's daily life rather than the idea.
2. Talk about what's already happened, rather than getting statements from the user about what might happen in the future.
3. Talk less and listen more.
4. Avoid the following questions:
    - Do you think it's a good idea?

This question must be avoided because you will get more out of gaining knowledge of the user's daily life than their personal opinion of the idea. Often the user will say that the idea sounds great, but they can't really decide whether they would use it.

- How much would you pay for the app?

    This question will often give misleading answers because there is a big difference between what people say and what they actually do in a buying situation.

FOCUS GROUP INTERVIEWS

Focus groups play a central role in a lot of literature on product development, and they are a significant part of the market analysis before large companies introduce products on the market. They can be anything from informal group discussions to very controlled videotaped sessions with tastings and so on. The method typically involves inviting 6-12 people to discuss a product (or in this case a problem you want to solve with an app). The discussion is led by one person, the moderator, who will seek to direct the participants' attention to different aspects.

Our experience is that focus group interviews are not suitable as a preliminary study of an app idea. Focus groups are very time-consuming both to recruit interviewees and also to conduct the interviews. However, the big risk is that focus groups are difficult to implement and that you can easily be turned in the direction of one or more strong opinions in the group. When an app idea is as vague as it is at this point, it may be particularly problematic to use focus groups because opinions are reinforced in the group. But having said that, focus groups are still used to identify a potential target group's needs and problems. However, we don't recommend that you use focus groups to present an app idea as such.

EXPERT INTERVIEWS

If possible, consider conducting 10 so-called expert interviews, which are not interviews with potential users or customers, but with experts who have a more general view of at the market. For example, academics, journalists and industry experts in large companies might help to spot trends in the market that potential users or customers can't see because they are set in their views on how their needs are addressed in the current market. It's often said that Henry Ford was against asking people what they wanted because, as he said: "Had asked people what they wanted, they would have said faster horses." Experts may have a broader understanding of a problem, but they can also be harder to arrange interview times with as they are often busy.

Jakob Jønck who helped start Endomondo said that almost none of his potential customers understood his ideas when he first presented them. Before beginning to study customers, you must formulate a hypothesis about their problem. The study first aims to find out whether customers actually have the problem or need you have formulated, whether they perceive the problem as significant enough to do something about it, and how customers currently solve the problem. If your research shows that customers actually have the problem that you assume, you can go ahead with your idea. It must be said that it's complicated to conduct these studies on ground-breaking ideas. Mark Zuckerberg, for example, wouldn't have been able to identify his users' problem before he created Facebook. And the question was, whether they even had a "problem". He instead created the need with his users. Instead of hypotheses, he had to test a preliminary version of Facebook to see if it made sense.

FROM IDEA TO CONCEPT

10. MAPPING AND SELECTING FEATURES

You've got an idea for an app. A lot of ideas about sleek design and cool features are rattling around in your head. You must now write them down and "translate" them into concrete thoughts about app views, features and user flows. In other words: What is your app going to look? What features will it have, and what happens when you press the buttons? How will the user navigate around the app? Which features should you prioritise?

Below you can see the process which, in our experience, examines the idea, concept and design phase, where your app idea becomes a concrete concept.

Chap. 6, 7 and 9	Chap. 10	Chap. 11	Chap. 14	Chap. 14
What problem do you solve for whom?	**What are the existing solutions? How do they solve the problem?**	**Which features are you focusing on?**	**How should the user navigate in the app (UX)?**	**What does the app look like (UI design)?**
• User interviews	• Mapping solutions • What works well with the competition? • What doesn't work well with the competition?	• Describe the features in words • Draw all app views (wireframing) • Map the navigation in the app from view to view • Have total control of what is happening with every interaction in the app	• Map navigation in the app from view to view • Have total control of what is happening with every interaction in the app	• Choose basic colours • Draw icons • Design all views

Figure 23. The idea and concept development phase.

There are some key questions that you could answer in each phase. In the idea phase, who are the users and what are their needs and problem? In this and the next chapter, we review the concept phase in which you must answer the question of whether there are competing solutions, and which features should be in the solution. Once you have analysed your way to the answers to the questions, you can begin to create your first user tests. The figure also shows in which chapters you can read about the individual phases of concept development.

MAPPING AND ANALOGUES

You are guaranteed to get new ideas when you look at the competition closely, and when you start to draw and design the app's user interfaces. How is your app different from others in your field? Which unique features will your app have? It's crucial to have carried out a thorough analysis of the so-called "analogue apps", i.e., competing apps or apps that have fairly comparable features. In that way, you can learn how they do and see what can be improved.

Carry out a thorough competitor analysis

John Mullins and Randi Kommisar (2009) give their take on how you can make comparisons with existing apps or digital platforms to move on from the concept phase to an independent concept. If you find parts that are comparable, it's called analogues. The objective of the comparison is to see similarities that you can exploit. If an existing app had success in an area that overlaps your idea, it might mean that part of the app has a good opportunity.

To map all the other apps in your "field" may take a long time and is usually a process you will have to repeat continuously. It's an excellent idea to follow technology media such as TechCrunch or by news screening services that can keep track of keywords for you. Also, follow the app ranking lists such as AppAnnie to see what apps are trending in your field.

You probably already have 3-4 apps or websites in mind – perhaps you have already been in and tried them. However, mapping is a systematic exercise that you must complete before you proceed with the selection of features, design and programming. See the example in Figure 24.

Understand and explore other people's associations with your idea

Your starting point is, of course, your existing knowledge of the field and the solutions that already exist. However, your first "user" interviews with friends, family and people in the target group can also be a great help to identify the apps or services that people associate with the solution of the problem. If your problem is a big problem for many people, then it's very rare that there is no existing solution to it in one form or another. But don't let that put you off. It's also very rare that you come to market with something new, and it's an advantage if you can explain your problem and your solution with regard to other products that people already know.

The first step is to read all about the solutions you know of and have heard about via your user interviews. Download apps, try websites, take screenshots and make a note of features and user flows. You will be able to find examples or references to other apps in articles or app stores that are reminiscent of the app you have in mind. In this way, you quickly expand your search to perhaps 15-20 apps, websites and services that in some way are concerned with the problem that you would like to solve.

Be systematic in your mapping

The primary sources of your mapping are "experts", who will typically be people working in your field or with apps. Perhaps you have been lucky and have already conducted some expert interviews. Then you can use them and possibly ask the expert what services he or she know. App stores are also primary sources and the best place to find references to other apps. Finally, you can find great analyses of apps in the reviews that are made in TechCrunch and other technology media.

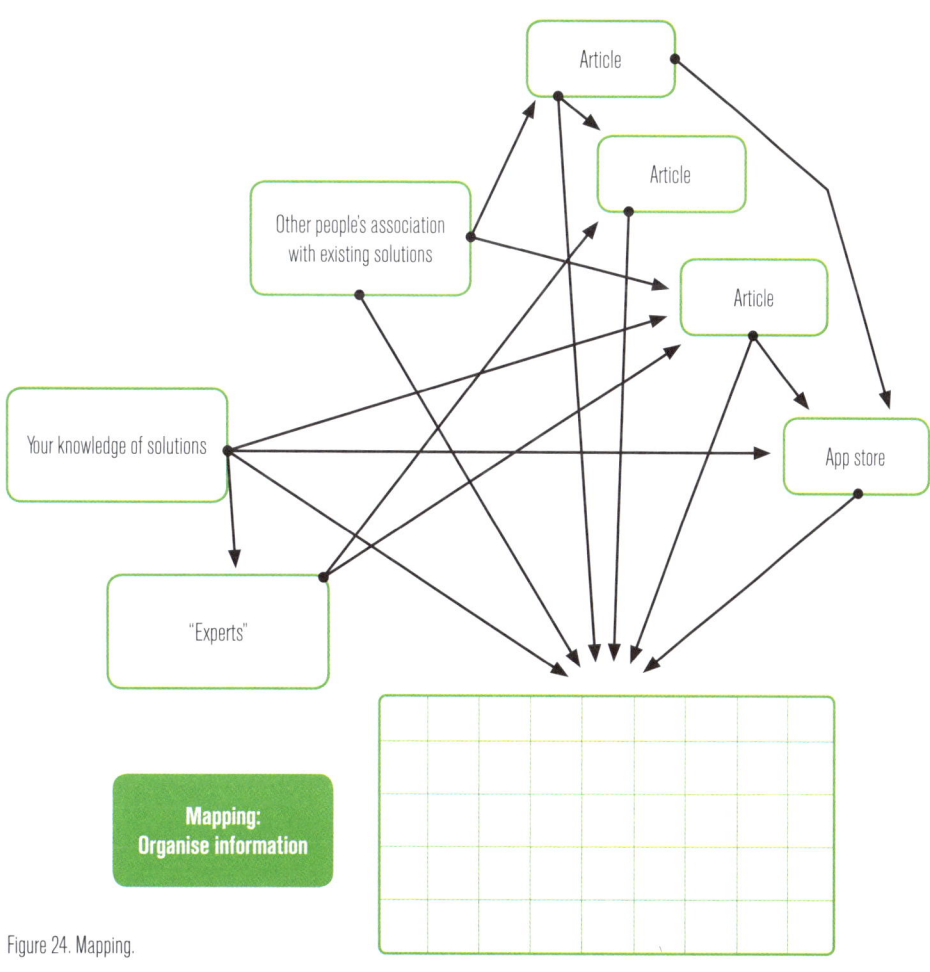

Figure 24. Mapping.

Figure 24 illustrates how you can have an explorative approach in your collection of information. As with the unstructured interviews, you must stop when you start to find the same apps again and again. In other words: If you can search on Google for an hour without finding any new app that resembles what you want, then it's time to stop. People you meet are guaranteed to give you some more names and new apps will appear in your "space" while you are in the process of development.

Keeping track of all the information can be difficult, and the systematisation of information is an excellent example of a problem that many apps have tried to solve. You can, for instance, choose to use Evernote or Trello, which provides two different solutions to the problem. A whiteboard with Post-its is also an option until you find out how you will systematise the information. But of course, we have a method that you can use. Here it is.

ANTILOGGERS

Once you have found some analogue apps, you must then try to find "antilog" apps. An antilog app is an app that has done something that your app shouldn't do. Typically, they are apps that have failed and therefore antilog apps are also harder to find and study. Not everybody behind a failed app has the time or inclination to talk about their mistakes, and you should, in any case, tread carefully and be aware that these people have invested a lot of time and perhaps money in a failed project. If you look down on their journey and their ideas or you are too self-confident in your manner, you can quickly destroy a precious relationship that potentially can provide you with a lot of data and knowledge about what you should not do with your own project.

PRIORITISE YOUR FEATURES

It's crucial with a mapping exercise to note all the relevant features that your competitors have, and, of course, the new ones you have thought of with. It's highly probable that at least 90% of the features come from existing solutions, but you might have small improvements to them. Remember to have it all documented.

You should categorise all features in a way that makes sense for your project. It can be done in many ways, but we recommend that you divide the features in relation to whether they are essential regarding creating value for your users. It's also good to organise features in the flow that your users are in when they get acquainted with your app.

No features in your app are random

Here we suggest that you use Trello (free) to systematise your information. You can create five columns ("lists" in Trello) in these categories: "Acquisition", "Activation", "Retention", "Referral" and "Monetisation". The five categories are objectives in the user's journey from potential user to superuser. The potential user must download your app before they can be activated and become a real user, and who subsequently becomes so fond of your app that they invite other potential users of the app.

You can organise the features under the categories that contribute to each objective. Figure 25 gives examples of a way in which to organise your features under each category.

Acquisition	Activation	Retention (key feature)	Referral	Monetisation
• Feature 1. Instant app	• Feature 1. App guide (from competing app 1) • Feature 2. Text activation (from app 2)	• Feature 1. Value-creating feature 1 (from competing app 8) • Feature 2. Value-creating feature 2 (from app 5)	• Feature 1. Facebook share (from app 4)	• Feature 1. Banner ad implementation (AdMob) • Feature 2. Payment to turn ads off

Figure 25. Categorisation of features.

All apps need to acquire users, and acquisition is primarily about marketing, but some features may be related to user acquisition. For example, "instant apps" make it more attractive for users to download your app when they can try it first. Activation is designed to help the user to start using the app, including registration, activation, and a user guide to the app.

Understanding the interaction between features and what they do for your users and your business

Retention is your app's key features that make the user remain in your app and keep coming back. Referral happens when the user invites others to use the app. Monetisation is any purchase that the user can make in the app.

Under each heading in Trello you can upload screenshots, write notes, create checklists and much more. You can easily move ideas up and down on your five lists, so the best is at the top, and those you might have to find more information about are at the bottom.

THINK VIRAL FROM THE START

It's vital that you consider from the start what features will work for the user together with other users, or which could give the user the desire to share your app with their friends. It's a great advantage for you if users invite other users because people are up to 10 times more likely to buy a product if it's recommended directly by someone they trust, compared to seeing an advert.[33] This means you save a lot of money on marketing, and as the indexed price for a download is around DKK 25, it's a necessity.

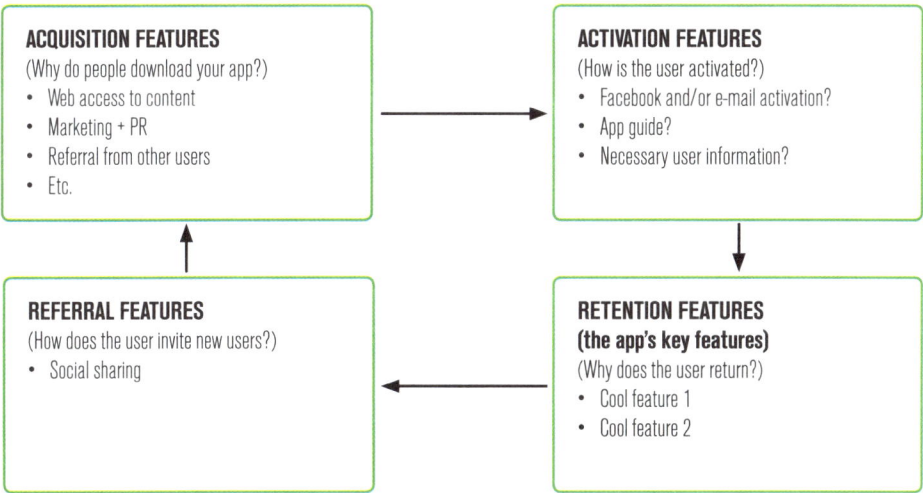

Figure 26. The interaction of features.

It's very difficult to get users to share your app on social media, and you must have a really good product before a user even considers a share. When a user is considering sharing something on social media, or verbally, they unconsciously consider whether they may intrude with their sharing or will look like a fool because they have shared, and so recommended an app that is no good, which can give the feeling of a loss of social status and capital.

Why would people share your app with their friends? Think about it!

So although it's easy to click "share" in the app, you should consider how to make your user look like a superhero when they share it on social media. Can they make cool graphics and post on Instagram? Can they make a funny picture and put it on Reddit or 9gag? Have they earned DKK 20,000 on the stock markets via the app? You need a "wow" to get shares, but before you can get shares, your app must be good enough that people like to use it. The first step is to find the few key features that your MVP app must contain.

11. FIND YOUR MVP FEATURES

You now have a long list of features. Now you have must select those that you believe will be the core of your app. These are the features that are included in the first app release and which are called "Minimum Viable Product" or just "MVP".

Be ruthless with the prioritisation of your MVP features

The features that are not part of your MVP are prioritised for the next version of the app. It will most likely be appropriate to move around and re-prioritise the different features, but right now it's important to understand how vital it is to choose correctly regarding the first features. At the same time, you must also have some idea of the features that must be changed, for instance, in a year. It's essential that your programmer has the opportunity to see where you want to take the app so they can make the right decisions in the long-term. Although your priority *always* trumps everyone else's priorities – because you know what users want – you should listen carefully if the programmers point out potential pitfalls with your priorities. Often it will be worthwhile to spend a little more time in the beginning to lay the right foundation for future features, even if it slows things down in the short-term.

MVP – MINIMUM VIABLE PRODUCT

What a MVP is depends on your product. The concept comes from the book *Lean Startup* by Eric Ries and is based on IT development in general. In the original definition, a MVP is the product version that in the shortest time can create value (and any revenues) for one or more users on a continuous basis.

Eric Ries' central idea was that you should make sure to get your product in the hands of the right people as quickly as possible because it's almost impossible to predict how users will receive and use the product. Eric Ries had even been involved in lengthy and costly IT development processes where products hit the market wrong, too late or not at all, because they hadn't got a "minimal" product off the ground quickly enough, but instead had held it back until it was completely finished and thoroughly tested.

The same consideration applies to apps. It's crucial to understand that for each additional feature there is an exponential increase in the consumption of resources (time and money), because of complexity and development time increases, and the project is riskier, there are further complications in the code and it takes longer to test the app. Therefore, you should think really carefully when choosing your MVP features.

> *Your chance of success typically decreases just as fast as the complexity of your app increases*

Figure 27 illustrates the problem: However, the numbers may vary from app to app. Some MVPs will be more advanced than others because they might not work without four key features.

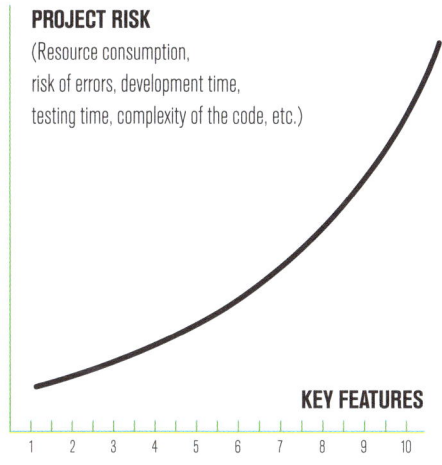

Figure 27. Project risk as a function of project complexity.

Another reason to think minimalist is that paradoxically, users often have a better experience with a simple solution. This is particularly true for mobile apps that appear on tiny screens while people are on the move. The requirements for simple design and simple solutions are therefore higher than for websites. It shows how important it is that you choose your MVP features with care. "Less is more" is a key principle when it comes to apps.

Let us also give an example.

> You want to make an app where people can trade on the stock and currency markets. In addition to trading, users must be able to talk in a small community, and they should be able to vote on shares, get real-time news, receive coaching from a professional advisor around the clock and buy advanced algorithms to predict the markets with. You have spoken with two programmers, and they estimate that it will take 8 months to build a "functional" app.
>
> You launch this app after 12 months. The programmers struggled to the end to sort out many faults with load in the system, crashes and design errors. Users' immediate feedback is that it is useful and nice. They use it, but not for very long. When you do follow-up user interviews, you find out that users think that the app is confusing and slow. Many users experience that the app

> crashes (because it's running too many processes at the same time). However, users may like the features, and you still feel that you gave them something they needed. But when you look at your user reach, you see that some user groups only use one feature while another user group uses a couple.
>
> The lesson from the example is that you could have had an app out after 3 months at 1/8 of the cost if you had focused on one user group (e.g. currency traders) and given them the one feature that they need most. The result might be the same, and users would wonder about the missing features, but you would have had the option of feedback, and you would not have wasted time building something that people didn't bother to use.

The "minimum" is very much up to you. Many apps are free, and revenue depends on a critical mass of users on the platform, such as advertising revenue that requires a lot of users. In such an app, the goal of your MVP is that users download and regularly return to your app.

On the other hand, if your revenue model is a subscription revenue model, you can earn money from your first users, so the MVP, in this case, is an app that can provide a service that people will pay for. You can discuss whether the payment elements must be there from the start, as it can ruin your chance to test all the app's functionality if people, for example, don't bother to pay for premium features.

CATEGORISATION OF FEATURES

It's important that you make clear prioritisation of your features based on five parameters:

1. Value to the user.
2. User motivation and ability to use the feature.
3. Development time of the feature.
4. What value does it create for your business?
5. The feature's "causality" in relation to other features.

Value to the user

Firstly, your features create value for the user. The user must be motivated to use the feature, i.e. they must save time, money, be entertained, find comfort or reduce pain or irritation. These are the typical reasons why we buy or start using something.

> *Know your users' needs and problems – that can't be said often enough*

The Be my Eyes app is used by the blind. Using the camera, sighted people (often volunteers) can help the blind to read things on packaging and so on. The app reduces all the annoyance and time for the visually impaired person. However, what does it give to all the volunteers who open the app for free to help to read what the blind need to be read aloud? It can be hard to figure out people's motivation to do something, and even big brands like Coca-Cola, Arla and McDonald's have committed huge product and marketing blunders, although they had done excellent preliminary work.

In Chapter 6, you can read about how you can come close to understanding your users' needs.

Your users' motivation and ability to use the feature

In Chapter 1, we talked about your motivation and used B. J. Fogg's motivation model. However, it's equally appropriate to use the model in relation to your users. The model has been illustrated below in Figure 28.

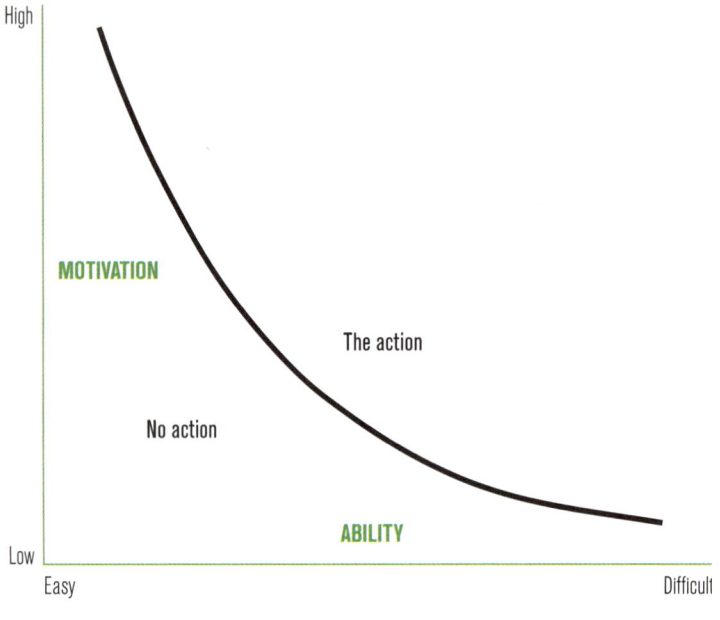

Figure 28. Action model.

The model illustrates how high motivation and excellent ability to use the feature results in the person acting. However, there must also be a "trigger" to initiate the action. The user must have an advert, a push notification, a message in the app or the like to initiate an action. We will return to triggers in the next chapter.

Next, the user must have the ability to use the feature. In the example with

Be my Eyes, one major challenge is that the app's buttons should be large and few. Otherwise a blind person can't find them on the screen.

Generally, people don't have the time and inclination to use "brain power" to get the app to do what the user expects it to do. A classic example in the field of user interface design (UI design) is the use of icons with or without explanatory text. There are surprisingly few people who know what standard icons in apps do, and therefore many choose UI designers to write what the icon does, although in principle it should not be necessary.

For instance, look at Facebook's "Like", "Comment" and so on next to the icon. And here arises another problem, since it's both expensive and difficult to translate apps. Facebook's "Like" becomes "Synes godt om" in Danish. The Danish translation is much longer, but Facebook has chosen the solution so that as many people as possible can understand and use the feature.

You must NEVER overestimate your users' motivation and ability to use your app

An essential fundamental condition for our ability to take action is the brain's limited ability to focus. The brain processes many impressions per second, but we are only aware of between four and eight of them. Most processes and impressions run "on autopilot" in the reptilian brain because this part of the brain doesn't believe that there are changes in our environment that threaten our life.

Daniel Kahneman, who is a Nobel laureate in economic psychology and author of *Thinking - fast and slow*, shows from his studies of human psychology how the human brain prefers not to make analyses and calculations because it requires more energy. Simply put: your average user is lazy and reluctant when they must learn to use your feature, and yes, maybe even physically and cognitively unable to use or understand it.

Development time for the feature

The third item on the list of priorities of features is that the feature, of course, should be programmed and designed within a reasonable timeframe. It's vital in a MVP that one single feature doesn't blow the budget or takes so long to program that the app never gets off the ground. It goes without saying.

Significance for the business

Fourth, you need to evaluate the feature's significance regarding what it does for you. Can you make money from the user using the feature? If the feature is secondary in terms of the revenue model, then it may be the wrong feature to focus on.

Features must support your business

The feature's relation to other features

The fifth and final item on the list of priorities is that the feature should be assessed in relation to the user's "journey" through your app and so the "causality" that is built into your app.

If we take Tinder as an example, the user can't use Tinder before they activate their profile. So, activation and creation of a Tinder profile is, therefore, more important than anything else, because other features are totally irrelevant without profile creation. A MVP version of Tinder might well have worked with a very stripped down profile, but there are risks of downgrading the first stop on a user journey, because users may not bother to move further into the app if the profile creation was very messy and poorly put together.

The next feature, which can be described as MVP for Tinder, is matching. The user should be able to match with other users before they can begin to chat and maybe go on a date. This means the match feature is more important than the chat feature because it comes before the chat feature on the user's journey through the app. In principle, a MVP of Tinder just reveals users' snap-name or e-mail address of the users that have matched, and in that way, it can quickly test if people even bother to download the app, create a profile and begin to match. A chat feature is a relatively major feature as it works in real time, but it also has to be scaled globally (still in real time) and preferably also integrated with push notifications.

PLANNING APP VERSIONS

Now you can start planning your MVP and subsequent app versions by reviewing the features you thought of in the mapping exercise in Chapter 10 and evaluate them based on the five parameters discussed in this chapter.

> *Prioritising your features is one of the hardest and most important ...*

You can then prioritise the features in the table below, where you relate the features to your app version and the user journey from a new user (acquisition and activation) to a standard user (retention) and superuser or ambassador (referral).

		MVP (initial release)	1st iteration + 3 months	2nd iteration + 3 months	3rd iteration + 3 months
Potential users (50%)	Acquisition	Feature 1			Feature 1
	Activation	Feature 2	Feature 1	Feature 1	
Core users (45%)	Retention	Feature 3 Feature 4 Feature 5	Feature 2 Feature 3	Feature 2 Feature 3 Feature 4	Feature 2 Feature 3
Ambassadors (5%)	Referral	Feature 6	Feature 4	Feature 5 Feature 6	Feature 4

Figure 29. Prioritisation of features.

The table gives you an overview of your features compared with your target group. The question is whether you trust that your MVP features can create users who love your product so much that they will act as ambassadors for the app and invite their friends to use the app. Most users are "core users", who like the app but don't love it. Can your MVP features keep people's attention on the app?

Then there is the large group of "potential users" who try your app but never become real users. Most will never return to the app. This group will probably be at least 50% of all people who download your app. But the question is, of course, which features motivate them to use the app again and again and become core users.

Most apps will never be more than MVP

Most apps never get their 1st, 2nd and 3rd iteration implemented because the MVP was not good enough, and the company runs out of money. Nevertheless, it's a critical task to describe future features, because programmers need to know whether they must lay the foundation for more demanding features. Therefore, look upon your list as a "feature roadmap", but remember that some of the cool features will probably be implemented in one or two years.

12. CREATE A COMPLETE USER EXPERIENCE

It's crucial to think transversely across features. When developing apps, it's easy to focus on features, design, buttons and other "tangible" elements of the app. But it's vital to incorporate the user's journey and the whole experience into the design.

How does the user experience your app before and after installation? Is the experience consistent? How does the user experience being contacted via push notifications? These are crucial questions to ask yourself and the user, as it gives you not only an insight into the user journey but also an understanding of how to create an app product that users want to return to again and again.

THE USER JOURNEY

Once you have finished with the initial studies, you can prepare a complete user journey that can help to give you greater insight.

Make a complete user journey

In a user journey, you describe your customer's journey before, during and after using the app. The purpose is to identify the most central interactions that a user has with an app, what we call "touchpoints".

You describe the customer's activities and experience on a timeline in relation to using and interacting with the app. In preparing the user journey, you must relate to the needs and difficulties encountered in the current way the potential customer does things. Before the preparation, you also need to decide whether you lack knowledge of something that you, therefore, need to explore further.

Start by selecting a potential customer that you think is typical of the target group that your app is aimed at. Set aside an appropriate amount of time for the user journey. Divide the user journey into phases (e.g. before, during and after).

The user journey is compiled through interviews with potential users. It's essential that the user journey is not based on your assumptions, but on potential users' actual experiences. This means that you go out and talk to them.

A user journey must be tested on potential users

There are different ways to learn how users experience the user journey. Specifically, you can conduct interviews or workshops with many users, where you ask users to tell about their encounter with what your app is trying to do better. Step by step. Enquire and ask the user to go in-depth with follow-up questions such as "What did you do?", "What did you think about it?", "What did it mean to you?" and so on.

User journeys based on interviews

- The user's journey, as it looks now, is pieced together from interviews with individual users. Emphasise describing the specific course of action and the needs created by the user along the way.
- Let specialists and users with knowledge in the specific area comment on the user journey and also make suggestions for changes, so it matches the user's needs better.

User journeys based on workshops with various stakeholders

- Invite various stakeholders, users and people in the know to a workshop.
- Let users put into words their needs and journey through the offer. Their input is pieced together to form a user journey. Possibly plot the process on a timeline that everyone can see.
- Then get different perspectives on the user journey so the needs of users will be complemented with contributions and feedback from the other stakeholders. Discuss improvements and changes with the parties involved about how the changes work in practice.

Interviews and workshops have different characteristics. Interviews are easier to organise, but workshops can create better results because there are more users and perhaps experts present and because the group dynamics can make the participants more motivated to provide feedback. For one interviewee, it may seem strange to have to describe their experience with the app if you aren't used to being a test subject. In practice, it may be difficult to get good information out of the interviews, because there is usually a relationship between the interviewee and interviewer that can mean that the answers are either more positive or negative than if they were given in a group where participants don't know each other.

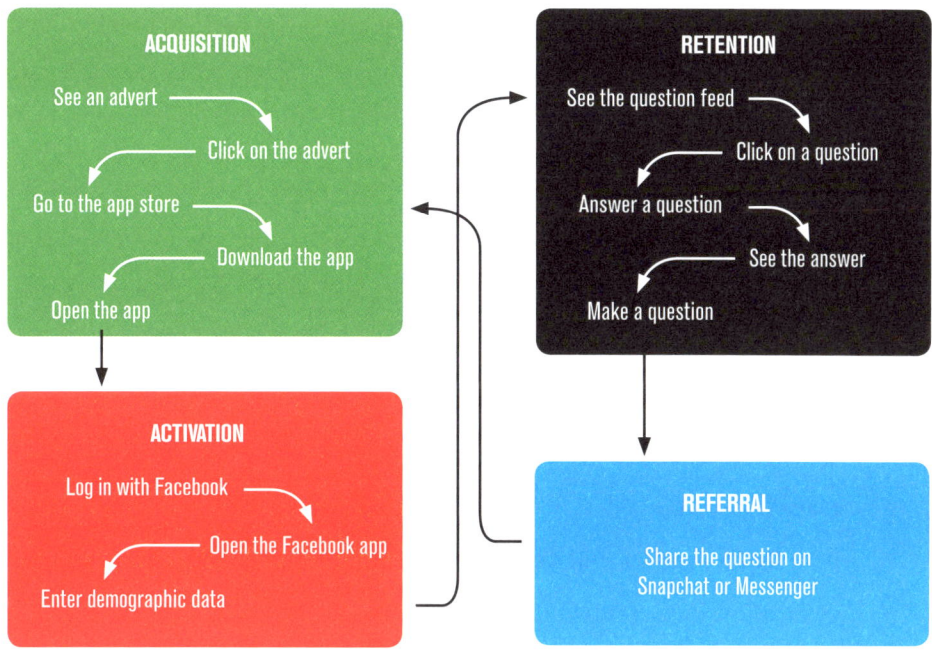

Figure 30. A simplified user journey as it might look like for the WHAT app.

Figure 30 is a simplified user journey in the WHAT app. It's not organised chronologically, but more concerning how users navigate in the app. After a workshop, you can draw the user journey with arrows from the various "elements" in the app. It doesn't have to be from view to view, but it can also be from features, for instance, from where users are activated in the app, or you can listen to your interviewees and take note of how they describe the various elements of the app. You can also make a chronological user journey: Where is the user after 30 seconds, 60 seconds, 90 seconds, etc.?

When you construct your user journey, you can base it on the following checklist:
1. Use a large piece of paper. Hang the paper up on a wall. Draw a timeline that stretches from before the user's encounter with your app and afterwards.

2. Use Post-its. What does the user do regarding the various touchpoints? One action per Post-it is put on the timeline in chronological order from the different touchpoints.
3. Mark the touchpoints. Touchpoints are points of contact between the user and the app. For example, the user is aware that the app exists and that they need the app. Then it's about downloading the app, using the app, returning to the app, possibly upgrading and possibly deleting the app.
4. Mark the user's actions in the app and record what the user was feeling and thinking at the time. What options does the user have at the given place in the app? What does the user think of the options? Should there be a fourth option that you hadn't thought of in the design, or are the current options confusing?
5. Communication. What does your user tell you along the way? Next to each touchpoint and action you place a new Post-it that describes your user's experience right there, both good and bad.
6. The problem and value prepositions. It can be just as important what your user experiences without encountering the app. If your app solves a problem, it's important that the user's encounter with the problem is also mapped. Does the app do what it promises? In the same way, it also counts with any download and the subsequent use of the app.
7. Focus on before and after. A user journey consists of the user's experiences before, during and after using the app, but it can also include other factors that influence the experience. For example, where will users typically use the app? In the bus, on the toilet or in front of the TV. This is crucial information.

Most analysis packages such as Google Analytics/Firebase, Applytics, etc., can give an overview of the user journey in your app once it's built. How many people went one way, and how many went the other? However, it's difficult to know the user's experience of the app if you can't ask them. That's why both workshops and interviews can be vital concerning a complete understanding of the users.

THE HOOKED MODEL

The Hooked Model is a tool from Nir Eyal's book *Hooked – How to build habit-forming products*, which is one of the main references for many app developers.

Is it possible to create a habit with an app? The answer is yes!

The model is illustrated below and consists of four parts: A trigger, an action, a reward and an investment. The idea is that as a product developer, you must get the user into the loop and get the user to complete the loop so many times that it becomes a habit to use your app.

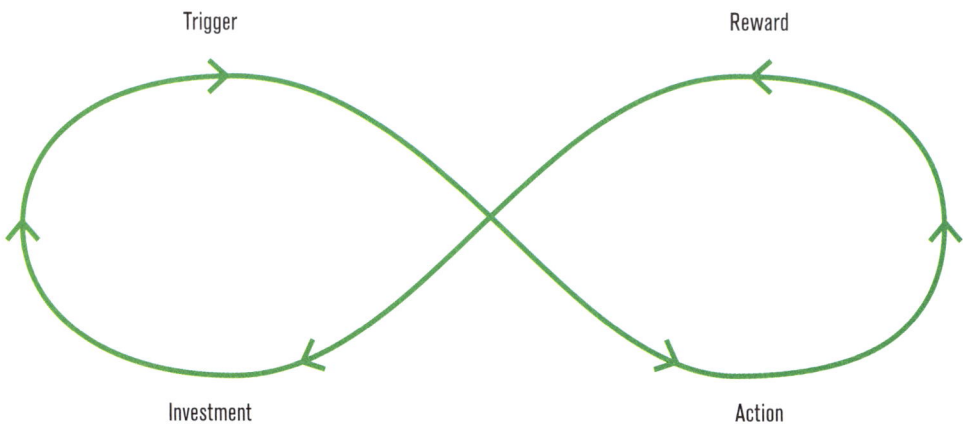

Figure 31. The Hooked Model.

It must be said that the Hooked Model is not applicable to all apps. However, it's particularly powerful for apps where you want to get the user to interact as much as possible with the app. For example, Google has a general principle only to develop products that users are ideally going to use at least twice a day. The idea here is that the products only become very powerful once they are a habit with the user.

The difference between whether something is a habit or not is absolutely crucial. If something is not a habit, you as a company must constantly make consumers aware of your product through advertising, publicity and marketing. It's called an "external trigger". It's expensive and inconvenient. However, if your product has become a habit to use, then the consumer is automatically triggered to use your product. It's called an "internal trigger". One example is Instagram that many habitually check while watching TV, waiting for the bus or taking a small break from everyday life, etc. The trigger is not due to an advert or a push notification, but simply that "you just need to check" when you are already sitting and watching TV.

Habits are created by repeated use and an expectation of a reward

If you want to make your app a habit that automatically triggers the user to use it, then it's essential to work systematically with the app's features. A systematic analysis based on the Hooked Model is a complete description of user flow, from when the user is triggered to download the app and until they are triggered to use it again and again and again. When the user repeatedly uses the app, it increases the chance that the user will become an ambassador and invite a new user to use it.

Figure 32 shows how this works for Tinder.

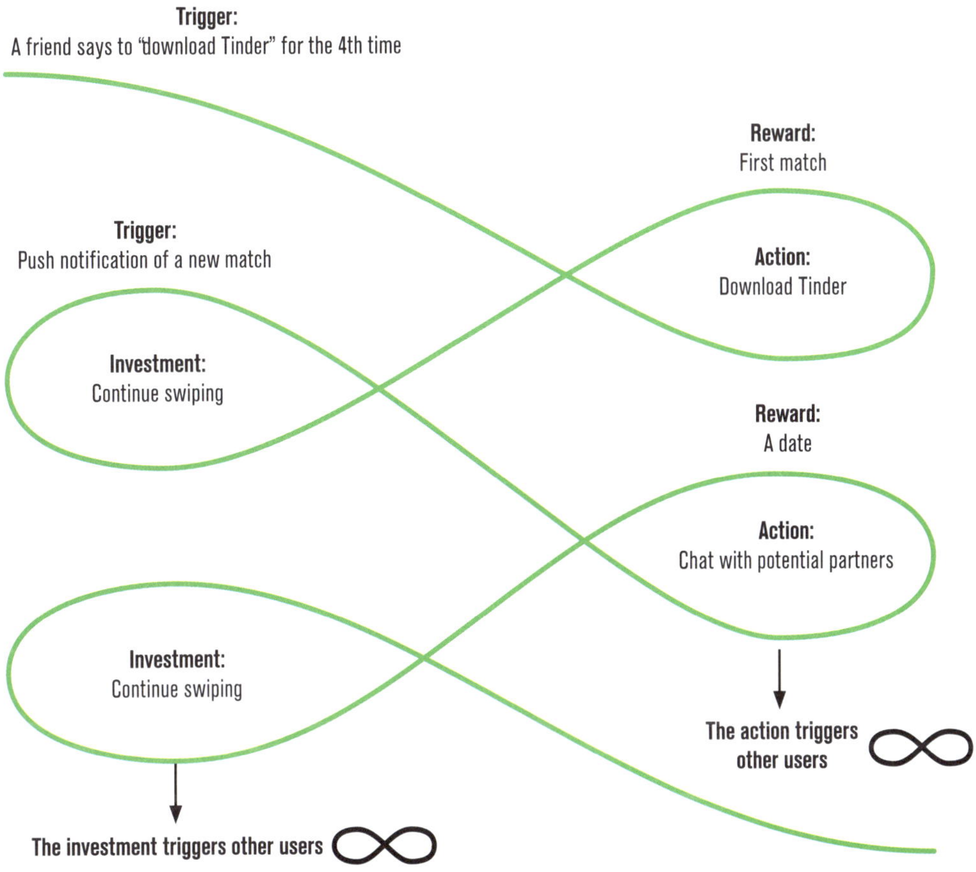

Figure 32. Tinder analysed with the Hooked Model.

In this example, a user has triggered the use of Tinder by a friend who says that it's the best way to find a boyfriend. The user could also have been triggered by an advert on Facebook. Then the user downloads Tinder (action) and will be able to swipe a lot of potential boyfriends. The investment is the time that the user spends creating a profile and swiping. After five minutes the user stops using the app and the loop ends.

At this important time, most users stop using an app. They are simply not triggered to return to the app, or there is not enough value to be gained by returning. It's imperative that you don't merely expect the user to return without a trigger. That only happens in apps where the user has invested heavily, such as money to buy the app.

Don't forget to provide a trigger to use your app

You can trigger the user to use the app again via a push notification, an e-mail or advert. In the example of Tinder, the user is matched with another user, and they both receive a push notification. So, Tinder triggers two users to return to the app and use it by swiping multiple users, who are then triggered with a push notification, etc.

Use of the Hooked Model

You can write your MVP features on the two tables below and so get an overview of how your app becomes a habit for your users. The first table is for the first time the user uses the app where the trigger of the user is external and based on marketing or publicity. The second table is related to the external trigger mechanisms that the app generates (push notifications, e-mails, text messages, etc.) which contribute to using the app eventually becoming a habit.

Where does the user come from?	Trigger	Action	Reward	Investment
Marketing or an invitation from a friend (virality)	• Advert • Social media • App store search for, e.g. "dating" • Search in a search engine (e.g. "dating app")	Download	Get access to a lot of singles	• Create a profile, upload photos (investment of time) • Swipe (investment of time)

Figure 33. Acquisition and activation.

It's crucial for Tinder that the new users create a profile that others can swipe. A profile is the content of the app, and a big part of the fun with the app will be related to "swiping" potential partners. "Content is king" for apps – content is key, because without content there is no retention of users on the platform.

Content is king

Next, it's extremely important for Tinder that the user starts to swipe other profiles. If the user doesn't, then Tinder can't match the user with another user. A match is the ultimate reward of the app, and it's crucial to give rewards to users to get them to stay on the platform.

Investment	Trigger	Action	Reward	Investment
No investment – i.e. no profile or swipe with the creation	• Push notification: "You need to create a profile so you can meet the love of your life" • E-mail: "You need to create a profile so you can meet the love of your life"	Open the app	Get access to a lot of singles	Create a profile + swipe
Profile	Push notification: "Swipe and find your true love"	Open the app + swipe	See lots of singles	Swipe
Swipe	Push notification: "You have a new match"	Open the app	See the match	Write to a match + swipe
Write to a match	Push notification: "[Name of the match] has written to you"	Open the app	Read the message	Write to a match

Figure 34. Retention.

Tinder's strength stands out when you analyse the app with the Hooked Model. The app has high value propositions for singles that they can find their (sexual) partner on the app. Love life is a primary human motivation, so the motivation to download the app is high and there are very few barriers to get started. The profile is simple to create as Tinder retrieves data and photos from Facebook. And finally, it's effortless to swipe, which is the action that gets a reward.

Most apps have more advanced "hooked loops", which is not a good thing. You should try to do something as simple as Tinder's "hooked loop", if possible, and it's a huge advantage if your value to the user is related to the user's basic needs, such as reproduction and social affirmation.

Variable reward

The general assumption is that people act to avoid pain and increase pleasure. However, the observation says nothing about how to design your app. In his book *Hooked*, Nir Eyal talks about three human and evolutionary traits that you can base the design of the app features on because they motivate people to action.

The expectation of a reward is as important as the trigger in the Hooked Model. The hope of getting a reward is what creates the internal trigger – that is creating a habit where the users trigger themselves to use the app.

Nir Eyal speaks about "variable" rewards because the rewards are quickly taken for granted if they are the same. When the reward is variable, it becomes more random what you get from opening the app. It's a vital element, as we know from gambling. If every time we put a dollar in a slot machine, we got 81 cents straight back because the return rate is 81%, then it quickly becomes boring to play and very apparent how bad a business gambling is. But when the reward is made variable, it then becomes more exciting and unpredictable.

Nir Eyal categorises variable rewards as rewards of the Tribe, the Hunt or the Self. The three categories should primarily be seen as tools that make it easier to remember them. However, they are of course tied to human behaviour and loosely based on research in psychology and sociology.

What are your variable rewards?

If we look closely at the different types, then the rewards of the Tribe are related to the human need for closeness to other people. We, humans, are pack animals and have survived and evolved in relation to the tribe, as Nir Eyal calls it. If primitive man was expelled from the tribe, he had little chance of survival, and therefore the closeness and acceptance of the tribe are so important that it has become an internalised motivator for most people that they seek acceptance from others and stabilisation of social relations. With the right features in your app, you can trigger this desire in people. The number of likes on an Instagram post is an example of a variable reward that is related to the tribe's acceptance of us.

The rewards of the Hunt are related to human curiosity. We constantly want to know what's around the corner. The variable could, for example, be your Instagram feed, where we are constantly being surprised by photos, funny quotes, memes, etc. Our feed is often an image of this "hunt" to find something that may surprise us and so entertain us. If our feed can't do this, we'll stop using it.

The Self is about the human urge to master and complete things and develop ourselves. An example is LinkedIn's permanent message that you need to complete 10% of your profile. You want to finish it. The reward is variable because you don't know what job opportunities may present themselves on the basis of a profile update. The same applies to traditional computer games with levels where you get better and better the higher your level is.

The three motivators are put into a table here:

	The Self	The Hunt	The Tribe
Explanation	The Self is linked with human intellect and social status. People get bored if there is no development.	People hunt to survive, and the Hunt is associated with enjoyment. It's related to curiosity, intelligence, strategy and tactics.	The Tribe is what has kept people alive for thousands of years. The Tribe is something you have to adapt to to survive, and therefore you are rewarded by nature by adapting and doing something "right", looking right and so on.
Examples of app features that reinforce motivation	The Self is related to game (gamification) mechanisms: • Scoreboards/leaderboards • Points • Completion bars • Levels • Learning • Prizes: gold, skins, etc. • Tokens The Self is also relational since you can develop as a group (role-playing game), or against an opponent. The Self is associated with social status, power and dominance.	The Hunt should not be understood literally, but more like: "What's around the next corner?" Curiosity and willingness to seek and search for surprises and entertainment: Feed – search for interesting content, profiles, sexual partners, or the like.	Social media is full of social mechanisms related to tribe mentality. Women react more strongly to tribe behaviour than men: • Likes, comments, photos, etc. • Upvotes/downvotes can be social, but also self-developing.

Figure 35. Variable rewards.

Many apps only have a few of the above three mechanisms built in. In the previous examples with a "trader app", it can be difficult to think how to make "cold" data from the world's stock exchanges into a bestseller.

But actually, there are quite a few possibilities: For example, you can incorporate search features in the app, so users search for the best prices and continuously return to the app not to miss a great trade. You can introduce points, levels and tokens so users can follow their self-development (social status compared to other traders in the app). You could make a mini-community where traders could establish "correctness" and strengthen tribal mentality by asking questions and commenting and so getting more points, etc. However, remember that these features are not MVP material and usually first appear in an advanced version of your app.

13. IS IT STILL A GOOD IDEA?

Is it now time to stop? What's your gut feeling? Are you still sure that your idea is so unique and good enough that it's better than the alternatives already on the market?

In the previous chapters you have done the following: You have mapped the apps that are in your field, and you have identified the features that are primary required to create an excellent first version of your app with the needs that you have identified.

Therefore, it's now possible for you to compare your solution (MVP app) with the existing apps on the market. Hopefully, you will discover that you've prioritised some features higher than them and so you have a good starting point to create an app that differentiates itself from other apps on the market. You'll be surprised how different the solutions can be for the same problem, and you must be very aware of this now when you re-analyse the competing solutions.

You will most likely be able to identify apps that have a very complex solution among the competing apps. If one or two apps are very simple and already have the features that you believe most in, then you should probably consider what you can do to compete with these apps. Look at their downloads and when they were last updated. Both figures are indications of popularity, but also an indication of whether the company behind the app could make money. Maybe you find an app with 10,000+ downloads, but the app is just living a quiet life on the app store without being updated. It's a sign that the company not only had no money for marketing, but also that the app had no viral mechanisms to continue its growth as the money for marketing ran out.

The better you know the market, the more you will notice the differences between the solutions

There will often be a solution that has been hugely successful that perhaps you get irritated over. However, the deeper you go into the analysis of service, the easier it will be to see how your idea differentiates itself or can differentiate itself. Perhaps it's now clear that you should target your app at a specific user segment that the great solution didn't manage to hit, and which requires a slightly different functionality. Perhaps the existing solution is very complex, and maybe you can go in and do away with 50% of the secondary features in your own app, and then give your solution away for free at the beginning such as Trello or Slack has done, and also as Tinder do.

After Tinder, there were lots of dating apps that implemented a swipe feature and in many ways were similar to Tinder. But many of them have some sort of unique feature that makes them strikingly different from Tinder. For example, the Bumble app that in 2017 became the second most downloaded dating app in the United States after Tinder. Bumble's unique feature is that after a match, women have 24 hours to write to the man.

If you try to analyse this feature with the Hooked Model, it's apparent that it's a bad idea. Many matches don't come to anything because the women don't write, and this hinders Bumble's trigger to get men to use the app as a match will mean less for them because they can't be certain that will women write. Apparently, it's not a problem for Bumble, but the feature is a barrier and you should always be aware of the barriers in your app.

The example of Bumble clearly shows that you can have a lot of success with an app in a competitive dating market. In 2017, Bumble was offered USD 450 million for the app at a time when there were 12.5 million downloads, and where the app was most likely not making a profit.

> *You can succeed without doing something unique.*
> *You just have to do it better!*

If your solution is very similar to existing successful apps, then you should focus on a few other features and solve some other problems for some other users. If your solution to the problem is significantly different, and no apps are similar to yours, then it's a good idea to be very certain that the few unique features you believe in, will also work. We will look at this in the next chapters when we start to develop and test your app design.

EXPLORE "KNOWLEDGE GAPS"

There are certain questions you can't answer by looking at existing apps or conducting user interviews. It's important that you try to define the crucial things that you *don't* know. We call it "knowledge gaps" – i.e. unexplored black areas on your map that can be critical to your success.

> *Explore "knowledge gaps".*
> *What don't you know?*

Knowledge gaps are important because they require particular attention. If there is something we don't know, we humans tend to make automatic and unconscious assumptions because it can be difficult to find the knowledge to fill the knowledge gap. And sometimes you don't have the time or resources to conduct market research that can shed light on all the unknowns in your project.

Therefore, you must work with questions and hypotheses to clarify for yourself what your main assumptions are. It's essential that you focus on the few crucial assumptions that you don't have any knowledge of, but which are vital for your success. One question for clarification of a knowledge gap might be: "Will the customer order a takeaway via my app at least once a week?" You're pretty sure that potential users will use apps to order food with but you don't know how often, and your budget relies on users ordering food every week. Your assumption and hypothesis are that people will use your app to order food on average once a week. Then this is the hypothesis that you need to work on getting tested.

What are your primary assumptions?

You can then make a list of your main hypotheses and describe how you would test them, and what the outcome was of any tests. It's a time-consuming process to test hypotheses, and sometimes some hypotheses are very hard to test, or where you have to rely on analogies to other apps or services – take a "leap of faith" – jump into the unknown and trust that you're right. Don't be afraid to do so, as you may scuttle your project and lose momentum.

You can compile a list of your hypotheses as follows:

Hypothesis	Testing	Result
Knowledge Gap 1		
The user will use your app to order food on average once a week.	Via a prototype displayed as a website, it's tested whether a variety of customers order food at least once a week.	25% ordered food at least once a week.
Knowledge Gap 2		
On average, users will return to your app within 14 days and reorder.	Via a prototype displayed as a website, it's tested whether a variety of customers return and order food within 14 days.	37% returned within 14 days.

Figure 36. List of hypotheses.

If the fundamental idea behind your app is new and innovative, it won't make sense to conduct a traditional market analysis to see if there is a market. It goes without saying that you can't make a market analysis in a market that doesn't actually exist yet. When you look at analogues and antiloggers, you will also automatically get a view of potential competitors.

If your primary assumptions are also knowledge gaps, then you have a problem

It's essential to reduce the number of knowledge gaps by using analogues and antiloggers, tests, interviews and focus groups. In other words, you must find ways to test your knowledge gaps. The process of analogues and antiloggers is carried out by a computer, whereas testing takes place with contact to potential customers or users. However, it's important that you don't think you should test all knowledge gaps before you can move on. You have to see it as a process where you might go on to design the app while you test the hypotheses that you have the opportunity to test. It doesn't make sense to test all hypotheses and you just have to rely on your gut feeling and start to build the app. It can take a long time to test and conduct experiments and although it's undoubtedly a good idea to avoid wasting time and money, you also need to move on.

TEST YOUR HYPOTHESES

There are many ways to test hypotheses before you build the app or make its MVP or prototype. Alberto Savoia worked at Google when he developed the *pretotyping* concept which is to test ideas before building your prototype or MVP. In its simplicity, it's about conducting simple experiments that verify the hypotheses that are fundamental to the success of a product in the market –

most products fail when they come to market. It's neither the great ideas nor the well-built products that are missing, but rather a focus on building the right solutions and not the wrong ones.

Below are some examples of pretotyping methods and other "hacks" that you can use to get some sort of market validation of your app. Note that you can't have pretotypes for all concepts, and you can't meaningfully test all hypotheses without building your app. Functionality that is very specific and requires hardware (camera, GPS, etc.), for example, are difficult to pretotype.

Make a mockup

You can build a "fake" app, which is on your or someone else's phone, where people can browse through the different views. We review this approach in more detail in Chapter 15. The method is not really pretotyping, because the user won't have the perception of a real app since it quickly becomes apparent that it's a mockup. However, the method may be used in conjunction with some of the other methods including, for instance, when people click on an ad for your non-existent app.

Use DKK 1,000 on AdWords or Facebook ads

To get an indication of the interest in your app, you can create ads with a photo or video of your app and see how many clicks and the price you pay Facebook for that click. If you can get the price of a click under DKK 5 on Facebook, it will mean that there is interest in what your app offers. You can also promote a Facebook page.

Make a Facebook page or landing page

Once you have posted your ads, you can link them to a Facebook page or a landing page. A landing page is a website with just a home page that you can create for free using, for example, Instapage or other providers. Here you briefly and invitingly explain what your next app is all about. You can, for example, ask users to click three buttons: 1) Fantastic idea; 2) Ok idea; 3) Bad idea. They could also answer a short questionnaire and it can give you an indication of interest. Most commonly, we assess people's interest by getting them to perform an action – usually to get them to subscribe to a mailing list that alerts them of when the app is released in the app stores. It's an excellent way to contact people again, and this is the litmus test of interest in your app because here you tell what the app is about, and people indicate their interest directly by giving their e-mail address to you.

Make a website

You can create a free website with, for instance, wix.com or WordPress. This is probably the closest you can get to a real app experience for your users, and so also a pretotype of your app. If you have success with your website, you may well consider whether you really need to make an app, or whether you should continue the success on the Internet. Do you really need an accurate and fast GPS location, accelerometer and other hardware on the phone for your service to work?

> ***It's is easier said than done to test your assumptions – but that doesn't mean that you shouldn't do it***

Use a competitor's service

Maybe there are Internet services that are similar to what you want to offer users, which you can then use to get an insight into how people are using the service.

Steven from WHAT used, for instance, quiz program QZZR and questionnaire program Typeform to see what people thought of questions and quizzes on Facebook, and what it would cost to get people to click on an ad to a poll. Users gave their e-mail address via the quiz program to receive more quizzes. In that way, Steven tested both his concept (partially) and collected 11,000 e-mail addresses that he could send newsletters out to.

Create a Facebook group

Here you can talk about the project and ask questions to the group members. You may want to create events that you post, which gives you an indication of how much your topic interests users. It's vital that you are active on Facebook, and here you can test what can activate and interest your users. It must be said, however, that in 2017 Facebook significantly reduced the organic reach that groups and pages could achieve. Therefore, you can use a lot of resources to build a community on Facebook, and it really depends whether your service lends itself to a Facebook group.

Check out Google search words

If you have a consumer concept, where you sell a product or service directly to end users, then you can check how many searches are made on Google for that product or service. It's a great way to check whether there is much competition on those search words and so how large the demand is.

Create a blog

You may think that you can't write, or that people won't read what you write. But try to create a blog anyway. If you've explored a small area, there will always be someone who is interested. When you create a blog and there will be some readers who give feedback, and you also learn how to formulate the values in your app more sharply. You will also need to reflect more on what will actually attract users. Blogging is excellent for generating traffic to your app or website in the long-term, but it's a long haul, and you risk getting fed up with it as it requires a lot of blogging.

Teach and hold presentations

If you have the chance, then offer to come and visit for free and teach or give a presentation. The presentation need not be about your app, but about something related that may be of interest to a group of people. It can be time-consuming if you are in the process of developing an app, but you will get feedback and you will again be forced to communicate clearly and directly.

In any case, it's important to involve the next potential customers as much as possible. Therefore, you must continuously consider:

- How can you involve more potential customers and strengthen existing contact?
- How can you and your team train your powers of observation if they make an interesting observation?
- How do you learn about customers' frustrations that relate to your app area?
- Can you and your team take photos with your smartphone when exciting things occur with a customer action?
- How do you get customers to return in the relationship with you?

Meet the users where they are

Try to be there where users are or gather them at events, which allows you to create a relationship with them, and you can give them incentives to go to your website. When Endomondo was founded in 2012, founders Christian Birk, Mette

Lykke, and Jacob Jønck went to running events throughout Denmark and handed out flyers telling about the exercise app.

You can't get users involved too early

Morten Resen was already known by parts of the public when he took the initiative to start the GoLittle app. GoLittle is an app that is similar to TripAdvisor but for families with children. He made a series of podcasts about the whole GoLittle process, and it turned out that these podcasts were the most played in Denmark in 2017. In addition to podcasts, Morten Resen posted on Facebook and posted short videos on YouTube, where he asked anyone who could recommend great places for families with children to write to him. He was very busy, as he wanted to reply to everyone personally. In return, he built up a relationship with hundreds of people who had written to him to suggest great places for the app.

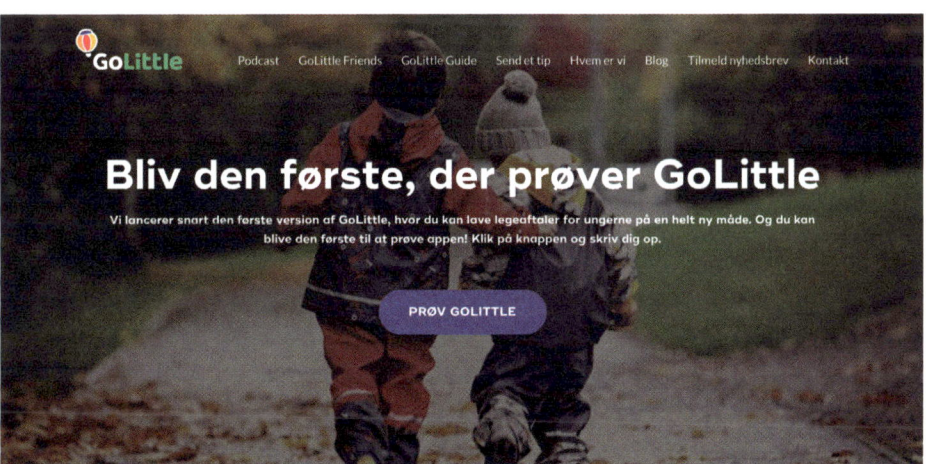

Figure 37. GoLittle's landing page before their launch.

Figure 37 shows GoLittle's website before their launch. When you clicked on "Try GoLittle", a page appeared where you could write your name, e-mail address and phone number, and you could also write the age of your children. Once you had filled in the form, you would be among the first to be allowed to try GoLittle. Morten Resen also posted a short video on Facebook that was seen 111,000 times in 6 months in December 2017. At the end of 2017, his podcasts had been downloaded more than 1 million times, after only running for about a year.

Why is it so important to establish early relationships with users?

When you have created relationships with potential users before the app is ready to be launched, it's to learn about user behaviour. Moreover, it's to get an indication of whether you are on track with the app and the value you offer. Finally, it's essential to have an enthusiastic group of users ready for the day the app is launched so you can quickly get feedback.

> Andreas and his partner from dating app Venyo thought it would make the most sense for them if they programmed their app early, so they turned to some developers in Ukraine and got a quote of DKK 95,000.
>
> They hadn't built any real relationship to potential users before programming began. They had been in contact with some students at Copenhagen Business School (CBS) early on, but it turned out that the main target group was to be found elsewhere than among students. After a while, they realised that it would create more value if the app were more closely linked to specific clubs.
>
> Only when the app was finished and almost ready for launch

did Venyo start the process of identifying users, but it was harder than they had expected.

They made agreements with clubs on, for example, a free bar until midnight if you downloaded Venyo. However, they soon discovered that they didn't quite hit the target group with these actions. Some people already had a boy/girlfriend and weren't interested in dating. They also went to parties at CBS and offered free beer if people downloaded the app, but they found out that people weren't interested in downloading apps when they're at a party.

THE DESIGN PHASE

14. DESIGN YOUR APP

Once you have determined that your app with its MVP features has a chance in the app stores, then it's time to draw app views with features. App design follows a logical progression from users' needs and considerations about the features that the app should contain, and then the app's architecture, navigation and interaction design.

Get a sharp design in place from the start

It's imperative that at this time you have agreed on what features the app should contain, especially if you work in a team. Of course, there's still room to change decisions on features based on sketches and brainstorming, but it quickly becomes more time-consuming to change once you're in the process of drawing in Photoshop or have a designer doing the job.

DESIGN IN LAYERS

The design phase is divided into five levels, each with their logic, and in which we have taken our starting point here. The levels are illustrated below:

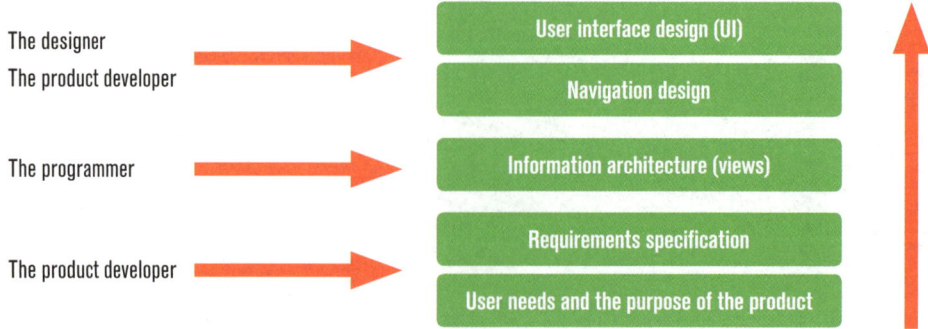

Figure 38. Design levels.

You read the figure from the bottom and start with the users' needs and the app's purpose, which we dealt with in Chapters 6-9. Against this background, we made a functional description of the app and its MVP features in Chapters 10 and 11. With these two levels in place, we are ready to focus on the top three layers that deal with app architecture, user interface design and user experience.

The advantage of following this model is that it becomes clearer how different disciplines affect the project. The model can be a guide for you in this early phase of the project where ideas, features and design are still not clearly defined.

Learn what "level" your designer and your programmer are thinking on

The lower two levels are the app developer's domain. The programmer must realise the app on the top three levels based on the requirement specification (level 4). Therefore, the programmer starts with the app architecture (level 3), which must be in place before they can effectively develop at levels 2 and 1. The app developer and designer will tend to focus on design details at the top level, which is more emotional orientated. These details are like furniture or painting a newly built house, i.e. the last thing you do once you have made sure that the architecture is in place, data flows, database and server setup is stable and so on.

The three upper levels are design, but it's important that you work from the bottom up. So, you start with an overall structure (views), and then you design each view and navigation between views. If you start by focusing on the upper level, which is the graphical elements of your user interfaces (e.g. icon design and animations), then you can end up spending too much time and get stuck in the details. If you don't have a designer, the top level of graphic design may be slightly too much of a mouthful for you. Therefore, it's better to focus on what you can do in the beginning. In this book, we have chosen to go into more detail with view design and user navigation between views, and we will focus less on the specific design.

The app's architecture and navigation

App architecture is about how information is presented to the user on a general level. Standard elements of an app's architecture are a main-view, top-navigation, bottom-navigation, possibly signup/signin view and a settings view. These elements are used in the major apps (Facebook, Instagram, WhatsApp, Twitter), but not in Snapchat, which doesn't have a top and bottom navigation where the user has a clear view of where they are in the app. Snapchat has received a lot of criticism for this, but the app is an excellent example that it's possible to think differently and succeed.

Meet your users' expectations for design

In general, we recommend that you use standard navigation and follow the design guidelines from Apple[34] and Google.[35] They are very well written and you can learn a lot from reading them. However, you must remember to stick to your own ideas, and that the two guidelines each represent their "true" design school for apps. If all apps were designed according to one of the two guidelines, it would be a boring app store, and there would be no apps like Snapchat, who dared to challenge the traditional way of doing things. However, your chances of success are obviously greater if you meet your users' expectations and design an app where the user instinctively knows where various information can be found.

Figure 39. Snapchat's main-view.

Figure 40. Instagram feed.

Snapchat starts in the camera and the largest button is the camera button. It's clear that the app suggests you must take a photo and send it to somebody else, and then that person is drawn into the app.

Instagram's main-view and navigation are entirely different. Here the user starts by seeing photos from other people, and so the app paves the way for you to consume the content and that you don't immediately make new content. With bottom-navigation, the user always knows where they are in the app, and the app can easily handle more features and views than, say Snapchat.

Stick to design standards
– it makes your life easier

Note that the bottom-navigation on an iPhone app is sometimes moved to the top of an Android phone because many Android phones have several built-in navigation buttons (including a "back-button") in the display or on the phone where an iPhone has only one button. It's these details that can make it very complicated to build apps when phones are constantly changing appearance, and since there are many standards specifically for Android phones.

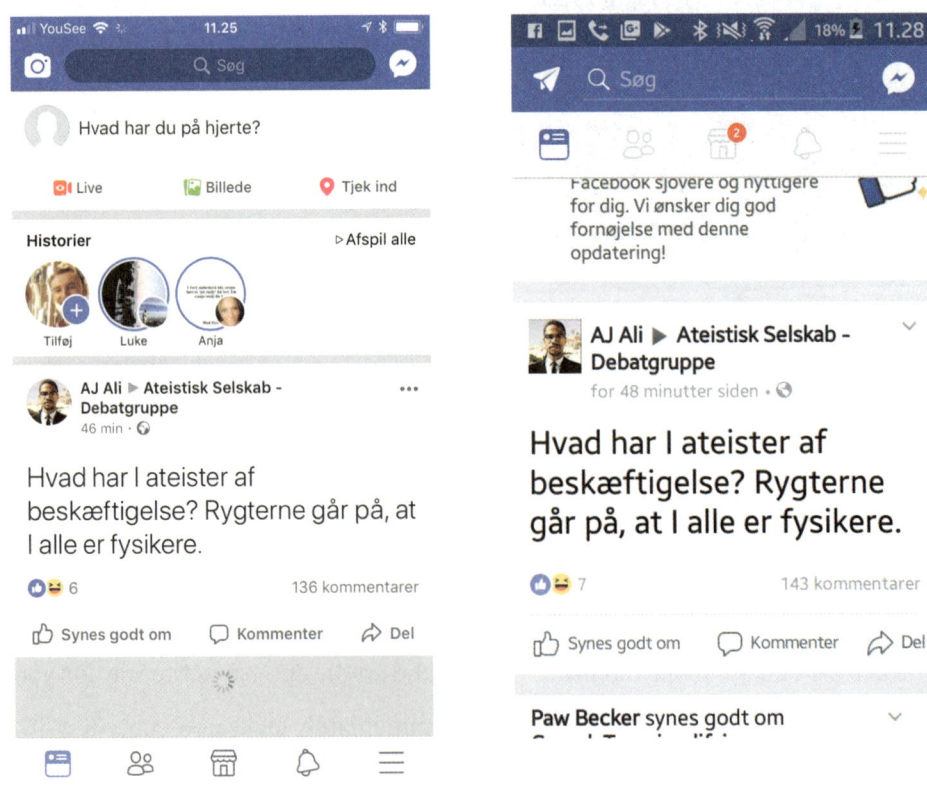

Figure 41. Facebook's main-view.

Figure 41 shows Facebook's main-view, i.e. right where Facebook wants you to spend the most time. Just like Instagram, you view the content of Facebook in their feed, where you will be updated on everything that has happened in your network.

Facebook's iPhone app (left) has a distinct top- and bottom-navigation, where the bottom is the primary, and the top is used for filters and a search feature. Facebook is used primarily to keep in touch and stay updated with your network, and this is probably why Facebook has put a search box in the top-navigation, as many people often use this feature.

When designing your app, you need to decide what should be in your main-view. What is the primary content that you want to show your users and to attract them to the app? How will the user navigate around the app based on the main-view?

Observe the rules in the app stores

Next, find out what features should be in your onboarding flow, i.e. the views that precede the user entering the main-view. Finally, you need to design a settings-view. Settings must be kept quite simple at first, but, in turn, will accommodate many settings as your app grows in complexity. For example, go into Facebook's or Snapchat's settings and you will see an incredible number of settings for using the app.

Note that there are some requirements for your app from both Apple and Google (mostly from Apple), compared to contacting a support page and Terms of Service. You must read and comply with the requirements of Apple and Google; otherwise you risk that the respective app stores don't approve your app.

Now you should have some "empty" views without content, other than (perhaps) a top- and bottom-navigation, a settings-view and an onboarding flow. You have a vague idea of how the user navigates around in your app, but you haven't yet put content in your views.

User interface design

In Figure 42, you can see an example of a navigation design of parts of an app. In practice, your app will consist of anything from 20 to 100 views, if you draw all the views that the user can potentially end up in. The arrows from the interaction elements (such as a button) are important because they illustrate your users' navigation through the app, and this is done in "wireframes" as seen in the example below.

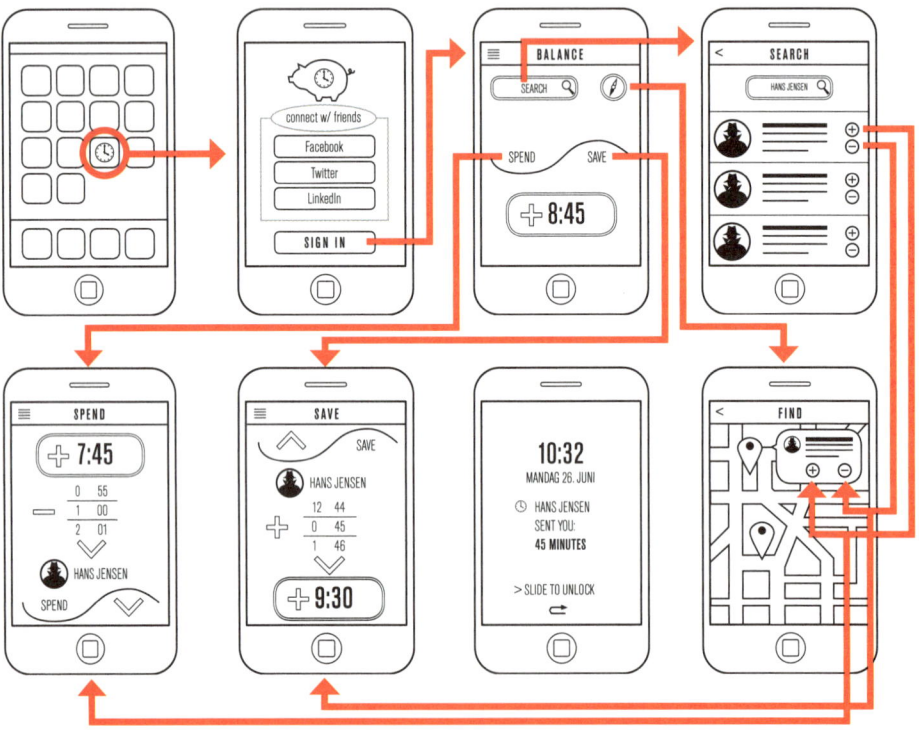

Figure 42. Navigation design with wireframe's navigation arrows.

Note how navigation with each additional feature becomes more complicated – it's crucial to keep it to a minimum. For instance, consider what one like on your content does to the app's complexity. The user should be able to press the like icon, but they must also be able to see how many others have pressed it. Next, all other users of the app must see that the content has received another like. Perhaps the content is displayed in more than one way, and then the like feature also has to be in these views.

It's a lot of work to make a complete drawing of your app's navigation, and it can be frustrating because many things can change when you modify just one feature. At the same time, you may have the feeling that you're going nowhere because there are so many unknowns. However, it's at this stage that you save yourself and your future designer and programmer a lot of questions, discussions and misunderstandings.

Draw your user interfaces by hand

We recommend that you draw on a whiteboard or a large blackboard to get a full overview of your app's views, and so you can move the different views around and get an overview of the navigation between views in the app. You can give the individual views numbers or names and draw them by hand. It's a huge advantage to draw by hand because you outline your ideas much quicker and throw the sketch away and start over. It's harder digitally, especially if you're not used to using design and mockup programs.

Navigation in your app is not just about communicating clearly to the user what he or she can do in the app. As in Snapchat, it's about you prioritising the features in the navigation that you want the user to use. We call it "objective-thinking" because you have to think of your app as some priorities that ultimately support your business model. The objective is linked to the user journeys that your users are going through, which we call "path-thinking" because you need to make sure that users make actions in your app as quickly as possible that meet the app's objective. Once you have your objectives and paths in place, it's ultimately much more straightforward to analyse how your app is doing, and where users drop off from a path towards taking decisive action.

Objective-thinking. What do you want users to do so you achieve your objective? You must think of your app as a means or medium where your users do what you want them to. When you define objectives with your users' actions, it becomes clearer if your app does what it's meant to do.

Objectives can be many things, but it makes sense to relate them to acquisition (an activated user), activation, retention (the user returns) and referrals (the user shares the app with other people). Therefore, objectives can be prioritised, since a user must be activated as a user in the system before they can start using the app and so fulfil the other objectives in the app. It's vital to keep this in mind and not, for example, use too much energy getting users to make an in-app purchase if the more primary problem is that users have never understood what the app can do in the activation process. You can run the risk of trying to solve a problem in the wrong place if you don't focus on solving the fundamental problems first, typically relating to activation, the first experience of the app, value proposition and so on.

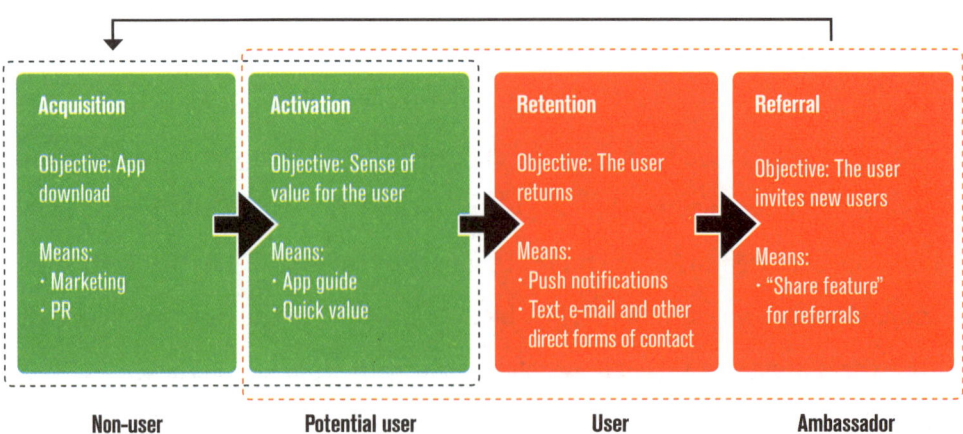

Figure 43. Overview of objective priorities.

Figure 43 shows your user's "journey" with you and your app from acquisition and activation (the acquisition funnel) to retention and referral.

Once activated, a person is only a potential user because a user (mostly) has to use your app regularly to be a "real" user (more on that in the next chapter). Only very enthusiastic users recommend apps to other users, so we choose to call those ambassadors.

Your user journey is comparable to the user journey in any retail shop. Customers must first hear about your shop before they go into it. When customers come through the door, you want to seduce them, and you want them to buy a product. If the customer is happy with your service and your product, then the customer returns, and if the customer has received a lot of value, they will also recommend the shop to their friends, and then you get more customers.

It's essential to have the entire user journey in mind all the time, although it may be tempting to only focus on getting app downloads. There is, in fact, an overlap between the different phases. For example, marketing and advertising design are dependent on the app's characteristics and value factors. At the same time, user and brand experience should be consistent from when the user sees the first advert to them using the app.

To activate (and validate) new users with Facebook login (or another third party service), it's also essential which options you have to retain users within the app, such as via Facebook, where you can get profile photos and friend lists, so it's easier for new users to find their friends in your app.

It sounds abstract, so let's look at an example.

> The WHAT app's business model is that users pay to get answers to questions from market research, and for this to succeed, it must be easy and fun to answer questions. The most important thing for WHAT's design is that it's easy for users to answer the questions.

Path-thinking. It's crucial that you see your primary and secondary objectives as if they were the end of a path that you have designed. Your objective is to keep users on the path by "luring" them and communicating with signs, etc., so they achieve your objective even though it might take a little time and maybe a little brain power. You must design a "path" for each objective you want to open in your app, and once again, it's probably best with an example.

Think of "paths" that your user must go along

WHAT has four paths with associated objectives:

1. **Onboarding-path** (objective: to get the user to the app). Onboarding is always a path that needs to relate to when you need your user to download your app and perhaps register and make other actions until they are in your app as a real user. WHAT is a social media where the user must register, which they must do for security reasons, among other things. Registration can be done with Facebook, which makes it easier for the user.

2. **Answer-path** (objective: to get the user to answer questions). It's important in WHAT that the user can easily and quickly answer the questions. Users participate in draws for prizes when they answer questions, and they see the answers to the questions they have answered, which creates an incentive for the user to answer.

> **3. Ask-path** (objective: to get the user to ask questions on the platform). To create a fun platform with relevant user-created content it must be easy for users on WHAT to make their own questions. It's very complex to make questions if you have to consider various answer categories that other users see when they answer a question. Should there, for instance, be photos with the question? There are many considerations here.
>
> **4. Share-paths** (objective: to get the user to share). For WHAT to go viral and become a major app, sharing relevant content has been designed into many of the app's views. "Share-paths" are not, therefore, long paths, such as the onboarding-path.

Your paths consist of some actions and considerations that your users have to go through. The idea is to reduce the complexity of these choices as much as possible, allowing the user to move quickly to perform the action in the app that provides value to you (and hopefully value to the user).

It's worth thinking about how to create value for the user with a reward for users to act in a certain way. In WHAT, the user sees other peoples' answers to a question after they have answered. See the Hooked Model that creates a loop in which the user gives something to get something.

Objective- and path-thinking helps you to not only focus your app but also to evaluate it. Analysis software such as Firebare and Applytics help you to visualise whether users follow your paths, or they jump off along the way. If they do, you can step in and perhaps in the long-term, modify a few things in the app to get more users to take the right action, so they proceed on the path towards making the decisive action. It may be that a purchase button has to be bigger or green to attract more attention and get people to make an in-app purchase of your service.

Below is an example of what it might look like when you have analysis software to show the completion rate for a path. The figure is based on all those who have seen the app on the app store (100%), and how many of them that then downloaded the app (85%), opened the app after downloading (80%), signed up (70%) and then made the first value-creating in-app action (50%).

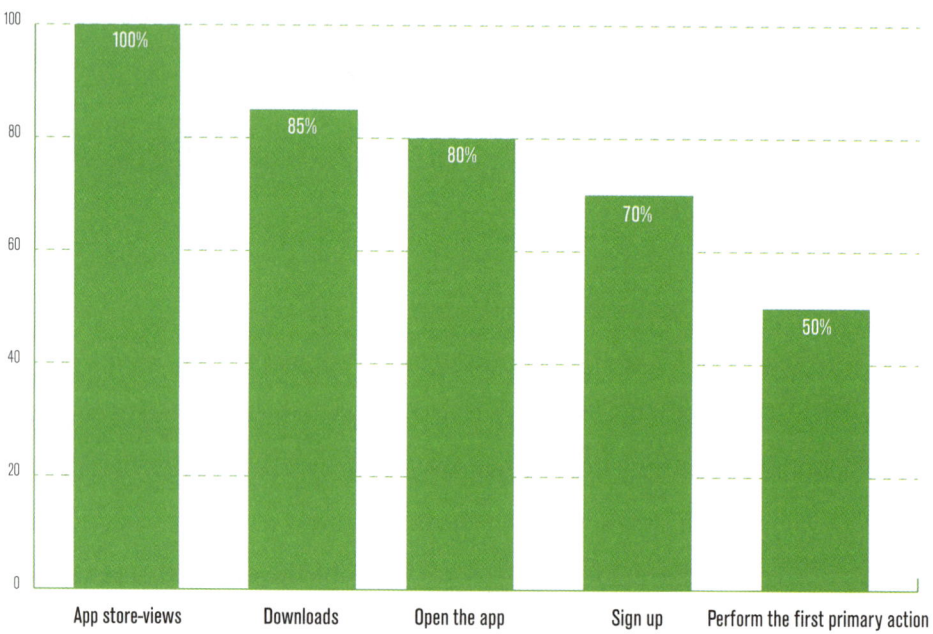

Figure 44. Analysis of the completion rate on a path with the use of software.

If you want to focus your views, you can try to answer the following questions for each app-view: What action would you like the user to make in this view? Ideally, the user only considers one thing in each view, so they don't get confused and might leave the path. And then you ask: Where should the user go when they make the (one) choice that you gave them? What do they get out of it? Why would they make the choice?

One pitfall is your own view of the app and its possibilities. It's very dangerous to assume that the user has a "memory" and takes actions based on information that the app has given the user previously. For example, you should never assume that the user has read the messages in the app's onboarding-views and remembered them, or that the user "can figure something out" based on information that is available in other views. Think of your user as a mouse that you have to get through a maze, where you must place a small piece of cheese at every corner because you can't count on the mouse looking around the next corner, if it's easier to go out of the maze again.

Anyone can create wireframes, but not everyone can design a cool app

If you're going to build a large global platform, then it's worth considering getting a professional app designer to design your views based on your wireframes. The designer will create a graphic identity with colours, buttons and app icons, fonts, images and possibly audio and photos. This process should preferably take place in close collaboration with the app developer, who is familiar with the users, their needs and problems. For large app projects, it's an advantage that the designer sits with the rest of the team.

If your app is simple with little functionality and not necessarily part of a broader commercial context, you can easily manage with icons and graphics from the Internet. There are many sites on the Internet where you can download finished views to Photoshop or Sketchbook that are ready to work with, and there are many services online where you can buy icons. Otherwise, you can hire a cheap designer online at 99designs or Upwork to adjust your design before it's delivered to the programmer.

Teach yourself Photoshop – it will save you time and money

In general, we recommend that you try to use Adobe Photoshop and Adobe Illustrator or Sketch. If you download the design or get a professional designer to make the design, you can save a lot of time and money if you can adjust the design before the programmer has to use it. There will invariably be a need for design adjustments, and it's a great advantage to be able to do some of it yourself. Although the programs are advanced, they are relatively easy to start using, and when you need to make something special, you can find everything explained on YouTube.

If you can work in Photoshop or Sketch, you get more control of your project, while you can release more of the designer's time to think about the user experience and make the cool details (e.g. icons), which is very difficult for you to make if you're not a designer. This gives you the most value for money and you don't have to pay the designer each time a comma needs correcting.

15. TEST YOUR PROTOTYPE

You've made wireframes and given them to a designer, or you've designed the app yourself with templates from the Internet or from scratch – it's now time to test your design.

There are many ways to test the design, and it seems to be one of the areas that many people skip, but which in practice is also quite difficult. You've already made a thorough competitor and user analysis, so why should you now test your design that maybe has been made by a very talented app designer? How long should it take to test the design and what does it cost?

However, it's important to test your design in relation to 1) the navigation logic; 2) communication clarity with icons, text and images; 3) the app structure; 4) the aesthetic qualities of the app. In short: Is the app visually coherent and is the brand (colour, line, tone, etc.) consistent in the app and possibly also on the company's website? Can the user navigate through the app, and is it clear what to do in different views? Can the user see the value of using it (the fun, the entertainment, the function, etc.)?

Design tests are not testing the app's purpose or the app's value to users, though it does overlap. It's important that you now focus on the design because you've already validated the quality of your idea. You must also remember that the design test is only an early "rehearsal", which can't possibly measure up to getting real users on the app. It's one phase of the app's development, which leads to the app becoming slightly sharper conceptually, and what the programmer must make is more clearly defined.

QUANTITATIVE TESTS WITH PROFESSIONAL TESTERS

If you are very thorough, have plenty of time and resources, then you can use InVisionApp or similar software to upload your app-views as image files and link them to print interactions in the photos. You can then download the "app" to your phone where it's on your home-screen with the other apps. When you click on the app icon, the app opens, and you can click around in it. You can share the link with others, so the "app" is also on their phones.

It's a smart tool if you need to present the app to investors or test it before you have a single line of code. There are many websites on the Internet[36] where you can post your link to the test version and where testers can test it for USD 1-10 per test. You can ask them specific questions and you can get video footage of the tests, where the tester tells of their first impressions of the app. The cheaper the test, the more mediocre and more inexperienced the testers. If you choose this option, you must have at least 30 testers and preferably 100-200, so you can see patterns in the data generated.

It's easy to get feedback on a prototype, but it's not easy to get useful and accurate feedback

However, there are many practical challenges in getting semi-professional testers to test your app design at an early stage. Besides it could end up being very expensive and time-consuming to coordinate, it can also be difficult for even a seasoned tester to relate to a mockup, even when it's made in InVisionApp or other professional software.

It can take a week to put the design into InVisionApp, and then it takes a few weeks to organise an online test and get the results. At the same time, the testers can become so confused that it's not a real app they are testing that their reactions and feedback can be reinforced in negatively. Although you can brief them about the app and its purpose, many of them will not have understood the purpose or know the area, and therefore their comments can be misleading, and the whole exercise may end up being a waste of time. The wow effect that your final app might be able to provide is guaranteed to be absent in a mockup test, where there are no fantastic animations and transitions, no dynamic updates of views, etc. It can also be difficult to find testers that match your specific target group.

You can always choose to use testers who offer their services for free, and that's often what ends up happening. But there is an even higher risk of you wasting your time with bad answers from people who don't quite understand what the prototype is.

QUALITATIVE TESTS

A cheaper way to test is to let friends, acquaintances and people in the target group open the app by sharing the link to your InVisionApp mockup. There is also software that can create session recordings such lookback.io or UXCam, but it's important that you or another person sit next to them and fill them in on how they test the app, pick up on their reactions and help them around in the app if the mockup doesn't quite work as intended. It's essential that you don't guide them through the app, but only help them get started and help them if they get stuck. You don't answer questions, but instead get the test person to talk about their experience while they go through the app. Experience shows that it can be extremely difficult for even technically savvy friends to open the app properly, keep their concentration and provide adequate feedback beyond "it looks really good".

The advantage of qualitative tests is that you have more time to explain the concept, which is often needed when the app still only exists as a mockup. Maybe your testers already know the idea, but now they want to see it materialise in the design, and you may experience the first eye-opener from your user group or your family members.

Qualitative interviews and observations are cheap and excellent methods

You will need about 20-30 qualitative user tests to get enough data to see patterns in people's answers. Perhaps some features are unclear, some views may be too messy and so on. The disadvantage of qualitative guided tests is, of course, that there may be a bias because the subjects are relatively few and maybe even know you. But tests can, in turn, be easily arranged, and in a week, you can conduct 20-30 tests in house.

EXPERT TESTS

The last option is to involve 2-4 "experts". If you have had an experienced app designer on the project, they're already an expert. But you can also ask other app or UX designers if they want to spend two hours looking at your app design. This may be the most effective way to test your app design, because a design expert knows all the many conditions that apply to the developer, on the various app platforms and so on. You can't explain those relationships to your test subjects.

Expert testers and friends are usually the quickest and best way to test your app concept

The experts can advise on iconography, copy-writing and navigation, and they know about app development and digital product development and how users behave in digital products. It's a highly specialised discipline and compared to other testers, there is a much higher chance that they understand the whole app product, including the business model, user journey, marketing, value for users in the concept and so on. And in our opinion, the overview creates more value at the current time in the app's development than quantitative tests that take too long and are too expensive and resource intensive, given the quality of the feedback you get.

Once you've tested your concept, you should be left with a solid foundation for developing your app. By prioritising, designing and testing the features of your app idea with mockups and good wireframes, you reduce the risk that programmers spend months on features that people don't understand because they are unnecessary, or merely because the user interface is poorly designed. The next section deals with the development process and choice of technology.

FROM TESTING TO APP

16. CHOICE OF TECHNOLOGY

An app is not just an app. Every app on the market differs in some way from the others in design or function – or, perhaps most importantly, in the choice of technology. Just the choice of technology is crucial and will have severe consequences for your options, costs of development and maintenance, and not least, the user experience of the app.

You can generally divide apps into three categories: native apps, web apps and hybrid apps (also called "shell apps"). There are pros and cons of each type, and you must make your choice based on what your app is intended to do, and what requirements there are for the app's performance (see the checklist in Figure 46). However, your budget partly plays an important role in both the short- and long-term, and partly it's your access to programmers with the right skills and your control of development cost is important in the long-term.

The question of which type of app is best has developed into an almost religious debate among app developers. Therefore, we advise you to focus on making a choice, then you 1) get your app out as quickly as possible, and 2) can get it developed for as little money as possible. If you make a gaming app, the choice is, however, already made for you. Here you need to choose a native app because of the high requirements on performance that games often have when they must run fast graphics on the phone.

It can be costly to make the wrong choice

Here you have an overview that gives you a picture of the pros and cons of each of the three categories:

	Native app	**Hybrid app**	**Web app**
Advantages	• Best performance and speed regarding graphics and access to the phone's hardware. • Can work offline (as a program on a computer). • Direct access to all hardware components on the phone, such as GPS, accelerometer, camera, etc. • Updates rolled out automatically.	• A code base that can be reused on both platforms. • Close to native performance (except for the fast graphic representation, such as in game apps). • Lower development costs than native due to code reuse across platforms. • Low maintenance costs due to code reuse. • Can work offline. • Access to all hardware elements of your phone, i.e. camera, GPS, etc. • The code base can be partially reused on your website.	• Lower development costs because web coding is less specialised than native coding. • Takes less time to develop. • Users don't have to download updates. • Easier (cheaper) to maintain. • Doesn't have to be downloaded from an app store. • No fees on sales through the app when not in an app store.
Dis-advantages	• In general, more expensive to develop because native development is more specialised. • You have to develop an app for each platform (Android and iOS), i.e. you can't reuse the code base. • Longer development time. • Must be constantly updated when there are OS updates.	• Must be continuously updated when there are OS updates. • Lower speed for complex data processing. • The cost quickly approaches native if performance must be matched. • Still dependent on native elements.	• Performance and speed are worse. • No access to the phone's hardware, i.e. camera, GPS, etc. • Doesn't offer user interaction with native gestures, i.e. tap, swipe, zoom, etc. • Only works with an Internet connection. • Doesn't offer in-app purchases, etc., like native apps do.
Examples of apps	Snapchat, Pokémon GO	Facebook, Instagram	Sarahah

Figure 45. Advantages and disadvantages of app categories.

NATIVE APPS

If you want to develop the best app, you need to develop it as a native app, which allows for the best performance and a superior graphics experience that is in high demand among users. A native app can communicate directly with the operating system on your smartphone because they speak the same language. In practice, this means that native apps are much more reliable and work better with the screen, GPS, camera, sensors, etc.

However, options and performance aren't free. It's expensive to hire specialised programmers for both an Android app and iPhone app because you have to build and maintain two code bases continuously.

Native is best – but also expensive

Native apps are called "native" because the code is "compiled" and interpreted into ones and zeros – the language a computer understands on the underlying hardware, in this case, the phone itself. To develop "native" can be compared to having the whole toolbox available that Google and Apple have developed. The programmer can press all buttons, just like recording a music album, where you rent a professional recording studio with huge mixing consoles, and every little tone can be adjusted.

A native app is the right choice if you make a gaming app, or your app requires fast graphic interactions to give the user the right experience. Snapchat is an example of a non-game app that also requires many graphic resources and high speed because of the advanced graphical display of the filters.

Another example of a native app is Pokémon Go, which utilises the smartphone to the fullest. First of all, the app uses GPS, so it knows your location relative to the Pokémons, PokéStops, Gyms, etc. Next, the app uses the camera to create Augmented Reality (AR), so you can catch Pokémon in the real world. AR places heavy demands on the processor in your smartphone, so here the app is heavily dependent on being able to communicate directly with the processor through the operating system. And the "native swipe gesture" that you use when you shoot your PokéBall at Pikachu is also a feature that wouldn't work as well on hybrid and probably wouldn't operate satisfactorily on a web app.

WEB APPS

Web apps are different from native apps because the browser interprets the code you write on the phone, i.e. the software interprets software, whereas the smartphone interprets native and hybrid apps. It gives web apps the advantage that they can run on all types of operating systems, as the phone just has to have a "compatible" browser installed such as Safari, Chrome or Internet Explorer.

A web app should therefore not be installed just like a native app. A web app is basically a website which opens on the phone as an app through your phone's browser (Safari for iPhone and Google Chrome for Android). Therefore, the app is also dependent on a stable Internet connection to function.

The code language is usually HTML, CSS and JavaScript. This means that a web app communicates indirectly with the operating system because the Internet browser will be a connecting link. The connecting link increases the complexity significantly, which often affects reliability, performance and attractiveness negatively.

The advantage of web apps is that they are cheap and quick to make. Therefore, it can be ideal to make a MVP version of your app if you quickly need to have many users on a simple service, or if your service is not very complicated. They can also be search optimised as Google can index the app just like a website. This makes the app easier to find since the user doesn't first have to enter a "closed" app store to find the app.

Are web apps the future? Maybe?

Google has launched "progressive web apps" that takes web apps much closer to hybrid and native. It's so new that we don't know of any or have experience with it. The coming years will surely make web technology so far advanced that it might threaten app stores and change the way we access apps on our various devices.

A web app is right for you if 1) your service doesn't rely on data from the phone's GPS, accelerometer and other hardware elements; and 2) if you don't display fast graphics updates. If you need one or both of these elements, you should choose either hybrid or native.

HYBRID APPS

Hybrid apps are, as the name might suggest, a combination of native and web apps. In practice, this means that the app's code is a combination of native and web code. Besides functioning much better with the different operating systems, because they contain a native element, the hybrid apps are also released and downloaded through the various app stores. However, there may be a huge difference in how much of that is native, and how much of that is web. Some would argue that hybrid apps have the best of both worlds, but this very much depends on the purpose of the app.

> *Hybrid is (perhaps still is) the best of the two worlds*

In practice, the web code is packed into a native and then called a wrapper. The wrapper acts as a connecting link that still interprets the code in a browser, but the elements of the code "talk" with the hardware, typically with elements of Swift and Java. This means that a wrapper must be developed for each operating system, but that the same web code can be used on both platforms, i.e. iOS and Android, which reduces the initial development costs significantly.

Wrappers are developed with special software called cross-platform development tools that are released by companies who are paid to give access to their specialised tools. The most well-known companies are Xamarin, PhoneGap and Appcelerator. Many develop open source as well, such as Cordova/PhoneGap plugins. But the downside is that a single update from, for instance, Apple can take several plugins out of play at the same time. If you don't have the development skills in-house or you don't know much about native code, you have to wait for the creator or company of the plugin, to fix an update of their plugin. Until then, it won't work. This could be a Facebook login plugin that doesn't work after a Facebook update, which means that no one can log in to your app. Of course, it's the same with native apps, but there your own developer hopefully understands Facebook's update and then makes the modification native.

Hybrid apps really took off in 2017, and many predict that web-based apps are going to be huge. In the past few years, hybrid apps have gone from mediocre performance to be nearly as good as native apps on most points. Even Mark Zuckerberg from Facebook decided that the Facebook app should be developed as a hybrid because he realised that development speed is so much faster than native. Instagram has also evolved as a hybrid app, but it can cheat a little because Facebook has so many development resources (Facebook owns Instagram) and programmers that have made the hybrid language (React Native), which the two apps work on (and which is now open source), and we don't know how much is native, and how much is web on the two apps. So just because large and successful apps are hybrid doesn't mean you can just assume that hybrid will be best for your own app.

You should consider a hybrid app if you don't develop a game app or an app that requires quick views of graphics, photos and sound. There are some frameworks you can use if you want to develop an app quickly – and if you're willing to make a slight compromise on your own design. Ionic is an option that many people use to make their first MVP solution. Ionic has design components and is based on Cordova Open Source, but there are others out there, and the landscape is changing rapidly.

WHAT TYPE OF APP SHOULD YOU CHOOSE?

The million-dollar question is, of course, which type of app should you choose? It can be costly to make the wrong choice, and it may very well ruin your progress and maybe your company. Development is moving so fast that the choices you make here and now may be right, but it's changed when you're ready to launch the app.

> *Your choice of technology is vital and represents a risk that you must learn to live with*

In general, two things must be in place before you are ready to choose: 1) You must have completed all your wireframes and design of your app, as well as your requirements specification of all your features for your MVP and ideas, which is a little more long-term. 2) You need to contact various skilled programmers in your network and ask them what type of system and technology they would recommend.

Furthermore, we've made a small checklist that can help you to assess how complex your solution is, and so how large the requirements are for the frontend, backend and the programmers and the team that in the short- and long-term shall make the solution.

You want to make an app that …	Your need	Put an X
… can be used worldwide.	All types of apps. Potentially involves many users and requires a potentially advanced server setup to handle the many users.	
… shows fast graphics, animations or AR like Pokémon Go.	Only native apps (iOS and Android).	
… displays content created by many user interactions like Facebook, where people post, like, comment, etc.	Native and hybrid apps. The database must be able to handle exponential development in the amount of data.	
… displays content that is dependent on data from API integrations with other services, such as financial data from the world's stock exchanges.	All types of apps. Can create a bottleneck regarding working with poorly documented APIs, and so takes a long time to integrate with.	
… makes money.	Payments always increase the complexity slightly.	
… uses GPS location, accelerometer or other "native" hardware.	Native and hybrid apps.	
… must be available for both iOS and Android.	All types of apps.	
… must also be released in a special edition for a tablet.	Best as native.	
Number of crosses		

Figure 46. Checklist to assess app complexity.

If your app only scores 0 or very few points, it's simple to make. An example of such an app could be an app made by a small company with an overview of their product range. Generally speaking, the more an app creates interaction between many people, the more complex it is.

Although web apps are the cheapest, it can quickly become costly if you expect to develop an app on par with native, and developers will soon have problems delivering what you want. The same applies in principle for hybrid apps, but you can get a lot further in complexity before developers start having problems.

The developers are also challenged when native apps increase in complexity, but the point is that you have all the tools. The only challenge is whether your programmer can figure out how to use them.

WHAT IS BEST PRACTICE?

In most cases, you can get far with hybrid apps, and as mentioned, many world-renowned apps started as a hybrid because it was vital for them to reach as many users as possible with as cheaply as possible. You must remember that you have the same needs – to reach as far as possible at the lowest possible cost.

Can it really be true? Yes, it can. Facebook, Instagram, Uber and Airbnb all started as websites, i.e. hybrid apps, and only later changed to native because it would increase the app's performance and user experience. Facebook and Instagram even went from native and back to hybrid because the development time was too long with native.

The point is that many of the companies that today we could never imagine would compromise, started somewhere else than where they are today. It's a good reminder that even if you're successful in the market and have a lot of money in the bank, it's still important to invest your money wisely, i.e. only when it makes sense.

Facebook and Instagram are hybrid apps

Another example is the ridesharing service GoMore that was a website before they made their native app. At that time, people were used to renting cars on their computers or phoning, so it made perfect sense. What about Jesper Buch's JustEat? The same story. They were also long established before they decided to develop an app for hungry smartphone users.

Many forget or don't realise it, but what really matters to your choice of type of app is the starting point of your company – What problem are you solving?

THE CRITICAL THING THAT NOBODY IS TALKING ABOUT – THE BACKEND

If you want to make an app, there's no avoiding having to relate to the importance of a "backend". Without getting too technical, the term backend describes a system that consists of a database and a corresponding communication module called an API. The database stores the data that users have access to in the app, such as timetables for flights, images or the weather forecast. The database also stores the data that users create themselves when they use the app, for example, user information, photos, history, friendships to other users, bookings at the fitness centre, etc.

For users to access and store content in the database, the API ensures that data is transported back and forth between the app and the database. The API is tremendously busy because it's responsible for handling all the data that users use.

> *Don't forget the "brain" behind your app – the backend. It's both more important and more demanding than you think!*

Generally, we use the term "frontend" to describe the part of a software solution that users interact with *directly*, i.e. an app or website. The concept of the backend is what we use to describe the part that users interact with *indirectly*, i.e. the database and the API.

If you have a very simple app that basically only displays information, calculates simple arithmetic, etc., then it can easily be handled solely in an app. However, as soon as there is advanced data processing, your app must have a backend, and the more advanced the processing, the higher the demands on your backend.

Let's look at an example. What actually happens technically when you press "like" on a fun post in the "Friends of Monty Python" group on Facebook? We've made the following list to illustrate the complexity of the action that would otherwise seem quite trivial.

You sit with your phone and press "like" and the Facebook app now gives you a choice between several emoji that assures you that you actually pressed the button. At the same time, your like is sent to the database, where it's associated with the unique post (ID3224nojlk2j34) that which you know as the "Friends of Monty Python" group, but in the database, it has ID number G2399348283784892ndknkn343iu2. Your like is saved and associated with a post in a group that is created by a person at a certain time and so on. All the data is in the database and is related to each other.

But we're not finished, because now you and everyone else who follows the "Friends of Monty Python" group can see that you've liked the post. The number of likes is updated, and your name is shown to other users. This is typically done by the backend updating your status, which is read by all relevant clients who then see the most recent data for the whole post.

As you can see, the Facebook app must ask or update based on a change in the backend (a refresh), for you to get a good user experience. It doesn't mean that you click "like" and it takes several minutes before the counter updates the number, and this is where the server setup is important. Facebook needs vast data centres to serve the entire world quickly and easily. Facebook is so big and has such a special need for speed and control that it can't use cloud services like, for example, Amazon. It has to have its own server infrastructure with thousands of server computers that are in massive buildings around the world, and it ensures that you and we can get a fantastic and fast experience on Facebook's frontend (Facebook app, Messenger, Instagram, WhatsApp, Facebook.com, etc.).

As you can see, your backend is extremely important. Without it, you won't have a usable app (in most cases). Fortunately, a "standard" backend setup (database and server settings) is relatively simple so that the frontend developer should be able to set it up for simple apps. However, you should carefully consider whether you need a dedicated backend developer, as the approach of a backend developer is different than that of a frontend developer. Your backend must be error-free because it can have detrimental consequences if your system is not secure enough, or if it's not built to handle the amount of data the system must process. It often takes time to think through the whole system, and it's not always the case that an "off-the-shelf" backend setup through Google Firebase or another free services can handle the features that you've planned for your app. Perhaps you quickly build a great app on the services, but suddenly there's a new feature that is unsupported, and then you have to start all over again.

A lack of security can very quickly ruin your company

Another important thing is data. Your backend must store data securely, so others can't use your API and so get hold of sensitive personal data about your users or vital trade secrets from your system. There are a variety of encryption technologies such as https or oath2. But data is also a huge resource, and it's worth considering how you store it in your system so that you can subsequently take advantage of more advanced analytics and machine learning tools to run tests on your data to optimise your service. It's often several years away for most apps, as it requires large amounts of data. However, it can be extremely valuable to have the option, and it's a shame if your data is stored in an inappropriate manner that is difficult to work with.

Where does the data come from?

If you want to make an app, then you should be able to say where the data comes from. You should be able to because the answer has significant influence on what it will take to realise your app idea. Imagine, for example, that you want to develop an app that allows users to get an overview of the opening hours of all the cafés in your city. In this context, you should be able to say where data about the cafés comes from. Most often it's a case that you have to collect and enter all data in a database, or there are already some databases that either fully or partially have what you require.

To answer the question in the example is that you must start by finding out whether you can access some lists with a complete overview of all the cafés in your city. The list should be as complete as possible as it means less manual typing for you. This means that the minimum content should have the café name, address and opening hours.

Imagine that after lying sleepless for a few nights you remember that the Danish Food Administration may have a list of all the cafés in your city because they have to make sure that the cafes meet special rules. You call them and after a few days you receive an e-mail with an Excel file of names and addresses, but no opening hours. It gets you off to a good start because you can contact all the cafés for their opening hours and then you have the data you need.

In the example above, you have created a so-called static database because it doesn't keep itself updated with the latest information. This means that if new cafés open or close down, then the database must be updated manually. If the database is dynamic, then it means that it's automatically updated with the latest information, which is obviously more valuable.

If there's no data, then you can consider the possibility of getting users to help you collect it. But remember that they must have a personal interest in spending their time on it. GoMore had no database of motorists who were interested in renting their own cars when they didn't use them. Luckily, for some motorists it was worth creating a profile at GoMore so they could earn money by renting their car and the principle is the same with Airbnb.

17. THE DEVELOPMENT PROCESS

A very common barrier to getting started with an app is that you don't possess the skills needed to make it. We can all see a need or an idea for an ingenious app, but few people have the programming experience, app design- and marketing skills needed to launch an app. Therefore, the consideration of a team certainly pops up early in the process.

You can get far without a programmer

However, you can actually get very far without a team. In fact, you increase your chances of success both with your future team and investors if you do solid groundwork. We will now look at exactly how far you can get, and when you might need the design, programmer and business development skills that we presented in the previous chapter.

For this purpose, we have made a table of the stages you will get through. You should read the table from left to right with a focus on each phase, where we describe the key skills you will need divided into three levels:

	Concept development	Design phase	Development phase	Launch phase	Operational phase
Relevant "layman topics"	• Brainstorming • Idea validation • Concept definition • Clear communication • Ad hoc idea feedback	• "Wireframing" on paper • Basic understanding of apps • Interaction design • Use of design templates for views and icons • Mockups in Photoshop	• Communication	• Communication	• Human empathy • Punctuality and order
Practice makes perfect	• Systematic qualitative user surveys with interviews and focus groups • Systematic studies of users and their needs	• Advanced knowledge of UX and user flows • Good skills in Photoshop or Sketch • Setup in InVisionApp • User psychology	• Understanding programming languages • Understanding programmers	• PR • Organic traffic • Facebook ads • AdWords	• Leadership • Management • Phone sales • Customer support • Communication
Expert level	• Quantitative user surveys with, for example, questionnaires • Understanding the needs and problems on an underlying psychological level	• Knowledge of design standards • Advanced understanding of user psychology • "Proper" use of Photoshop, Sketch and Illustrator	• Programming and understanding of new technologies	• Programming and troubleshooting • Google Analytics	• Building brand equity • Advanced communication • B2B sales • Legal, audit and administration

Figure 47. Phases of the development process.

We recommend that you only get reinforcements and build a team when you need expert knowledge from the bottom row but try to get as far as possible on your own. By team, we don't necessarily mean a full-time employee. It can also be help from a friend or outsourcing the task to a freelancer.

WHEN DEVELOPMENT STARTS

Now you need to decide if you should get a programmer on your team, or whether you can hire a freelancer. It depends a lot on the app's complexity, which we have described in the previous chapter. If your app is very complex (>5 score), then be sure to get a programmer on your team. You must get on well because you will be working closely together over the next year.

If the app is not as complex (<6 score), you can consider getting it done by a freelancer or agency. We recommend that you choose developers in close physical proximity to yourself. If you don't have the development experience yourself it is important that you can meet the developer and establish a trustful connection with the developer. IT development processes are notoriously difficult to manage. Think of the many IT project scandals in the public sector, where billions have been spent on unusable software. Why has this happened? You can compare these IT projects with a major construction project like an apartment building or a bridge. There are many people involved at different times. The complexity is high, and requirements for performance and appearance can be huge, while material standards, etc., evolve during the process. It requires incredibly efficient project management to succeed, and it's the same with IT.

The programmer will ask about the requirements specification. Some choices and some deselections have to be made, and it must be done together. If things should go quickly, then it typically affects quality and performance. Refer to our complexity test in the previous chapter to see some of the key questions that will crop up in the first conversations with the programmer. Are you building a small app for internal use in a small company, or do you want to conquer the world with the new Facebook? How confident are you that the users have a real need?

Before you hire a programmer, you must have wireframes and a detailed requirements specification in place. End of story!

We recommend that you start small and have an app built with the core functionality first. You can be sure that you will learn a tremendous amount from watching the first people who use it. You don't know how they will use it until they have it in their hand. Therefore, you should consider very carefully whether to leave out some features in the first version. What is the single most important feature of the app? Take that and build an app around it, and then add what follows as updates to the app.

In the development phase you are entirely dependent on the programmer. If they are experienced, and your app is not complex, then together you can set deadlines and milestones for when the app and features are to be finished. If the app is complex and the technology is new to the programmer, then it can be very difficult for them to say when it will be finished.

It may be a good idea to break tasks down so you can get an overview of what the programmer is doing on a weekly basis – hold at least one short status meeting a week. It doesn't have to be more than 10 minutes, where you hear what was made for the app last week and what the plan is to make for this week. The same applies if you have hire freelancers, and a useful tool is Trello, which easily keeps track of the various tasks.

While the programmer works pretty much in isolation, it's important that you take steps to prepare for a launch. It's a massive job, and it's vital to be as prepared as possible – we look closer at this in the book's final section.

DEVELOPMENT PHASE

All phases of development are different, and therefore you can only get inspiration from another companies' development. You must be careful not to reflect and compare your own development too much with the development of other companies or lack thereof because the development process is too complex with too many variables for there to be a reasonable basis for comparison. Perhaps the other company has more capital, a better programmer or a more experienced team. Perhaps there was some spin on the story before it came out in the press. The most crucial thing is to focus on you and your project and get the best out of the resources you have available.

It's generally a good idea to focus on one thing at a time. When you're in the development phase, it's all about the product, product and product. Your product is only good enough when you have product-market fit, and it always takes longer to achieve than you bargained for.

> *Only hire people to solve problems if it is critical to the company that they get solved*

A classic startup mistake is to scale the organisation too quickly, which means that you hire people before you need them because you want to be at "cruising speed" when you need them. The problem is that you can't predict precisely when you will need skills that are not directly related to product development. A basic rule is that you only hire people when there are critical things in your company that aren't being made.

In startups, you often compensate for the lack of capital with free or cheap labour. It can work really well, but it can also take all the focus from key people in the company, and it doesn't matter if you're 15 people if quality work isn't being done. If a software development team is too big, there is a risk that the code becomes fragmented and perhaps has to be written again. In marketing and communications, you can easily use trainees, but it can take trainees several weeks to familiarise themselves with a concept, and so it doesn't matter if they leave after a month or two. As a rule of thumb, trainees must be with you for at least for two months before it makes sense for both you and them.

Best to say things once too often than once too little

In the development phase, it's imperative that the team communicates well. Ideally, there is an informal tone in which the various disciplines on the team come into play. As the product developer, a key task is to make sure that there are no communication barriers on the team, and it can be a bigger challenge than you think.

In general, it's very important that you like to work with the team. Trust is paramount when it comes to doing business together in what will probably end up being several years. This is supported by the productivity research that Robert L. Sutton has conducted. "The no asshole rule", which basically says that an organisation must get rid of employees who have a poisonous and bullying behaviour, as they destroy long-term productivity by, for instance, scaring good employees away.

There's no room for idiots in your company. Going to work should be fun!

DEVELOPMENT NEVER STOPS

Your app is finally finished. It's probably taken too long, you think, but it doesn't matter, because it's a big day, and now remember to pat yourself on the back!

As we've said repeatedly, you shouldn't expect to launch a completely "finished" app. If the app feels "finished" then you've launched too late. There will typically be a lot of work for the programmer in the months after the launch to improve your app's performance or implement the features that you didn't include in the first version. It's normal that users will contact you with suggestions for improvements or send bug-reports about the app crashing or behaving strangely. So, there is no sharply defined boundary for where development stops and the launch begins. In reality, the phases overlap each other.

An app is never finished

The app is to be launched and to avoid it becoming a tame experience without users, it's essential to do thorough groundwork. It's mainly about getting users of the app (acquisitions), which we have written a lot about in Chapter 21. The groundwork is best carried out by a business developer. Marketing and PR must be done, and the network must be activated to get people to the app.

Before the launch, it's crucial that you have tracking software in your app, so you can learn how people use it (e.g. Firebare/Google Analytics, AppSee, Amplitude). It's standard on websites and in apps, but to the outsider, it might sound a little sinister that you should be able to look over people's shoulder.

However, it's no more sinister than that all user interactions with your app are collected in your database, and that you then use software to visualise this data, the number of clicks, measure the average time in views and other relevant data. If you shop at the supermarket, you should also expect that your purchase will be recorded.

The business developer has several tasks in the launch phase in addition to getting new users to the app. It's also their job to interpret the data you collect from the first users. Have you achieved the objectives of the app that you set for yourself? By analysing the data, you can see what has gone wrong and how users have behaved differently on the app than you had expected. It's no secret that most apps have great difficulty in retaining users. Can you make small design or user interface modifications, so users get a better experience? Or do users disappear because the app keeps crashing? It's pertinent to find out quickly so you can correct the bugs.

When you get the first user data, you may find you have to go back to the drawing board and adjust your product and hypotheses about the users' needs. Do you assess that the app can become a business from what you know now? It's normal that your underlying assumptions are wrong in the face of reality.

18. SKILLS YOU WILL NEED

It's rare that a person possesses all the skills needed to succeed with an advanced app. In this book, we've chosen to focus on three key competencies: software development, design, as well as product and business management and development.

The three competence groups cover huge professional disciplines, each of which we don't have time to go into detail in this book. However, Figure 48 can give you a basic understanding of the primary and secondary skills you may need in different stages of your project.

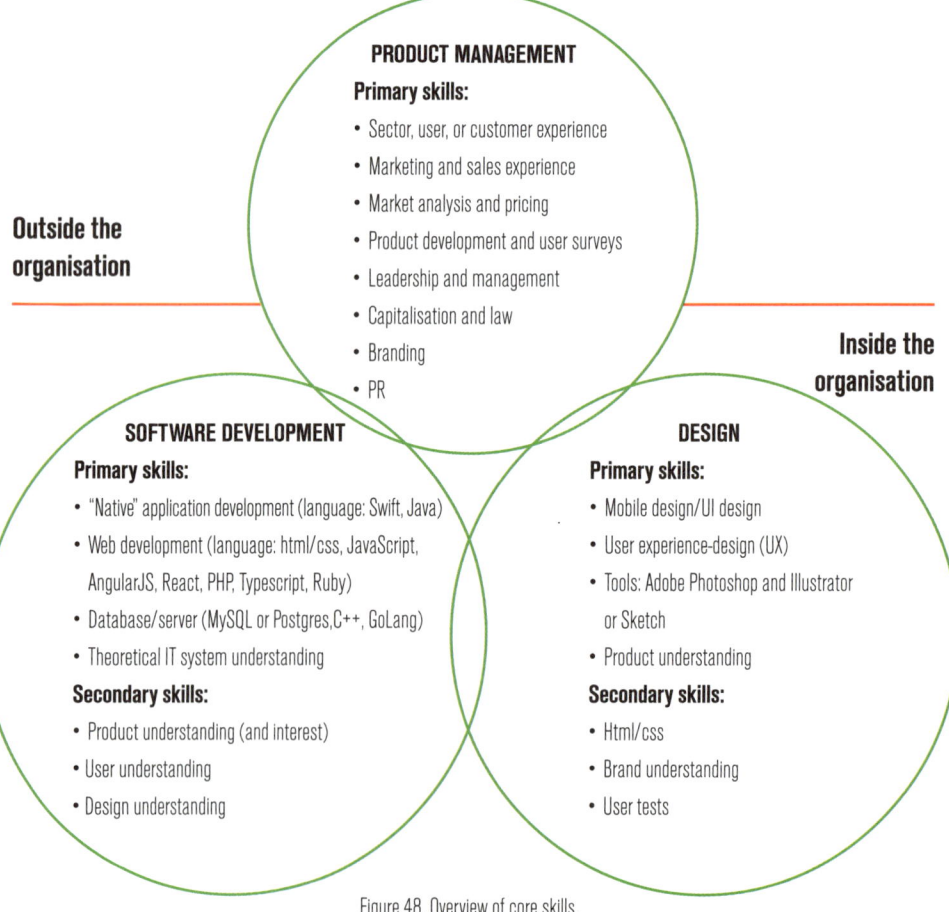

Figure 48. Overview of core skills.

THE PRODUCT MANAGER WITH MANY HATS

It started with an idea for an app, and before you realise it, you're suddenly the business and product manager, sales manager, marketing expert, director, legal counsel and investment expert. Or to put it another way, these roles will very naturally become yours, unless you're a software developer or designer – one of the two other core skills that you need for your app project.

What does the product manager do?

Your primary job as a product manager is to understand the social and economic reality that your app will work in. In other words, it's you who talks with and understands users, organisations, the media and other players outside of your little app business.

You are responsible for spotting and identifying a need correctly. You have the answers to all the key questions: What is the need? Who has the need? When did the need arise? How great is the need? If you've made a mistake here or been careless with the analysis, then you're wasting your own and everyone else's time with the app project, since there is an imminent risk that no one will use the app. (Perhaps reread Chapters 6-9, where there is good advice to identify the needs of a market).

> *You need a product manager – and that's always the business developer*

Since you know the needs and problems of the market, it's also you who is most qualified to find a solution to the problem. You should be able to devise an app with the features that are needed, so you solve your target group's problems satisfactorily. This problem is solved in close collaboration with the programmer, who can qualify the different ideas regarding how long they take, whether they may be smarter and so on. You must also be able to evaluate and generate new ideas to improve or modify the app if the early attempts fail, which they probably will.

On top of that, you need to find out where your app is positioned in the market and if it's going to make money, who will pay and how much they will pay. Can it be a sound business? (Perhaps reread Chapter 6 and 8). Next, you should be able to market and sell your app, as well as do the PR and find a logo and build a brand that your users will love. You will be using a designer for this, who should have some ideas in that direction.

As a product manager, in the end, you are typically also responsible for raising funds for the project (after all, it's your idea ...) and taking care of formalities such as company creation, pay, accounting, VAT, etc. You're a generalist in the team, so if a task is outside for your team's skills, then you are almost certainly the one who will have to pick up the ball.

If you aren't the product manager

We have primarily written this book with a product manager and business developer type in mind. However, if you don't belong to that category, what type of person should you look for if you need to find one?

The product manager's skills have to range from management and administration to business development, sales, marketing and communication. No one can be an expert in all of these areas, which either requires many years of experience (e.g. management) or which changes from month to month (e.g. online marketing).

However, we will generalise slightly and say that there are two types of product developers: a judge of character and a business person.

A judge of character – focus on the product

A judge of character is motivated by togetherness and learning about other people's lives and culture. It's typically a person with knowledge and interest in the social sciences, design, psychology or the humanities. The person possesses the thoughtful insight and empathy needed to understand the people you are building your app for. Therefore, the judge of character is focused on user-driven product development and value creation for users.

> *If you need to develop products for people, it's good to be interested in them*

The judge of character is an excellent profile in the first stages of a company, where the product is developed with a focus on iterations driven by user feedback. A crucial ability in this phase is a critical attitude towards assumptions about human motivation and behaviour patterns. It's dangerous to be complacent about user analyses and believe that you know what people want. A user's needs are seldom solely primary, such as food safety or sleep – in our affluent society where we have an almost free choice from all shelves. The modern service economy is much more about feelings, and Web 2.0 (the social web) showed that we use IT to be social just as much as making transactions.

Needs and user analyses are complex affairs, as data is often qualitative and answers point in all directions from the few potential users you talk to on the street, in your network and on Facebook. Imagine that you were the product developer for Apple's iPad before the first launch, and you were going to ask people on the street whether they would buy an oversized iPhone that couldn't make phone calls. It would certainly not be encouraging data that came out of the meeting with users. However, the judge of character's strength is precisely to understand and analyse the complexities of your first user feedback, interview responses, e-mail feedback, user videos, focus group data, etc., and condense the essential information so that you make the right product decisions.

The business person — focus on business

The other product manager type is the business person. They are motivated by the competitive element of running a company, achieving growth and making money. Therefore, their profile is also better in a later phase, where you may need to have capital, and especially when you start to make money. The business person also focuses on the economy, costs, management and administration, and getting the "machine" to run is something that motivates them.

> *It's a great strength knowing how to make money*

The business person typically has a commercial background, and their strengths lie in seeing opportunities to market, sell and make money. They know the disciplines that belong to traditional business development (not necessarily product development) such as pricing, competitive analysis, sales and market differentiation. They know the language that investors use, and they can formulate messages for the perfect presentation (the so-called investor-deck or pitch-deck) so that investors understand your business.

The business person and judge of character are generalised personalities, and you'll need all the skills they each possess. If you're in the idea stage, we still believe that user understanding and product development should be the focus. Therefore, you should look for a profile that can primarily strengthen your product by having detailed knowledge of the people who will be using it. Focus on sales and marketing comes second. First A then B – one step at a time! If you require early capital for your project, then the business person is still a good choice because they can sell the idea to investors early in the process.

THE SOFTWARE DEVELOPER

We've written this book for entrepreneurs who don't necessarily know much about app programming, and it's our experience that there are far more potential entrepreneurs with great ideas than there are people with the skills to implement the ideas. There's a high likelihood that you need a good app developer. So, what do you do if you're in that situation?

Your app has a house, and it must have a proper foundation

You can usefully think of software developers as engineers who have to build your house. A house is complex with insulation, water pipes, central heating, foundations, load-bearing elements, roof construction, a (beautiful) facade, bright and pleasant living rooms, ceilings, drainage, a cellar and attic, as well as the driveway and so on.

If even one of the above is missing, you would probably not be happy with your new house. Neither would a good engineer and they wouldn't accept that "their" building collapses after you've moved in and begun to use the house. So, bearing structures, piping and all "vital parts" will be their primary focus. In return, they will be more broad-minded and ensure it's a pleasant to stay in the house, the walls are the right colours, whether the style is Feng Shui or Scandinavian minimalism. This is where you and the designer have an opinion.

Your app is like a house. It's your role as a business and product manager (builder) to describe to the software developer (in a requirements specification) how many rooms you want, where the toilet should be and what type of bricks are to be used on the facade. It's also your job to find the money or resources to pay the software developer and to cover the expenses that otherwise might be related to the development.

An engineer without resources or the right skills can easily build a mud hut with a fireplace on the floor. It's a house, but perhaps not exactly what you had in mind. You typically get what you pay for.

It's also important to understand that IT has evolved in many different directions, just as web and mobile technology has become widespread. Since the evolution of the Internet has gone really fast, it's become harder to find skilled software developers within the many highly specialised fields. At the same time, there are also now many people who "can develop" something for you, as technology has become more accessible. However, that doesn't mean that the basic knowledge of technologies for that reason has become more widespread.

The simpler your app is, the easier it is to find a developer who can make it

A general rule is that the simpler your app is, the easier it is to find software developers who can make it. It's the difference between the type of house that's delivered with everything on a lorry, and sky scraper, with 250 floors, 1,000 rooms, pool on top etc. In the web and app world, the basic rule is that the more your app does, the more complex the IT infrastructure will be that allows the app to work in "the background".

What should you look for?

The ideal solution is to find a software developer who has experience with programming the type of app you want to develop (see Chapter 17). The developer profile you're looking for depends on whether your app is complex (score >5 on the complexity scale in Chapter 16) or more standard. The more advanced your app is, the fewer developers there are that would have worked with precisely the technology that you need, and with the technology in the details that your app requires.

Perhaps you're considering making an app that can give financiers advanced real-time analysis of the financial market based on machine learning from historical data and real-time input from your users. Your database must be built to handle machine learning and large amounts of historical financial data, which many computers will have to work concurrently with to enable your users to get a good and fast app experience. It'll require a backend developer who has an excellent understanding of and preferably experience of doing something similar. However, finding such a skill, i.e. a developer who has worked with roughly the same data under the same conditions on a startup budget, will be very difficult.

If your app is complex (scores 6-10 on the complexity scale), then you likely need to have several developers on your team. Complex apps require a large and sophisticated IT infrastructure, and the bigger the project is, the more maintenance there is on an ongoing basis. If you build a large detached house with a lovely big garden, it's expensive and requires more maintenance than an allotment shed. If you haven't built the house properly from the start, it may turn out to be a nightmare to maintain.

If you don't have many resources, you have to try your luck with the people and skills that you have available. If you want to make a web app that is written in AngularJS (e.g. Ionic-Framework,), a hybrid app (React Native) or native app (Swift/iOS or Java/Android), then you're looking for entirely different skills. It will generally take an experienced programmer 3-10 months to familiarise themselves with any of the above programming languages/frameworks. It's possible that they have to proceed by trial and error, but a skilled programmer with a sound theoretical understanding of programming can relatively quickly learn another programming language and advanced technology.

If your app isn't complex (scores 1-4 on the complexity scale), then you should look for a developer or an agency that has made that kind of standard solution many times before. If you're sure the app is not to be further developed, this is the optimal solution, and you can get a robust app on time. No matter what, we will always advise against choosing agencies abroad unless you have experience as a programmer and can describe in technical terms what you want. The prices may look tempting, but it can quickly become costly if you misunderstand each other, or if the quality is terrible – and unfortunately, this is the story you often hear from those who try their luck with cheap foreign agencies.

If you don't have the DKK 100,000-150,000 that a good Danish App agency will cost to make a web app with a simple database setup, you can also program the app yourself. It will take you about six months with 25-35 hours of input each week to learn how to code. You will make a lot of mistakes, but it will be instructive and useful when you intend to perform updates and maintenance.

Unless you have lots of energy or you are already technical minded, we would advise against you programming the app yourself. There is a high risk that during the six months you will get fed up with it and lose track and drop the project, which would be a shame. There's also an imminent risk that you do something wrong. A typical mistake that untrained "developers" make is that they forget to consider the implications if your solution must be scaled stable when, for example, there are many users of the app.

THE DESIGNER

Design is the last of the three major areas of competence that we have chosen to focus on in this book. Unfortunately, it's the skill that is underestimated most when app projects start up.

If the ideas man isn't a designer, then there's a tendency for the design to be under-prioritised. This is because you focus on the programming, which is a "hard skill" that you either have or don't have. When it comes to design, it's generally believed that everyone can design to some extent, which is true with modifications, but it's true that the vast majority have a relationship with design, colour and form. We've all tried to "design" something, and therefore we feel that the design skills are closer to – and perhaps within reach of – what we can already do. However, you must be very careful not to devalue the design profession, as the design is the feeling of your brand and decisive in how people are going to perceive you, your app and everything it stands for.

The designer is the artist on your team

It seems entirely logical that the app must be built before it makes sense to think about the design. You can have an app without design, but design alone doesn't make an app. Therefore, the programmer is often prioritised over the designer. Similarly, in a construction project, where the engineer often draws the longest straw, as the house must, of course, be built before you can begin to paint and decorate it – and it's certainly hard to argue against that. Nevertheless, in this and the next chapter, we will call for the design being give a higher priority and incorporated into your app project as early as possible.

THE APP DESIGN, BRANDING AND EVERYTHING IN BETWEEN

For most people, design can seem a little distant and perhaps unimportant, but when it comes to apps, the design is insanely important. There are so many apps on the market and design is a way to stand out. However, what's even more critical, as a new app in the App Store, you have abysmal chances of survival if the user experience (UX) is not of the highest quality from the start. And it requires not only good visual and graphic design, but also a well-designed user interface and interaction.

It's not only icons, buttons and "views" you have to design. You will most likely also have created a visual identity on social media, online advertising, a website and so on. And have you got a sharp photo ready for the journalist once you've finally gotten through to Metroxpress? Is your brand consistent? One of the key elements of branding is that the expression in text, sound and images is consistent, which can be difficult to achieve without access to a skilled designer who has mastered many design disciplines.

WHAT IS A GOOD DESIGNER?

Let's look at the skills you need. There are very few app projects that are large enough to make it perhaps necessary to hire a full-time designer. It may be relevant if your service also has a sophisticated website, content marketing and so on, but otherwise, you should instead focus on getting an experienced app designer involved in the project as a project employee, freelancer or part-time.

Experience with the app format

A designer should at least be able to make wireframes, design mockups and the finished app design for the software developer in Adobe Photoshop, Illustrator or Sketch. They must also have designed an app before and preferably have experience in web design, but web design experience is not quite enough to understand the very different user experience on a mobile phone.

A designer may have experience and interest in different types of design. One graphic designer will be good at icons and branding, and another works with user interfaces (UI) and interactive design as we know them from the Internet. It can be extremely difficult to find a designer who is good at icons when we come closer to the art and the subjective. The "quantitatively orientated" designers are also rare – those who are in line with marketers that think about how effective the design is in relation to strengthening the attraction, retention, sharing and business on the app.

Find a designer who has experience with app and UX design

User interface design is based on a large number of varying strong conventions for how to design user interfaces. Conventions are based on thousands of studies into how people use websites, and therefore the designer can base their design on this knowledge. Although conventions constantly change slightly, most people probably have the ambition to create an "ingenious" new design that changes our understanding of the interaction with a smartphone. Just think of Snapchat that was the first mainstream app to start with the camera immediately, and to do away with everything that was surplus to requirements, so there was only a large round button at the bottom-centre of the screen to take photos with. The button was quickly implemented in many other major apps and is now more or less standard. Tinder's swipe is another design that has been copied a lot by other apps.

A good app designer relates to many things that you might not think about if you don't know about app design. They can see a lot of possibilities and details that you can't see unless you're used to working with apps. Perhaps you immediately imagine that colour is the essential design element in an app. However, if you start by thinking a little more about it, most successful apps contain a lot of details where aesthetics begins to merge with function.

An example of such details are designed animations. We often don't notice them, but they're there and they're designed to focus our attention and/or convey a message. Just think of the "spinner" that is now standard when communicating to the user that the content is being loaded to the page. If the spinner weren't there, you wouldn't know if the app worked or had frozen (whether it had lost connection to the server or the like).

Another example is icons. Icons symbolise features, but nearly every other Internet user doesn't know what the most used "share" icon means. A good designer knows "standards" but can they create icons that will make your app look unique, and avoid using the designs that many people download free from the Internet. Next is the interaction with the icons or buttons. For example, note how the icons change colour when you press them – it can be done in many different ways. If they didn't, you wouldn't know if you had pressed the button, and then you would press it again, which would send another request to the database in the backend.

Imagine, for instance, a "like" icon that doesn't change colour slightly when you press it – you would then press it many times. In addition to the database having to make a lot of changes, it must also update the same view of all the other users of the app to show them that you've liked, not liked, etc., the post you're pressing. It's an example of how good design and small details can make a huge difference to the user experience and for your IT system as a whole.

There is a great variety of options to guide the user through an app and make sure that the experience is inviting and feels natural. If you don't know these options, you will tend to think more "statically", and it's obviously important to ensure that the app doesn't end up like a website from the 1990s with a wealth of information and a lot of crazy colours to capture the user's attention. Design, style and function are alive and changeable, and it's vital that you use the options that are available today that exactly suit your users – your app should feel "right" to your target group.

Knowledge of the target group's psychology and sociology

A good designer knows about the user's behaviour, environment, culture, trends and so on. However, it's also imperative that they know the smartphone format and the user situations that are entirely different than on websites and desktops, where you are typically sitting down while using them.

When using apps, it's usually on a smartphone with a much smaller screen, and the user can be on the move and have very little time to make decisions. Therefore, the app must make it easy to make quick decisions (preferably only one choice between two options at a time), and designed to help the user to go further into the app. However, you must be very sharply focused on the specific target group. If, for instance, you design an app for teenagers, it might be a good idea to place a vital button on the screen near the thumb, as users may have slightly shorter fingers, but in return, they are accustomed to increasing using a smartphone with one hand.

Therefore, it's very important that the designer doesn't just think of the visual expression. They will need to also show a well-developed understanding of the app's target group and user experience (UX). Understanding the user experience is closely related to human psychology, and an app designer must understand the mechanisms in our brain that causes us to act on stimuli from the app. It involves an understanding of the more cynical approaches to users, as we know from, for instance, marketing when it comes to "getting people to make a certain decision". In other words, it's not enough that the app feels stylish and looks good – it has to work for users.

Brand design

If you build a complex app (>6 in complexity), there's a high chance that you also need a design for branding, websites, videos, online marketing, PR and so on. It's a great strength if it's the same designer who does these things. Otherwise, you can easily come to confuse the consumer.

> *Think of your brand from the beginning. How do you want to be "experienced" by your users?*

Think of a "powerfully" managed brand like Joe & The Juice. Close your eyes and you can picture exactly what it's like to stand in a Joe & The Juice. The feeling created by a very consistent branding strategy, where everything is designed. Now think of apps like Tinder and Facebook. Which app has the best branding? Both companies have clear design guidelines, but because Facebook is a social media, their brand is also affected by what your friends post. The actions you make in Tinder are simpler, and the universe and brand experience are more consistent and not as susceptible to how other users are using the app. The same applies to Instagram. None of the three apps "speak" to you with a personality – but Snapchat does, which uses ghosts to create a brand personality.

WHO IS GOING TO BE YOUR DESIGNER?

App designers typically come from digital design or art academies or the technical universities. You can also be self-taught since all the resources you need are available on the Internet.

Design is more subjective and artistic than product development and programming. Therefore, all designers have their own style that they probably won't change much, and consequently, it's essential that their style fits with your style. All designers have a portfolio of the previous designs they've made, and if you like the designs, then there it's probably a good match. You must give the designer and their style and professionalism space, but it's important that they also understand the product that they must design – you're not interested in a "standard solution". Therefore, it's a good idea to see if they understand and are interested in your target group, their needs and the problem you want them to solve.

Designers also have preferences for what they want to work with. Some web/app designers would rather not work with physical things (setting up reports in InDesign, etc.), or graphic logo design, while others are more into video and animations. If you need several different design solutions, it's crucial from the outset to determine whether the designer is willing to leave their comfort zone and engage in learning new programs.

19. DEVELOP AN APP WITH A MOBILE AGENCY

To develop an app, we recommend you have an informal chat with a mobile agency because even if you haven't yet decided on whether to use an agency, you can benefit significantly from their many years of experience in the industry.

To give a local example, the three largest mobile agencies in Denmark are Trifork (established in 1998), Nodes (2008) and Shape (2010), but there are also smaller companies like Greener Pastures (2011), Makeable (2011), Touchlogic (2014), Ideal Development (2011) and House of Code (2014). Every country has a market with good mobile agencies.

The hourly rates vary depending on the size of the agency, their reputation, their existing clients, as well as how long they've existed. However, you can count on a range from DKK 500-1200 per hour + VAT. You may be able to negotiate a discount, but be aware that agencies often favour well-established clients because there is a greater likelihood of long-term collaboration, that they pay their bills on time and that they succeed with the app.

COLLABORATION

Although there will be differences in what it's like to work with each of the agencies, it's worth knowing some of the common denominators in advance.

Common to them is that they act as "hirelings", i.e. that they are paid to do a job that is agreed in advance, but this doesn't mean that you can expect them just to do what you say, because you pay them. Instead, you should give them space and expect them to actively contribute with an opinion about how things should be done because they are the app experts. It's also important that they're very responsive to your idea and what you want to achieve with the app. Sure, they're the experts in app development, but it's you who must decide whether the result meets your expectations.

App development is a process that you need to be involved in

The process is another common denominator to be aware of because even if you hire an agency to be responsible for the development of your app, the process has a significant influence on how satisfied you are with the end result. In this context, we recommend that you make sure you have continuous insight and influence along the way because your involvement is vital. This means that you must be able to actively participate in the project, which mainly means the start-up and design phases because it's difficult to involve non-developers in the programming phase. However, you can reasonably expect that along the way you will be able to try test versions of your app so that you can give constructive feedback from the side-lines during the programming phase.

It varies whether each agency makes use of milestones in their project planning, but you can usefully agree on milestones for the project so that it's clarified in advance when to meet to review specific progress.

An app development process will usually include the following phases:

1. Sales phase where you agree on what needs to be made, what it will cost, and under what conditions you buy the service, i.e. contract terms and conditions.
2. Start-up phase where you meet the agency's team so that together you can talk through the project and plan to align expectations and achieve mutual understanding. Before the meeting, there's usually some form of research conducted on the project.

3. Design phase where the app's design takes shape, and the agency regularly presents ideas to get your feedback.
4. Development phase where the app's design is implemented in the code so that it can run on a smartphone. It may also be now that the backend is programmed so that it can store data and ensure that data can be sent to and from the database.
5. The test phase is where the app is thoroughly tested, possibly with external users.
6. Release phase where the app is released on the respective app stores.
7. Evaluation phase where you and the agency evaluate and complete the project.

When you are about to enter into a partnership with a mobile agency, you can look at it like a new romantic relationship in which chemistry is an essential prerequisite for getting to know each other and over time building trust in each other. Therefore, it might be a good idea to proceed cautiously and use some energy to find each other. And of course, you're busy, but rather invest too much time in your partner than too little because you are repaid positively in the form of a good process and an app that you're happy with. Remember, it takes two to tango, so be aware of how you as a client contribute constructively to the dance.

Hire developers just like you would hire contractors to build your house

It can be difficult to determine which agency is the right choice, so here are some danger signs, but also good signs that you can usefully make a mental note of.

Typical danger signs:
- The agency doesn't answer your questions but is in a hurry to get you to sign the contract so they can get started on the project.
- The agency can't explain how its project process is going to be and it seems unstructured.
- The agency's designers have no direct experience with designing apps and can't provide examples of app assignments that they've done previously.
- The agency doesn't listen to your points or just tells you what you want to hear.
- The agency is focused on making your app more comprehensive, even though you can argue the sense of why you want the opposite.
- Previous clients haven't been satisfied with the process at the agency.

And after the start of the project:
- The agency won't let you meet the team who have to make your app, which may be due to your project being outsourced to foreign countries without you being informed.
- The agency can't/won't show you anything concrete, i.e. wireframes, design or test versions of the app during the project.
- The agency replaces team members on the project along the way.
- It's difficult to contact the agency.

Typical good signs:
- The agency takes the time to explain to you how they work and what their contract terms and conditions mean.
- The agency takes the time to understand your idea in depth and gives constructive advice on how you can do it better and maybe even cheaper.

- The agency makes a point of agreeing on milestones for the project and regularly informs you of progress. They take the time to explain different things and involve you in important decisions.

And after the start of the project:
- The agency is more focused to deliver and live up to your expectations than to send invoices and minimise the time they spend on your project.
- The agency communicates both good and bad news effectively and quickly.
- The agency's staff are knowledgeable and are working with great commitment to your project.
- The agency makes an effort to stay within the agreed framework and offers constructive suggestions on how exceeding the budget and missing deadlines can be avoided.

START SMALL

It can be difficult to know in advance which agency matches you and your project best. If you would like to test your match, it may be a good idea to arrange a short intro process that gives you an opportunity to work together. You should still expect to pay for such a process, but your money may be well spent before you both commit to a bigger agreement. Such an intro process could be a one-day workshop plus preparation, where you work together on a specific topic, such as mapping competitors, identification of possible revenue models, or how to get hold of potential users when the app is finished.

If you're a bit crafty, you can ask the agency if you can make a special agreement that you only pay for the workshop if you subsequently don't want to proceed with the app project with them. However, if you proceed with the app project with them, and you're obligated to pay a more substantial sum of money, then they give you the workshop as a discount. In this way, you're both investing in the collaboration in a way that's fair to both parties.

Depending on their process structure, you can also ask them if you can agree to divide the project into phases, so you have the option to walk away at a particular milestone if you pay up to that phase. It may mean that the project as a whole is going to cost a little more, but it may conversely be excellent security for you to be able to walk away ahead of time if it should be necessary. However, be aware that there are often significant costs associated with changing horses midstream if you need some new app developers on the project. There's a likelihood that a new team has to start all over again because the former team used some unconventional code tools and structures.

FIXED PRICE VERSUS HOURLY RATES

One contract condition that you need to be very aware of is the price structure. You can choose to purchase the project at a fixed price, or the alternative is at an hourly rate.

Fixed price means that the agency offers to develop your app for a price that you agree on in advance. It requires that you agree on what the app should do, called the specification, as well as which platforms the app must be released on, and what the development process includes, e.g. design, test and release. Based on the agency's experience, they estimate how long the app project as a whole will take them with everything included, e.g. 500 hours. But because it's they who bear the risk with a fixed price and so the risk of the estimated number of hours being sufficient to deliver the app, then you should expect that they put a buffer on top to cater for any unforeseen circumstances that require more time than expected. In this example, we can make a calculation in which the agency adds 25% on top of the buffer (i.e. +125 hours), and you get a price of a total of 625 hours multiplied by the agency's hourly rate, e.g. 625 hours x DKK 1,000/hour = DKK 625,000. While this may seem a little unreasonable, then you should look at it as you pay extra for them to take the risk to deliver the agreed app at the agreed price.

The advantage of the fixed price is that you're almost 100% certain what the app project will cost and that it's the agency which bears the risk, so you know that you get the app at the agreed price. The downside is that you often end up paying for more than you get because you're also paying for the buffer that the agency is forced to add on top. You must also be aware that you will be working with an agency that is focused on keeping within the agreed framework, which means time and specification. In practice, it may mean that you must argue more to have things made as you want them because it often means that it takes the agency additional time. It's not always the case, but you should be mindful that these dynamics can easily occur, and that it may be harmful to the collaboration and the end product.

Make a detailed requirements specification

The truth is that it's impossible for both parties in advance to make a full 100% specification of the app because it's incredibly complex to describe in words what an app should do and how it should do it. The agency also needs to have a certain degree of autonomy in their work, and although it's possible to get close to a full description, particularly if the app's design is finished, then along the way you will find that you need to adjust the agreed specification, because your understanding of the app changes. Precisely this can sometimes be a challenge because it creates a real need to make changes to the original specifications, which often leads to an increase in the fixed price. It's extremely frustrating if you've counted 100% on the fixed price and you may not have any more money.

Our best advice is that you should never enter into agreements where you spend your entire budget. Although it may be difficult when it's about such relatively large amounts of money, so make sure as a precaution to always have more money up your sleeve for changes.

Hourly rates, also called "guesstimates", means that you pay the agency for precisely the time they spend developing your app. As with a fixed price, the agency starts by estimating the hours spent in advance, but unlike a fixed price, the estimate here only serves as a guideline because the agreement is that you pay for the time that the agency actually spends on the project. They estimate, for instance, 500 hours, but end up spending more or less, then you should only pay for the hours they end up using. With hourly rates, it's you the client who bears the entire risk of what the project ends up costing.

The advantage is that you only pay for the hours that the agency actually ends up spending on the project, and not for the extra buffer that is added to a fixed price. The downside is that you don't know in advance what the app will end up costing. Here, it's you who bears the full risk, which for some can be quite anxiety provoking because they don't have full control over how the agency's time is spent. In other words, it requires that you have great confidence in the agency, and you must be aware that you will be working with an agency that is not restricted by a rigid frame. In practice, it may mean that you need to make sure to check their project planning and time consumption regularly, so you have a full overview as the costs evolve in step with the progress you've agreed. You will in turn experience greater flexibility to accommodate your wishes for changes, but just remember that it's your responsibility to keep track of the impact changes will have on the total cost.

Be aware that you can usually agree on a ceiling with the agency for hourly rates to put a limit on how many hours they can spend on your project. It can give you reasonable assurance that the project, and so the bill, doesn't go entirely off track.

Payment terms is another contract condition that you should be aware of. Many agencies will generally require a relatively large payment from you before starting the project, e.g. 30-50% because they have to ensure that you actually commit yourself to your agreement. Since it may involve relatively large amounts of money, some agencies also ask you to get your bank to confirm that you are good for the money.

When you pay to get your app developed with a mobile agency, the code they develop in connection with your project belongs to you because that's what you pay them for. There may be cases in which the agency makes use of some specific code elements that belong to them, but if they make use of them in your project, then it should state in the contract that you always have the right to use the agency's code elements when it concerns that app. The agency's own code elements can mean savings for you because when agencies develop and reuse the same features for different clients, they save time and money for you. The agency, however, wants to ensure that their competitors can't use the same code elements, even if they get to see them if, for example, you switch from one mobile agency to another.

There is also no reason that you should worry about or spend money investigating whether you can take out a patent on the code to your app. A patent won't be able to protect you against others making the exact same app. The reason is simply that it's easy to make two identical apps with a completely different code base, and since a patent only protects you against someone else using the same code base, then it won't have any effect, because others can easily bypass it without violating your patent.

MIGHT THEY DEVELOP IN RETURN FOR A SHARE OF OWNERSHIP?

To put it bluntly, there is unfortunately very little chance that an agency will develop in return for a share of ownership. The explanation is that agencies are focused on developing apps for others, which means that their business is not built to run apps for success. For them to get their company to make ends meet, they need to focus on getting new projects and solving them so that they can pay staff salaries, rent, etc.

But are there any examples? Yes, indeed there are, but there are remarkably few of them compared to how many apps are being built by agencies. Does it hurt to ask? No, it'll never do that, but you must prepare yourself to get a polite no thank you.

20. INVESTMENT – HOW DO I FINANCE MY APP?

Once you've an idea for an app, it's the development of the app and marketing that usually require capital. Before you get there, you've done a lot of groundwork, as we've previously described.

No one will pump money into an app that's not validated

Many entrepreneurs mistakenly believe that investors will be interested in investing in their app based solely on the idea. What they don't understand is that ideas – even good ideas – are meaningless unless they are validated, for instance, in the form of downloads, active users or actual sales to customers. Therefore, you must have your idea validated – no one will invest money into an app that's not validated.

Investors know all about the fact that many ideas are similar, but the difference lies in the execution. So, if you can show that you can execute, then you have a better chance of raising money through business angels or venture capital. Of course, there's also the option that you have the necessary capital yourself, or you have a close family member who will invest in the app. But even if you don't need venture capital, it's still important to validate the idea. Experience and research show that investment too early, i.e. investment before the app is validated, increases the chance of failure. The reason is that the development of the app is started and completed too early and without enough contact and feedback from potential customers along the way.

There are advantages and disadvantages to getting investors involved in a startup. The big advantage is, of course, that you can continue working on your app, and you get capital to cover the costs of development and marketing. Another significant advantage can be that you might get investors involved, who have a vast network that you can draw on, and years of experience, so they can give you advice and coaching. The disadvantage is that you must surrender your influence.

HOW MUCH IS YOUR APP WORTH?

Investors typically get a share of ownership in return for the money they invest in the company. To determine the percentage of the business they can get for their investment, you make a so-called valuation of the company in advance. It's vital to know that no answer book exists when we talk about valuing companies. In a traditional context, we often use a valuation model called "Discounted Cash Flow" (DCF), which is about calculating the present value of the total cash flow that the company expects in the future. The model isn't beneficial when the company is in such an early stage that it hasn't yet generated revenue and the future consists of only limited accounting figures and fragile budgets. In such cases, the valuation often ends up as a matter of appraisal where the individual investor looks at some factors affecting the outlook for the company's future value positively and negatively. The valuations will often vary from investor to investor because they weigh the factors differently.

If your app creates revenue, you're in a strong position for valuation because it's evidence of demand

According to the Danish entrepreneur network Keystones, the following factors affect the valuation of startups. (NB! We have replaced the "rights" factor with "growth potential" because we do not believe that rights are relevant in a app context):

1. Problem/need in the market: Investors look at how clearly the problem or need is defined, and the extent to which the problem or need is evidenced in the market. Investors will consider whether there is demand in the market because it will reduce their risk.
2. Growth potential: Investors will assess the company's growth potential in the market, which means that they will look at how large a target group the app is intended for and how often users are likely to use the app – is it many times a day or only once a month? They will also look at whether the app has global potential, which can often be extremely crucial because one of the advantages of the software is that it can often become global without increasing costs significantly.
3. The team: The composition of the team plays a vital role in such a way that their skills complement each other rather than overlap. Their involvement, i.e. full-time, part-time or spare time also plays an important role. The same applies to previous experience within the company's area of focus, but especially previous experience in entrepreneurship. It's also a great help if the team have worked together previously. Investors are often very interested in the company's team because they know from experience that it's easy to change the company's plans, but almost impossible to change the people behind it.

4. The development stage: Here, investors will assess which phase of development the company is in, how they got there and what the prospects for its further development look like. It's about getting as far as possible from the idea and concept level. This means, for example, that a fully developed MVP that has confirmed some of the company's key assumptions in the market is a good step towards a higher valuation. The same applies if you already have users, especially in the case of paying users. Generally, it's important to the company's position in the development phase to be backed up by concrete figures. Analysis tools play a crucial role here because they can do much of the work for you.

5. Market position: Investors will assess market awareness of your company and look at the presence of competitors. It's very common for investors to make a simple analysis of your company's advantages and disadvantages in order to compare them with competitors. Investors will typically look favourably on you if your company has established partnerships with companies that have a strong market position, and they will also look kindly on cases where there are reputable companies among its customers.

> *Investors see you at the outset as a 100% risk – the better you can explain why the risk is less than 100% – the better the valuation*

Based on a comprehensive analysis[37], Keystones have concluded that the valuation is the leading cause of the startup and investor not agreeing in their negotiations. To help both parties on the way, Keystones has taken their starting point in the realised early-stage investments from 2012 to 2015. On this basis, they've developed their so-called "Høker Calculation[38]", which aims to give Danish entrepreneurs an idea of what to expect in connection with a valuation.

DKK	0	500,000	1,000,000	3,000,000	5,000,000
Problem/ need in the market:	• Problem/need in the market is unclear	• The solution is "nice to have", not "need to have"	• We document the savings/benefits level at 10% in relation to the current solutions	• We document the savings/benefits level at 25-30% in relation to the current solution	• We document the savings/benefits level at +50% • "Disruptive"
The team	• Idea phase, no one involved full-time on the project	• 1 founder/owner & full-time	• 2 founders/owners & full-time	• 3 or more founders/owners with technical, commercial and professional experience	• Capital track record: Previously generated exit for investors
Phases	• The idea and concept are described • Technology under development	• Proof of Technology • It's proved that the solution works, e.g. beta level	• Proof of Concept • X number of customers have implemented the solution and have solid buying interest	• Proof of Business • X number of paying customers use the product/solution • Turnover DKK X	• A large number of paying customers • Capital needs primarily for sales and marketing
Market position	• No knowledge in the market of the company	• The first x number of potential customers and decision-makers know us	• Concrete dialogue/ pipeline and negotiations with the players in the market	• Strong customer and partner relationships • Established as a major player	• Market leader in a specific niche • Documented growth figures
Rights	• No possibility of patent/protection/ rights/licences	• Assessment/novelty study done with a positive indication	• Application submitted/ negotiations commenced	• Positive response to applications/ negotiations	• Patent granted, protection in place, licence agreement signed

Figure 49. Keystones' Høker Calculation was developed on the basis of concrete business angels and venture capital investments in Danish startups in 2017.

When Morten Resen started to develop the GoLittle app, he turned to the mobile agency Shape. They initially offered to help him develop a business plan, concept and MVP of the app for 10% ownership in GoLittle. Besides sharing Morten's belief in the idea and business potential, Shape felt that because of his strong personal brand, among other things, Morten had a particularly good chance of succeeding with the app. Therefore, Shape ran the extraordinary risk of stepping in as an investor, which is otherwise unusual among mobile agents in Denmark.

Since then there has been a number of positive developments in GoLittle that have, among other things, led to two of the "lions" from DR's programme *Løvens Hule* choosing to invest in GoLittle. So, both Jesper Buch and Birgit Aaby have become investors. It remains unknown whether GoLittle will be successful, but less than a week after his launch in March 2018, Morten celebrated having received 5,000 users of his app and was named by Apple as "App of the Day".

It's also worth noting that Morten ended up launching an entirely different app than he'd initially planned. In his podcast[39], which documents his entire journey up to the launch, you can hear how he got there and the many other difficult decisions along the way, and you can also hear how GoLittle's valuation has evolved through the investment rounds.

It's about testing the problem and proving that there is interest in the app, which GoLittle managed to do. Before launching their app, they created a website where 10,000 people gave their e-mail address, and that's pretty clear evidence that the problem exists and an indication that their solution was in demand.

There are several options for raising money for an app before you go to investors, and here are some options to get started:

BOOTSTRAPPING

If it's possible for you to bootstrap your app idea, do it. Bootstrapping means that you save money through your existing jobs, savings, investments or alternative businesses. If your start date is less than six months away, you can start paying a little each month. You won't end up with a huge sum, but it will be enough to get started. It's very difficult to bootstrap an app development – unless you yourself are developing – and certainly not if it's a complicated app, but if it's a web app and maybe a hybrid, then you might.

This is because there aren't enough developers. You might be fortunate and find one that will work for free full-time in return for a share of ownership of the app, but it's very hard.

> *You have to be able to look your friends and family in the eye and live with them even if they lose their investment*

FRIENDS AND FAMILY

Contact your friends and family members who believe enough in your idea to invest money in it. Get them involved and tell them about your plan – show them your Business Model Canvas. Friends and family are often more patient than professional investors. In turn, you can offer them a share of your profits. However, keep in mind that you have to be able to look your friends and family in the eye and live with them even if they lose their investment.

CROWDFUNDING

It may be an excellent first step to try crowdfunding for financial support. Crowdfunding has many advantages. First of all, you retain full ownership of your business, and it also allows you to use social media with a large number of users. Small payments are welcome, which opens the door for future major investments. You get PR, while also getting an indication of how many of the site's users believe in your idea.

Crowdfunding sites follow one of two models. The "All or nothing" model provides funding for projects if and only if the predetermined minimum funding target is reached or exceeded. Alternatively, the "Keep it all" model allows you always to keep the money that is raised at the end of the funding period, regardless of how much comes in.

A successful crowdfunding campaign relies to some extent on luck.

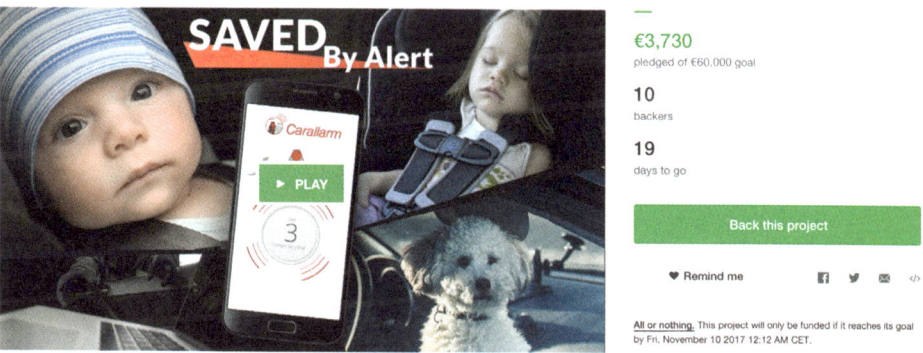

Figure 50. Here is an app for a car alarm that has been put on Kickstarter. The target is EUR 600,000, and there are 19 days left and only EUR 3,730 has been raised.

The challenge with crowdfunding for apps is that there is rarely a physical product or a value that you can offer crowdfunders going forward. Of course, you can offer a subscription, but crowdfunding works better for physical products, so you should really think twice before spending time on a crowdfunding campaign because it's a demanding process.

LOAN

It's extremely difficult to borrow money from a bank for a business idea unless you can provide collateral in the form of a house, for instance. However, we would advise you to avoid this if you can because it requires you being willing to risk losing your house and home if your company fails.

BUSINESS ANGELS

Business angels are individuals who invest in companies they find particularly interesting. Often you will see that business angels are willing to accept a greater risk than, say, private equity funds, which means that they frequently invest in companies that are at an early stage in their development. They do this because, among other things, it gives them more significant influence over the company's direction and that their share of any future returns will be higher.

In the Danish context – and according to a recent survey by the Danish Growth Fund (Vækstfonden)[40] – there are just over 4,000 active business angels in Denmark. The best way to get in touch with them is to get someone to introduce you. If you find a business angel who shows interest in your app, it will work best if you present a prototype (first version) or a solid mockup of your app – it will show that you're serious and that you want to put something on the line. If you get the opportunity to obtain investment from a business angel, it will be a great advantage if he or she has experience investing in apps.

According to Thomas Marschall[41], there are seven key questions that a business angel should ask themselves before investing in a startup:

1. Do you think the key person/people behind the company have the energy, experience, motivation and the drive that is required for the next 3-4 years to execute and overcome plenty of challenges and problems?

2. How long will it be before the company requires money again?
3. How much money do you think will be needed in the future from you and other investors?
4. What progress can be achieved with the money you contribute, which may increase the value of the company?
5. How long will it be before the company's revenue and expenses balance?
6. Is it realistic that you can get 3-10 times your money back in a few years?
7. What's the company's uniqueness? The technology, speed, timing, customers ...?

If you're looking for investment from a business angel, try to prepare answers to these questions.

VENTURE CAPITAL

It's very difficult to get venture capital for an app at an early stage – venture capital aims to get a 10-fold return on the investment. However, you'll only receive venture capital if there is "recurring revenue" (revenue at the time of investment) or approximately 1 million users if there is no revenue at the time of investment. Therefore, there must be the potential for a big market, which means many potential users. Football app Tonsser that appears in the following case, initially had a relatively small market when there was talk about football players in Denmark. However, the market could be extended to many countries in Europe, which it since has. It's crucial that the app is scalable, i.e. it has the potential to spread to many countries easily. Tonsser made sure of this, but expansion also demands that partnerships have been made with clubs in the country it expands to.

Case: Tonsser

Tonsser is a social football network that brings youth football and amateur football together in a hybrid between the Football Manager app and LinkedIn, where players' performance also comes to life after the game. The current football sector in Europe has a huge shortage of structure and finds it difficult to track down and identify players. There is little transparency in the world of football, and there is great interest in following one's own and local teams and players, which is often not possible. It's precisely this problem that Peter Holm and Simon Hjære, two passionate footballers and entrepreneurs, decided to solve by starting Tonsser.

For many months, the app's initiators sat in a cellar and worked six days a week, sometimes seven, often to past midnight. Kasper Hulthin, the founder of Podio, together with Martin Elbæk and Phil Chambers, invested the first money in the company, which the boys stretched as far as they could with a modest salary[42]. In 2013, Tonsser received three new investments[43]. After a month, Tonsser had 6,000 users. The reason that Tonsser relatively quickly received investment was that they could show that the number of users grew rapidly. Later, they received an investment of EUR 1.8 million (about DKK 13 million), which came from the Danish equity fund SEED Capital that invests in startups, the German venture capital fund Wellington Partners and some prominent European business angels. Tonsser now has more than DKK 34 million in investment and it currently has over 400,000 users.

> However, Tonsser had the same problem as Endomondo. They had a hard time finding a good revenue model. Tonsser has partnered with Nike and several sponsors, but they haven't yet found a truly sustainable revenue model.

PUBLIC-PRIVATE EQUITY

Many countries have public-private financial mechanisms to support entrepreneurs. In Denmark, there are four innovation centres that invest in startups at an early stage. They typically invest DKK 2-4 million for a share of ownership in the app company. The innovation centres are often more willing to invest in apps if they are rooted in the local communities where the centre is located.

Figure 51 below shows an overview of the common sources of finance, as well as in which phases of the company's development they typically occur.[44]

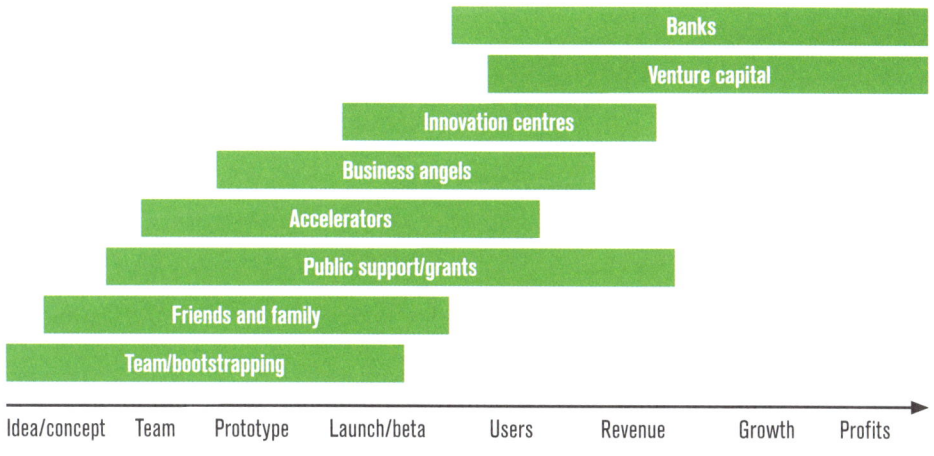

Figure 51. Development phases and possible financing sources.

Investors assess investment in apps based on the perceived risk (high/low) and possible return (high/low). It varies what they're looking for – not all investors are looking for huge returns. Some will be satisfied with less if the risk is also less. Therefore, it's very important that you prepare yourself thoroughly if you want to have investors, and part of the preparation is finding the right type of investors.[45]

PITCHING YOUR CONCEPT

To make a good pitch for your app requires training, and it may take several attempts to have an engaging presentation that hits the mark. You need to pitch your app in many contexts, and it may be for potential investors or customers. A pitch must, of course, be targeted at the group of people you're talking to, and you must accept that it probably won't be particularly good the first few times. It's very much about personal charm and commitment, and there are also some things that you should be aware of when making a pitch.

Your story should show how your app will solve the problem it's going to be created for

1. Tell a story

Begin your pitch with a compelling story. It will immediately get your audience engaged, and it's even better if you can make your story directly relevant to your audience. Your story should show how your app will solve the problem it's going to be created for.

2. What value do you provide for your customers?

You must concisely articulate your app idea and tell what it is, what problem it solves for the customer and to whom it provides value for – in short, formulate the app's value factors. It should always be at the very beginning of a pitch and so you set the stage for the rest of the presentation.

3. Your successes

You need to show your credibility early in the presentation. Tell about your previous experience, which contributes to the app being realised, and you must convince the audience that you and your team have the skills it takes.

4. Customise the length of the presentation

The process of making a good pitch can take a long time and be tough. As an entrepreneur, when you've been immersed in the development of your app and experienced both highs and lows, you very often think that many details are relevant and crucial to understand the background of the app. However, the audience doesn't always think so, and especially not for a pitch where they mainly want to understand the business idea and get an overview of the app's potential. Therefore, it's worth remembering that "less is more" – if the presentation is too long and heavy, the essential messages drown in the "filling".

5. Focus on customer needs, rather than what the app can do

As a starting point, briefly describe the app, and it can often be a good idea to showcase a prototype that can provide an immediate and intuitive understanding of what the app can do. If you want someone to invest in your app, you must have a fully designed prototype. The app market is still relatively new, and for many investors it can be difficult to understand how the app works if they can't see it. Having a design prototype shows that you're serious. Anyone can come up with a good idea, but it's the execution that matters. If you aren't willing to devote time and money to creating a design prototype, why should an investor be willing to invest?

Many entrepreneurs focus too much on technology in their presentation, and you often see some presentations with slide after slide of specifications and technical features, which tells about all the amazing things the app can do, but without going into what problem it solves, and so what value it brings to the customer. It's imperative to be able to connect the product's features directly with a solution to a real problem that the customer has, and so highlight the value that the app creates for the customer.

6. Remember competitors

Many entrepreneurs have an unrealistic relationship regarding their app's "competitive edge", i.e. the feature that's unique and relevant to the segment being targeted. Very often we hear that "my app has no competitors", or "my app will create a whole new market". However, this is rarely the case. Firstly, you're always in competition with something – either another app or a site that does something similar. And secondly, the attitudes of potential users are that "we do just do what we usually do" or "we do nothing" are examples of behaviour that's often much more dominant than you as an entrepreneur imagine.

Therefore, make sure to present potential competitors. You should also know your own limitations and recognise competitors' skills so that the presentation isn't an unrealistic picture of "they're bad" and "we're good".

One of the best ways to communicate your app's value relative to your competitors is to tell them about the competition in a matrix format, where you can list your competitors.

7. Be realistic regarding market potential

Many don't have a realistic picture of the actual demand for their app. Sometimes we see that a plan for an app is built around ideas and assumptions, such as "I've found out how big the market is for my product. If I can just take 1% of the market, then I'll make a big profit next year."

It's ok to give an overall perspective on the opportunities and potential, but it should always be supplemented with the starting point in the customers who actually have shown an interest in the app, and so it validates that there is a market. One way to construct a possible future scenario is to assess the value of customers based on the customers' own statements. Then you assess how many of these customers there are, and then divide the market into smaller segments that can be "attacked" one by one. In this way, the business case is built both "top-down" and "bottom-up", and it gives a more nuanced and realistic picture of the app's market potential.

Finally, it's crucial to make sure that potentials and value are well-prepared and interrelated.

THE STRUCTURE OF THE PRESENTATION

You can use the following structure for your presentation to ensure that the review of the messages makes sense – listed here slide by slide:

1. Name of the app/company and the speaker.
2. Value factors.
3. The market and the customer's problem.
4. The solution.
5. How is the app unique?
6. Competitive situation.
7. Revenue model.

8. How does the app get out to customers?
9. Financial overview and forecast (for investors).
10. The team behind the idea.
11. Timeline and status.
12. Investment needs and use of resources.
13. Why invest in the app (for investors)?
14. ROI (the time when the investment is paid back) and exit (sale of the company) opportunities (for investors).

LAUNCH

21. HOW DO YOU GET USERS?

The app is finished and now you need to get some users ("acquisition"). However, before we go into the details of how to do it, remember Chapter 14, where we introduced path-thinking. The primary path in your app's acquisition path, which has the objective to get an activated user on your app (not just to download the app), and this is the most important path as all the other paths in the app are dependent on you having users on your app.

THE ACQUISITION PATH

Figure 52 shows your acquisition path, which we touched upon in Chapter 14. Here we go deeper into it since it's absolutely fundamental to the success of your app. From left to right, the potential user is aware of your app on one or more of the marketing channels that you use in your marketing.

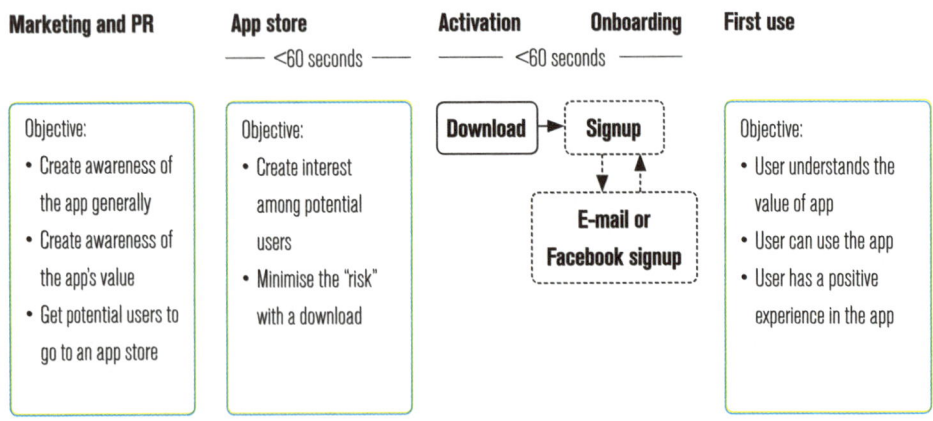

Figure 52. The acquisition strategy.

About 30% of downloads are from links to an app store, while 70% surprisingly come from searches in app stores. It says a lot about the importance of organic marketing such as word of mouth and PR, but also how important it is to optimise your page on the App Store and Google Play Store (ASO – App Store Optimisation).

Therefore, you must firstly ensure that your brand is consistent across all platforms – in other words, your images and designs must be sharp. In marketing, one convention says that an average consumer has to see your brand seven times before the product is perceived as an alternative to other products. The point is that the more times a user is exposed to a brand, the stronger the brand is, for better or worse, in the person's consciousness. Therefore, your brand design, etc., have to be professional with a clear visual identity, so it has the authority, seems authentic and not shabby and inconsequential.

So, before a user even gets to pressing "download" in an app store, the potential user has probably already become aware of your brand repeatedly. A download should lead to the user opening the app and possibly activated as a new user. In your acquisition path, you can focus on downloads as objectives, but we recommend that you focus on activating users (Facebook or e-mail activation) if users need to be activated to use your app. If they have to, then your objective for the acquisition path is that users open the app for the first time.

ATTRIBUTION AND CONVERSION

Two concepts are essential to the acquisition path: attribution and conversion. Ideally, you will want to know *where* your users are coming from (attribution), and *how many* download the app (conversion). Do your users come from your Facebook advertising, your Instagram profile or from an event you attended? Most sources can't be traced and you just have to accept that.

What is your average price per conversion for each source?

Ideally, you can find out where people are coming from, and how many converts there are from each source and the cost of each download. In practice, however, this is extremely difficult. You can always give people a general or unique tracking link to your app, so you can see where people come from. However, it doesn't solve the problem when you're at an event or give a presentation. Should people sit down and type the link into their browser or download a QR scanner app to scan your QR code with your unique link? No, most likely the audience will just type the name of your app in the app store, and then you will only see that the user came via an app store search, although they really came from your event.

If we look at the price in the example, then you've perhaps spent DKK 2,467 on transport and participation at the conference, where you gave your presentation. You've got 10 downloads, and so the cost of each download is DKK 246.70. On paper, that's really bad business, but maybe you found an investor at the conference or had the opportunity to present the app to a lot of students at a large school? This is just an example that there are many cases where, in practice, you can't use tracking links, and where it doesn't matter because you may only get very few new downloads.

The advantage of advertising is that you often get quite good options for attribution of the downloads to sources and an exact price per download and conversion. The best example is Google, which owns AdWords (Google advertising), Play Store and Google Analytics/Firebase, which you can install for free in your app tracking. Google has an overview of the entire process, from when someone sees your ad, clicks, downloads, installs and performs one or more actions in the app – it doesn't get much more precise than that.

Attribution is difficult in practice

But what if you use AdWords (Google) to advertise an iOS app? Yes, Google tracking "loses" track in Apple's App Store, and so Google can now only see that a user clicked on the ad and that someone downloaded the app (activated Google Analytics/Firebase). However, Google can't attribute the download to the person who clicked on the ad. So even the most advanced data-driven advertising providers lose significant attribution options when the user, for instance, uses an iPhone.

It illustrates very well how difficult it is in practice to track where users are coming from. But, of course, you can always put a unique download link on your website, a landing page, your Instagram bio, etc., and tracking will be simple. It quickly becomes a lot harder with PR and influencer marketing, where through a well-known (or not so well-known) person you get access to their followers on social media. For example, many influencers don't put a link in their Instagram bio, because that space is reserved for their blog, their agent or their YouTube channel. So, you can't track whether it was them or another influencer that generated traffic to your page.

DOWNLOADS AND USERS

We recommend that you understand acquisition broadly and take activation and onboarding into the equation – it's the difference between getting a download and a user. A download is worth nothing if you don't get a user, i.e. someone that makes an action in your app and actually uses it.

When a potential user has downloaded your app, they usually have to activate it with Facebook or an e-mail. It sounds trivial, but you may be surprised how many app and web applications forget to create a good flow in this process. In addition to communication to the user, there are several places where the process can go wrong – especially with e-mail, where the three major service providers (Yahoo, Google and Microsoft) have different spam weightings for activation e-mails. If your users need to be activated by e-mail, you should therefore carefully test whether your e-mails that land in the spam filter are quickly forwarded and so on.

A good activation and onboarding conversion is 90%, which means that 10% drop out just after the download and before the user actually enters the app. Typically, the number is much higher, and the main barrier is activation by e-mail, where the user gets a message that they should open in an e-mail application. They click a link, and then they have to return to the app to complete the onboarding. If you allow Facebook signup, you can count on about 70% of new users will use this option. If you don't allow registration via e-mail, you can, in turn, assume that a large proportion of the 30% don't go to your app because they either don't use Facebook or because they may not want your app receiving data from Facebook.

ACQUISITION – HOW?

Getting users to your app is usually a question of spreading a relevant and enticing message to as many people as possible either through marketing or PR. Marketing is many things, and the field has been developing rapidly since Google and Facebook revolutionised online marketing and made it possible for even a small app company to do advanced Internet advertising.

There's plenty of literature on traditional marketing models and channels such as TV, press advertising, radio and so on. The literature contains many points on user segmentation, communication, etc., but it's incredibly poor in its descriptions of how to do things in practice.

Marketing is many things and the field is developing rapidly

PR hasn't changed at the same pace as online marketing, and PR is therefore still about "selling" your story to a journalist, who along with their editor, decides whether your story is worthy of being shared with the media's readers, listeners or viewers.

Influencer marketing has become huge in the last 5 years. The principles, however, are the same as PR or press advertising, namely that you can pay to get publicity for a more or less well-known person's followers on social media. Just like PR, you may be fortunate to be so relevant for the individual influencer that you can collaborate.

Marketing channels: "Owned, earned and paid"

There's an important distinction between marketing channels that you "own" or you have "earned", and marketing channels you've paid for.

Owned channels	Earned channels	Paid channels
• Website. • Facade, stickers and other physical displays. • Blog. • Facebook page. • Instagram account. • LinkedIn account. • Other social media accounts. • Mailing lists. • App store profiles. • Company profiles on AngelList, Crunchbase, Gust, The Hub, etc. • Other channels that can reach people with publicity for your product.	• PR, articles, reviews, etc. • Publicity and sharing on social media. • App store reviews. • SEO (Search Engine Optimisation) of your website. • ASO (App Store Optimisation) of your App Store accounts.	• Google/AdMob or other banner advertising on the Internet or mobile apps. • YouTube ads. • Facebook and Instagram ads. • Advertising on other social media (Snapchat, Pinterest, Reddit, LinkedIn, Twitter, etc.).

Figure 53. Marketing channels.

Your marketing mix

Each app will have a different combination of marketing channels. What works depends on the skills you have on your team, how much money and how much time you have, how big your network is on social media and so on. But it's important to say that marketing is a time-consuming and challenging task. It may take months of daily work to build a "following" on Instagram or Facebook. It can also take months to find just the right advertising platform that can provide cheap app downloads, even though you spend thousands on advertising.

Test as many marketing channels as possible – you can't predict what works for you

You should consider the following when choosing your marketing channels:

- How much time and how much money can you spend?
- How "tested" is the channel?
- How much reach does the channel have?
- How "repeatable" is the channel?

Of course, you have an interest in using channels that are cheap, doesn't take time, that works, and which can reach as many people again and again. Unfortunately, there is no such channel. There's often a trade-off between the channel's efficiency, for example, as measured by the click-through-rate (CTR) or conversion rate and reach. With a good Facebook ad you can hope for a CTR of 10%, but a conversion rate (app downloads) of only about 0.1%, which means that 1 out of 1,000 people who have seen the ad, click on it and download the app. You can try to apply the same logic to your friends and family. If you ask your friends and family nicely, the conversion rate might be around 25%, while you might expect it to be around 50%. You'll be surprised at the many excuses that your friends and family may have for not downloading your app.

The model is generalised and illustrates the relationship between the reach and speed of one part, and the conversion rate per consumption of resources. PR stands out a little because the reach is high in a very short period, and the conversion rate is good compared to the consumption of resources because, among other things, you spend less time talking with journalists. However, you must remember here that PR is mostly one-off and so it can't just be repeated unlike Facebook ads, where you can control whether you want to put more money into an ad and attract more users.

Influencer marketing takes a really long time to administer, and both tracking and conversion can be terrible. In turn, the users you get will be much better because they associate your brand positively with the influencer they already follow and love. Influencer marketing is probably the most uncertain, but the market is becoming more professionalised, and the price has also increased accordingly. An influencer with 10k followers on Instagram can earn DKK 500 to make a post on Instagram with link sharing in their bio. It's essential to see how much engagement there is on an influencer's posts to estimate how many of their followers genuinely and actively follow them – activity between about 5% and 10% is good.

If you don't have much money for marketing, then it's most natural to experiment with marketing through your own channels such as through your Facebook or Instagram page. You can also blog or even try to do PR. All these efforts may take a very long time, and you have to measure the effectiveness and conversion on the different channels constantly.

ASO (App Store Optimisation) is essential and an easy way to get some organic (free) downloads through searches in the app stores. App stores work just like Google's search engine, and many will find your app by searching on search words. Your app's name, descriptive text and keywords are essential to your app being easily found. Note here that one of the great advantages of creating a web app or a mobile-optimised website is that users don't have to go through app stores before they can use the website. Websites can be SEO optimised (Search Engine Optimisation), which gives them a huge advantage because there are many more Internet searches than on app stores that are a bit like silos compared to the rest of the Internet.

ASO is a science in itself, and you should familiarise yourself thoroughly with how searches in app stores work, and which keywords are trending and which keywords have more traffic. It's important to use keywords that have high traffic, but which aren't used by too many apps. Then you might be among the first 10 apps that appear when a user types, for example, "flashlight" or "fun game".

ACTIVATION

When a person has downloaded your app, then it means that your value proposition has been compelling enough that the person has spent 30 seconds to perform the downloaded and focus on your app rather than anything else exciting. After downloading, you can count on having 30-60 seconds more of their attention as they have already invested something in your app. However, it's vital that you use this time wisely because otherwise, you lose the people in your acquisition funnel.

There's a big difference between a download and an active user

The purpose of activation is that the user knows how to use the app, and so becomes a "real" user, whether it involves performing certain actions in your app or just to get through the activation process. When a new user has taken the time to download your app, they are probably prepared to spend some time to understand it and get value from it. If the process is too time-consuming, then the user disappears and you never see them again. At worst, they speak negatively about your product. Therefore, it's a trade-off between the time it takes to get started using the app, and the amount of information that the user must have in order to use the app. The trend is towards apps being self-explanatory and that users have less time and patience to perform long activation processes.

How long a new user is willing to spend after downloading your app for the first time depends on:

1. How much investment the user has already made.
2. How much value the user expects to get by using it.

If you pay DKK 300 to download a game app or an advanced navigation app for your car, then you will be willing to spend several minutes to understand the product. However, we also all know that after 10-15 minutes with an expensive product that doesn't work, we will be particularly annoyed if the product doesn't live up to our expectations.

We are also willing to spend time on a product if the value of the product is perceived as high. If all your friends are on Facebook, and you know that they've all received an invitation to an important party that you didn't receive because you're not on Facebook, then it could be reason enough to spend time creating a Facebook account. The same goes for LinkedIn, where you typically spend hours creating your profile if you've just graduated and are looking for a job. The value of getting a job is high, and therefore you're willing to spend time increasing the chances of getting one by being on LinkedIn.

Signup

The most critical part of activation is the signup, which is typically done with Facebook or e-mail. Many apps don't have signup, just because it takes time in the activation process, or because the app doesn't need it. For example, a torch app isn't necessarily a signup, while a social media or a game typically has the need.

Take control of your signup process

There are two main reasons to require a signup and possibly activation via e-mail. The first has to do with security. Most apps need to know who their users are, or that their users are "unique" to associate them with an e-mail or Facebook account. If an app doesn't have activation with Facebook or e-mail, the app becomes vulnerable to automated users or "bots" that can very quickly ruin the experience for the right users, or at worst, "to mine" your app for real or virtual value, overload app servers, devalue the app's value through false traffic and so on. Secondly, as an app developer, you typically have an interest in being able to contact your users via e-mail or Facebook, WhatsApp or the like. A signup with Facebook makes it possible for direct marketing to the person who downloaded the app.

Information for the user

State-of-the-art in onboarding is about giving information to the user when they need it. Game apps do this best with small pop-ups at the right time during the game. In practice, it may be difficult to do, and so many apps remain a simple swipe guide, as we shall see in the example below. Whether it's one or the other depends on the app's complexity. The objective is, of course, that the app is self-explanatory.

Once the new user enters the app, it's normal to guide the user to the app's features, and at the same time, the information can be used strategically to point users in the direction of the in-app actions that you want them to perform.

Good activation of a new user is 1) as fast as possible, and 2) as precise as possible. When it comes to informing the new user, it must be short and sweet, and when the user needs it. However, it's easier said than done, and a good guide with, for instance, pop-up banners, etc., can feel like an unnecessary luxury if your team is already struggling just to get the core functionality in place for the app's launch. For the same reason, many choose to make apps with 3-5 views over the signup button, which you can slide back and forth between.

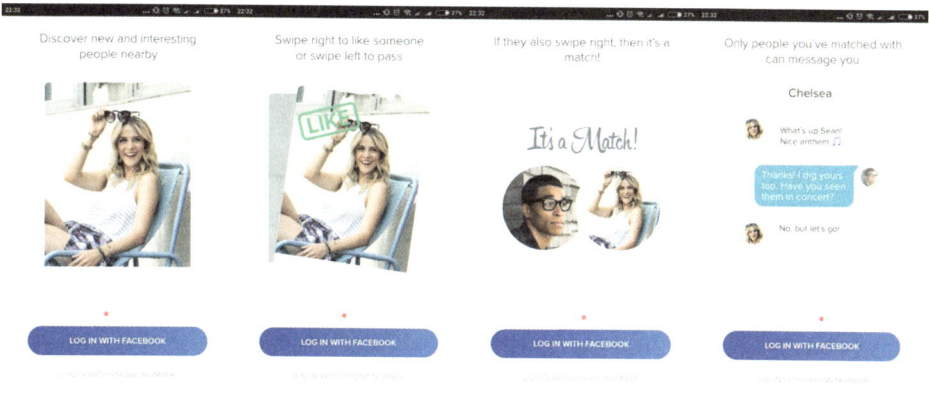

Figure 54. Tinder's onboarding guide.

Figure 54 shows Tinder's onboarding guide. Note that you can only get on Tinder with Facebook, and the button is on every view in the guide. The button is the key action element in every view it has a distinct colour and size that makes it very visible. Tinder uses Facebook's social graph data to find matches, and so it's vital to Tinder that you log in with Facebook. Since the app is free and it has a powerful value proposition, if the user is single, Tinder has chosen to let

Facebook be the only way users can log in. This makes it much easier for people who don't mind logging in with Facebook, but there is also a group of people who don't have Facebook and don't want to log in with Facebook, and Tinder loses them by making that decision.

22. RETENTION AND REFERRALS

Acquisition and retention go hand in hand. You can't have retention without having acquired any users – that goes without saying, and so acquisition should also be your first priority. Roughly speaking, you can always pay for acquisition, whereas retention is the true expression of what people think about your app. If you can retain your users, then you've done something right, and then you just keep going, but getting there can be a long and challenging process with many small steps along the way.

You must have users before you have to worry about retention

Just like acquisition and retention are inextricably linked, referrals are also closely associated with retention because without retention there are no referrals. This makes sense because it would be very rare for someone to refer others to your app without them liking it and using the app reasonably often. There may be exceptions to this rule, for example, a flashlight app that you typically use very rarely. However, in general, the case is that the user has to have gained a lot of value from your app before they become an ambassador for it and names it when referring others to it.

If your users don't refer other users to the app, and/or your app doesn't make money, then your marketing budget will run out at some point, and then you can't make any more acquisitions, and then your app dies a slow death. Therefore, it's essential to have a significant budget for marketing your app because you basically can't count on either retention and/or revenue through your app. The marketing budget must be your sustenance that keeps you going once the first iteration of the app has gone live, and where you can still adjust the app to the users and where you haven't quite found your "product-market fit" yet. In that time, you need to continually get new users to the app so you can test your modifications.

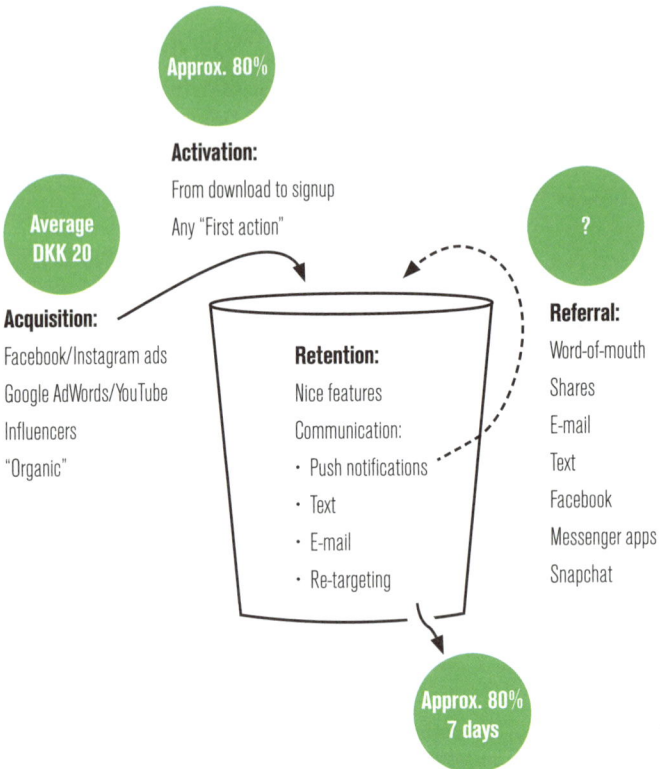

Figure 55. Key performance indicators.

Figure 55 shows the relationship between acquisition, activation, retention and referrals. You can look at your app like a bucket with a hole in the bottom, and the more water you pour into the bucket, the more water comes out the bottom. The water is like your app's users. If you spill water when you pour, you lose users in your activation. The larger the hole in the bottom, the more water pours out of the bucket again. Therefore, it becomes very apparent that if there are no referrals to the app from the users themselves or other channels, then, in the end, you can't pour any more water in, and slowly the bucket with active users will empty as users disappear over time.

People must love your app before you can hope for it to go viral

The figures vary greatly depending on the source, but one app download from the Western world costs somewhere between USD 2-4 on average, and 80% of downloads will result in an activated user. Of these users that were activated in one week, about 20% of them will use the app the following week. Even the best apps don't have much more than 5% of their users sharing the app with others.

The figures should hopefully serve as a good indication of the numbers that will apply to your app. What's defined as "good" numbers vary depending on the app you've made, but also what your strategic objectives are with your app – whether it's to earn money with downloads, from in-app purchases or to be sold to Facebook for millions. However, the figures should also tell about the hard reality where it's extremely difficult to make an app that people love, and that you can make money on. We're not trying to discourage you, but we aren't going to paint a rosy picture of the realities of the market.

Below is a standardised graph of the retention rate for Android and iOS as a percentage of users over days. For an average iOS app, there are 25% left on the first day after installation.

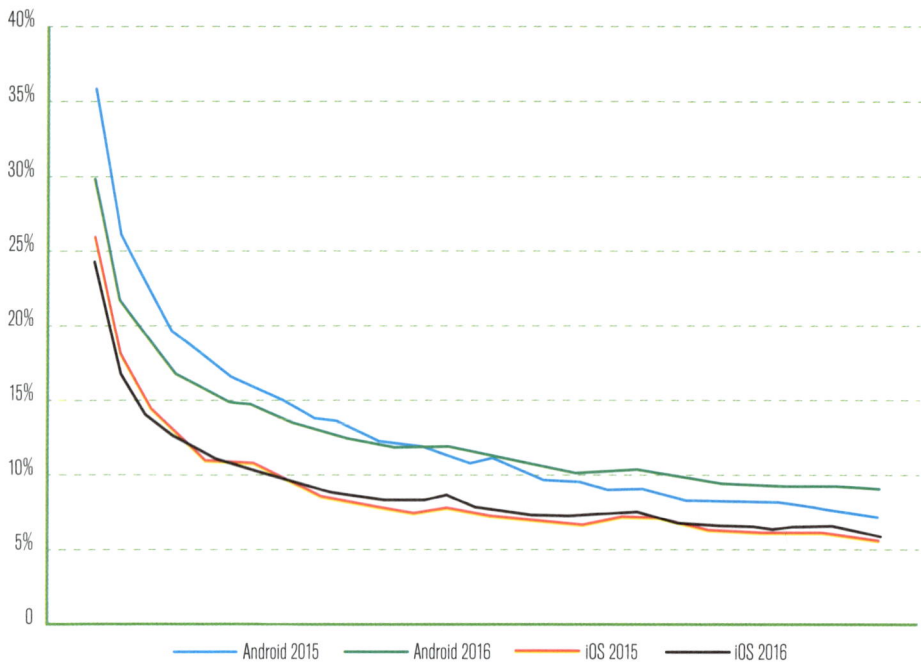

Figure 56. Retention rate over 30 days.

You can calculate the retention rate in many ways, but the most common is on days 1, 7, 14, 30, etc., or weekly cohorts. Cohorts take into account more varied usage patterns, and you see how many new users from a certain period (e.g. week #1) still use the app in week #2 or week #3 and so on. It could be that users don't use the app every day, and so it's an advantage to determine the retention rate in this manner.

RETENTION — WHAT DO I DO?

There are some things that you can do to retain your users, but basically, it's about you conducting thorough user analyses and meeting a need and solving a problem. We've gathered some useful tips that can help you to work with retention easily and intuitively.

Don't promise more than you can deliver

Firstly, it's vital that there's consistency between the value that the user was promised before they came to the app, and then the value that they get from the app once when they've downloaded it. If your advertising and your app store description promised gold and green forests, and the app turns out to be a shallow experience, then the user will obviously be disappointed and won't return to the app.

Control of the activation

Next, retention goes hand in hand with good activation. Therefore, we'll mention it again: If the user doesn't really know how your app creates value for them or how it works, they have about a minute to figure it out before they become impatient and choose to leave your app. Therefore, you must improve activation before you improve other things in your app. The best indicator of successful activation is a high activation rate (over 90% of app downloads to activation are completed), and it indicates that users can use your app. For the WHAT app, for instance, it's that users answer questions and find out how to ask questions.

Push notifications

Push notifications are the obvious way to increase your apps retention rate, and so you must have a handle on your push notifications. On average, 50% of all users accept push notifications, but those who have accepted them must receive relevant push notifications that don't come too often. The user can accept many push notifications if they're relevant. Just think of apps like Snapchat or Messenger. It would be strange if you didn't receive a push notification when a friend sent a snap or a message in Messenger.

    Push notifications is a complex area, where you have to watch your step. Many analytics software packages can handle push notifications in your app, and they can be useful, depending on how complex your app is, and which push notifications are to be sent out, when they should be sent out and so on. You have to carefully consider what "triggers" push notifications, and how to avoid that your app doesn't start to spam users. Instagram sends a push notification when you get a new follower, but how do you deal with it if the user is suddenly followed by hundreds of users? Do you then get hundreds of push notifications? Will there be 234 "new messages" on the app icon on your home screen? What effect will it have on the user?

The counter on the app icon

Many believe that the little red icon with a number in the app's icons on your home screen comes automatically with push notifications. But they work independently and can be related to what you like and have nothing to do with push notifications. However, the counter has a powerful effect on human psychology because most people find peace by completing things and they don't like it if things are left "unfinished". It can feel stressful, and so users open the app just to get rid of the little red symbol, and it will improve the retention rate. However, the symbol should be related to something new thing (follow, message, or the like) inside the app. Otherwise, it can be irritating for the user not being able to see what new things have happened in the app after they've clicked.

Note that the trend is for apps to just display a "1" on, even though there may be more "new" things inside the app. The reason is that people become irritated by large numbers on the app icon, as it can feel stressful. We again look at the example of Instagram and the hundreds of new followers – would it make sense if there were "243" in the little red icon? Many people know it from their e-mail app, which typically shows a high figure because you haven't deleted all the spam e-mails you've received over time.

Text and e-mail

Text and e-mail are alternatives to push notifications. If you've asked users for their phone number, you can send them messages. It's considered to be very invasive and it should generally not be recommended to exploit people's trust to spam them with irrelevant information. If you ask for a phone number, then it's a good idea to write explicitly what messages the recipient will receive. For example, it may be relevant to the user if a stock market app is allowed to send text messages if the market goes down significantly or if there are other important updates in relation to one's stock portfolio.

E-mails are much less invasive than Text because they "just" land in your inbox along with other spam. For the same reason, e-mail is not a particularly effective method to get people to return to your app. You should be happy if more than 20% open your e-mail, and if more than 0.5% click on your link. Figures vary, but market figures are somewhere around there.

Re-targeting with advertising

Both Facebook and Google offer options to send advertisements to the people who have already installed your app. It can be an effective way to draw attention to your app again and get people to return to it. However, you should spend some time familiarising yourself with both platforms and make images/videos and the layout of ads that have to be replaced regularly. As with push notifications, it's important that people don't receive the same ads over and over again, just because they've downloaded your app.

In-app notifications

Contrary to what you might think, studies show that in-app notifications improve retention. The pop-up messages that appear when you use the app, and tell, for example, about a new feature in the app or shows who the most active users are.

In-app notifications can get the app to appear more vivid and rich in content, but they can also be irritating if there are too many of them or if they come at annoying times with irrelevant content. With regards to implementing core functionality, in-app notifications will also be "nice-to-have" and so something that many apps don't manage to refine before they don't exist anymore.

Other factors

Retention is fundamentally dependent on your app's value for the users and so different features or minor modifications increase the chance that people stick with your app.

Most apps can be "social", although it often requires a lot of your backend. People are social, and if you get a push notification when a Facebook friend has come to the app, then most people will go in and see the person's profile on the app. People like to snoop, and profiles and information about other people can be appealing and retain users.

Competition between people or with themselves can also be a robust retention mechanism. Gamification of your app can work very well if the right features are implemented such as scoreboards, points, prizes, batches, levels, etc.

REFERRALS

The starting point to getting the coveted referrals is, of course, that you make it possible for people to share and invite others to the app. So, there must always be that option somewhere in the app, but don't count on getting any shares if the user doesn't get something out of sharing. Think about when you share something on Facebook. What does it take?

As a basic rule, people only share apps and other things on the Internet if they get something out of it. It can be points, bonuses, money, levels or other things of value, but it can also be subtler and more social. If people can share something that makes them seem clever, funny or a good person, then there's a chance. But it's rare that it's so simple because as a user, you risk losing "social capital" – being ridiculed, contradicted, seen as less intelligent and so on when you share. Therefore, it's easier just not to share.

You should consider referrals as your "growth engine" and you should preferably have several ideas on how to increase virality and the network effect of your app. There are some prime examples of how other services have done it, as we will shortly review, but it's rare that the excellent examples can simply be copied by other apps.

Dropbox grew by making an extensive promotion where users could get an extra 500 MB of space if they shared a link, and when their contacts used the link to create an account themselves. Referrals increased Dropbox sign ups by 60%. Dropbox exploited the fact that they had a value in terms of storage space to offer, but not all apps have such a tangible value. It's also relatively complex to make the system to provide users with unique links with associated discounts. If you don't make the system properly it can be abused. When giving value away, you have to be sure that you don't just suddenly owe more than you can give.

Hotmail is another example. The e-mail service wrote merely "Get a free Hotmail today" at the bottom of all e-mails their users sent. At that time, you had to pay to create an e-mail in most places, so the value was clear.

Farmville, like many other game apps, was known for sending annoying Facebook notifications through a special notification API that Facebook later partially closed down as the spam effect was excessive. The games gripped people so much that they were willing to spam people for more life, levels, etc., rather than having to pay for the "upgrade" that they needed in the game. So, Farmville, Candy Crush, etc., spread incredibly fast.

Sharing also depends a lot on the platform which you share on, and some platforms are more informal than others. Texting is perceived as something private. Try to imagine receiving an invitation to Candy Crush by Text, and it may well be that you want to send an angry text message back to the sender. On the other hand, it's not so bad to get a Facebook notification because the channel has been abused so much that you don't always check anyway. In this way, the channel loses its effectiveness, just as e-mails have also done.

Shares on your Facebook wall or Instagram are also perceived as very private, so it's a big decision for people to share there. On the other hand, it's easier in a Snapchat-story because it disappears again. The barrier to sharing something on the Internet is typically in contrast to how many people the share reaches. The more it's shared with, the more careful people will be to share a post. However, it's not always the case that each channel needs to be analysed separately.

It's also necessary to analyse sharing as a communication process with three different players: the app, the user and those that the user's app referral is directed at, or who see the referral. If your app can be shared on Facebook, what should be in the message that's going to be shared? The message must initially be acceptable for the user to share, and then it should be interesting to click on for others. It's a balance that isn't easy to find.

You can map the sharing process and the players and determine which sharing channels to choose. Overall, you must answer the following questions in this order to decide which "referral channels" to choose for your app:

1. What value does the user get from sharing?
2. What value does the share promise those who see it?
3. How high is the barrier for sharing on the platform? Will anyone share at all?
4. How effective is the channel with respect to its reach to many people?
5. How effective is the channel relative to being seen and engaging users who are being shared to?

Creating an effective viral loop is extremely difficult because the communication goes in different directions, and because sharing the right content at the right time and on the right platform can also be a demanding technical exercise.

If you analyse what happens when a user shares content, it looks like this:

1	2	Sharing 3	Download 4
The user sees:	**The user clicks the "Share":**	**7)** The share's photos/text attracts attention.	**Non-users download the app:**
1) Valuation	**4)** A sharing menu appears, or another app opens.	**Non-users notice the sharing of the app or app content:**	**11)** Sees the app/shared content.
2) Call-to-action			
and	**5)** The user sees (maybe) what the share looks like, and analyses again the advantages and disadvantages (see point 3).	**8)** Valuation	**Key factors:**
3) Consider (instinctively) advantages and disadvantages.		**9)** Call-to-action	If it's the content, it's very important that the new user via deep link routing is taken directly to the shared content. Otherwise, the app (and the person who shared the content) doesn't deliver what it promised to the new user and the user can't find the content.
What do I get out of sharing?		and	
Do I have the relative resources to share (time now, time later, money, capacity)?	**6)** The user should (perhaps) make a positive action, such as writing a message (e.g. e-mail or Facebook), find a place to share a link, select recipients (Messenger), take a photo (for example, Snap-story), etc.	**10)** Consider (instinctively) advantages and disadvantages.	
How will I appear in the eyes of others when I share this content (risk of losing social capital)?		What do I get out of downloading the app/seeing the content? (including social capital by showing the sender that you have clicked on the link).	
Other drawbacks and risks (e.g. cheating and deception, the risk of spamming, etc.)?		Do I have the relative resources to share (time now, time later, money, capacity)?	If there hasn't been any shared content, then it's important that the relationship between the person who shared the app and the person the app was shared to is strengthened as much as possible in the app.
Key factors:	**Key factors:**	What are the risks associated with clicking (e.g. cheating and deception, the risk of spamming and the risk of losing social capital if I don't click)?	
The value must be tangible for the user.	The contents to be shared must be as personal as possible. Preferably with name, text and a photo that is personalised or specifically for the content that the user pressed the "Share" on.		
Communication should be clear and action-orientated.		**Key factors:**	
Example from Dropbox:		Photos and text must be catchy just like an ad.	
Share Dropbox and get 500 MB for each referral that signs up. Your friends get 1 GB of free cloud storage.	The barrier for the user (time and brain power) should be as small as possible for the user.	The value must be tangible for the non-user.	
		Communication should be clear and action-orientated.	

Figure 57. The referral process.

On social platforms, the landscape is changing all the time, and you will have to keep an eye on the platforms and go with those that best meet the points above. For example, there are almost no young people who want to share something on Facebook anymore, whereas the older generation still does. On the whole, there are very few young people who share content because the risk of losing social status is experienced as greater during adolescence. There are also considerable differences in the platforms used by different segments. Boys and girls will use different apps and have different perceptions in relation to sharing.

Getting control of your "growth engine" and creating virality are success criteria for most apps, but for the same reason, it's also one of the hardest. For some time now the trend has been that app developers have focused solely on virality at the expense of retention. For example, the TBH ("To Be Honest") app that was acquired by Facebook for an undisclosed sum, although it's believed to be around USD 100 million after just 9 weeks in the app store with 5 million downloads. It later turned out that the retention rate of the app was abysmal, and that the app was only designed for growth through Snapchat shares.

Although you've designed an effective growth engine for maximum virality, it's still not certain that's enough. The app market has become so competitive that money for marketing and ASO certainly makes a big difference. App companies typically don't reveal how many resources have gone into the marketing of an app, and so you can see apps that magically reach the top of the app store rankings. These included the Sarahah app, which many believe was a more inferior version of ASKfm, but it still managed to get about 100 million downloads during the summer of 2017.

There's no doubt that retention and referrals are extremely difficult, especially because each app idea has its pros and cons. It's more natural for social apps to go viral, but usually, they don't solve a specific need for new users, and so they can be fun to share, but they aren't good at retaining users. Apps that solve a specific problem, such as MobilePay or Torch are perhaps permanently on the phone, but we still only use them when appropriate – when we need to pay for something or we need to see in the dark.

Your app is unique and you should therefore try to think outside the box with your retention and virality through referrals. It's most likely your ability to innovate in these areas that determine the success of your app.

EPILOGUE

Now that you've read our take on what's important to know about the process from idea to app, we hope that the book has lived up to your expectations. We want to take this opportunity to say a big thank you for taking the time to read our book, and we particularly hope that the book has enabled you to decide whether you should take the first step in realising your app idea or whether you should just bury it in the back garden.

Although the process we've described from idea to app can seem both tricky and financially challenging, we hope that the reality hasn't scared you from going ahead with your idea. Our ambition has been to describe the process without pulling any punches or trying to paint a rosy picture of what it takes to "just" design, develop, release, maintain and make money on an app. As with all entrepreneurship, success requires hard work, a good network, common sense and a little luck.

If you've decided to go ahead with your app idea, our best advice to you is to get as much clarity as possible about your concept before hiring a programmer to program the app. Concept and designs have to be tested in the market, and you must have a detailed requirements specification on hand to avoid wasting unnecessary time and money. Better to postpone the development phase and give space to ensure a market-related match than to start too early and end up having to start all over again.

An essential element in the concept development is the selection of the key features in relation to the problem that you're trying to solve. The choice of technology follows on from this, and here it's imperative that you deal critically with whether you really need an app, or you can instead settle for a mobile-optimised website, for instance. The difference in cost and development time on a native app and a mobile-optimised website can be huge. As we've mentioned, web technology made a strong comeback in 2017, while app technology has come down to earth a little. At the time of writing this, web technology for mobiles is developing in an extremely advantageous direction. Therefore, in all cases, we can recommend considering – and to get help deciding – whether, for example, a mobile-optimised website or web app will be an attractive option in achieving the objectives you are aiming for. Keep in mind that the aim is to get as far as possible for as little money as possible, and technology is only a means to achieving an end, not an end in itself.

The book's content is based on our own experience. Consequently, it doesn't reflect a "truth" about app development or the development process, but our subjective attitude to what you should do. We started to write the book because we felt there wasn't a brief and practical non-technical guide for people with an idea for an app. We often get questions about app development from friends, family and people we meet. So, we hope that by answering the most common questions in the book, we've also answered any questions you may have had before reading the book.

Should you still have questions, please feel free to write to us. We're always interested in hearing about app projects, and we would also like to hear from you if you have feedback on the book.

You can write to us through our website www.idetilappbogen.dk

Thank you for reading and the best of luck with your idea!

RECOMMENDED LITERATURE

About the entrepreneurial process and planning

Blank, S. (2013): *The Four Steps to the Epiphany.* K&S Ranch.

Blank, S. & Dorf, B. (2012): *The Startup Owner's Manual.* K&S Ranch.

Mullins, J. & Komisar, R. (2009): *Getting to Plan B.* Harvard Business Review Press.

Osterwalder, A. & Pigneur, Y. (2010): *Business Model Generation.* John Wiley & Sons Ltd.

Ries, E. (2011): *The Lean Startup.* Crown Pub.

Sarasvathy, S. (2008): *Effectuation.* Edward Elgar Publishing Ltd.

Thing, M. (2016): *Startup! Fra ide til virkelighed.* Akademisk forlag.

About funding

Marmer, M. et al. (2017): Genome report, https://s3.amazonaws.com/startupcompass-public/StartupGenomeReport1_Why_Startups_Succeed_v2.pdf

Marschall, T. (2017): *Angel Business.* PubliShare.

Nielsen, N. H. (2017): *Startup Funding.* NHN Ventures.

About habits and motivation

Eyal, N. (2014): *Hooked – How to Build Habit-forming Products.* Penguin Books Ltd.

Kahneman, D. (2018): *At tænke – hurtigt og langsomt* (Eng. *Thinking: Fast and Slow*). Lindhardt og Ringhof.

Pink, D. H. (2015): *Motivation – den overraskende sandhed om hvad der motiverer os* (Eng. *Drive: The Surprising Truth About What Motivates Us*). Akademisk Forlag.

About launching on the market

Moore, G. A. (2014): *Crossing the Chasm.* HarperCollins.

Rogers, E. M. (2003): *Diffusion and Innovations.* Simon & Schuster Ltd.

About methods

Barker, E. (2017): *Barking Up the Wrong Tree: The Surprising Science Behind Why Everything You Know About Success Is (Mostly) Wrong.* HarperOne.

Berkowski, G. (2014): *How to Build a Billion Dollar App.* Little, Brown Book.

Fitzpatrick, R. (2014): *The Mom Test.* Founder Centric.

Sims, P. (2013): *Little Bets: How Breakthrough Ideas Emerge from Small Discoveries.* Simon & Schuster.

INDEX

A
acquisition 129, 130, 142, 152, 264, 273
activation 129, 130, 142, 268
advert 152
AdWords 163, 209, 262, 263
Airbnb 36, 56ff., 86, 202
Amazon 56, 204
analogues 125, 162
Android 28, 29, 40ff., 66, 71, 75, 118, 176, 195ff., 201, 223, 275
Angry Birds 54
antiloggers 128
app architecture 174
Apple 13, 37ff., 45, 47ff., 54ff., 58, 59, 61, 63, 73, 174, 177, 196, 199
App Store 28, 37, 39, 41, 42, 226, 261, 263, 265, 268
attribution 261

B
backend 58, 59, 68, 69, 75, 200, 204, 205, 223, 280
blog 165, 263, 295
brand 230
Bumble 84, 159
business angels 250
business model 16, 100, 101, 179, 181
Business Model Canvas (BMC) 100ff., 109, 110, 248

C
certainty 87, 89, 91
Chrome 197
collateral 250
conversion 261, 262, 264, 267
costs 101, 102, 108
crowdfunding 249
CSS 197
customer relationships 103, 107
customer segments 104

D
design 16, 22, 35, 55, 75, 106, 124, 126, 135, 139, 144, 160, 172ff., 179, 181, 185ff., 190, 194, 199, 200, 208, 215, 216, 219, 225ff., 234, 235, 237, 238, 261
designer 75, 185, 225
design phase 172
development phase 209, 212
Dropbox 52, 54, 60, 281

E
ecommerce 55, 56
Endomondo 54, 62, 64, 104, 166, 253
Evernote 54, 128
expert tests 190

F
Facebook 26, 35, 36, 43, 50, 62, 64, 73, 84, 92, 95, 97ff., 106, 113, 122, 130, 139, 151, 154, 163ff., 174, 177, 181, 182, 195, 199, 201, 202, 204, 209, 210, 219, 230, 261, 263ff., 269ff., 275, 279, 280, 282, 285, 295
Farmville 282
Flipboard 50
focus groups 114, 121, 162, 209
freemium 47, 51, 52

G
GoLittle 109, 167, 168, 247
GoMore 36, 56, 58, 86, 202
Google 13, 27ff., 32, 33, 37ff., 44ff., 54, 55, 58, 59, 61, 63, 66, 73, 87, 104, 128, 148, 150, 162, 165, 174, 177, 196, 197, 205, 209, 214, 261ff., 279, 294, 296

H
Hooked Model, The 149, 151

Hotmail 281
HTML 197
Hybrid-app 195
hypotheses 90, 110, 112, 122, 160ff., 215

I

Instagram 35, 36, 43, 50, 62, 64, 84, 103, 132, 150, 155, 174ff., 195, 199, 202, 205, 230, 261, 263, 265ff., 278, 282
interviews 84, 88, 114ff., 122, 126ff., 145, 146, 149, 162, 190, 209
investment 152, 153, 242
iOS 66, 71, 73, 75, 195, 198, 201, 223, 263, 275
iPhone 42, 73, 176, 177, 196, 197, 219, 263

J

JavaScript 197
JustEat 36, 56, 58, 202

K

knowledge gaps 160, 162

L

LinkedIn 43, 50, 252, 265, 269
loan 250

M

mapping 124ff.
marketing 102, 152, 264, 265
marketing channels 260, 265, 266
market potential 257
Minimum Viable Product (MVP) 69, 132ff., 140ff., 152, 157, 158, 162, 172, 173, 197, 199, 200
mobile agency 67, 70, 76, 77, 80, 232, 234, 240
MobilePay 85
mockup 163, 179, 188ff., 250
monetisation 130
motivation 22ff., 67, 91, 137ff., 153, 156, 219, 250, 289

N

native apps 194ff.
navigation 172ff., 191

navigation design 178
need 16, 24, 48, 52, 54, 61, 75, 76, 82ff., 94, 97, 100, 102, 105, 118, 119, 121, 122, 125, 136ff., 144ff., 154, 155, 158, 172, 173, 185, 186, 201, 202, 204, 208ff., 215, 217, 219, 231, 237, 238, 251, 255, 276, 285
nemlig.com 56

O

observation 114
outsourcing 77
ownership 20, 21, 76, 247, 249
ownership share 76

P

pitch 254
platform 40, 43, 57, 66ff., 92, 96, 102, 104, 107, 119, 183, 185, 195, 198, 283
premium 47, 48, 103
problem 22, 24, 33, 36, 82ff., 105, 112, 114, 117, 121, 122, 125ff., 139, 148, 158, 159, 162, 180, 203, 231, 252ff., 276, 286
prototype 118, 161, 162, 187, 188, 250, 255

R

references 127
referral 130, 142, 180, 273, 274, 280, 281, 285, 286
retention 130, 142, 273, 276, 280
revenue model 103, 107, 257

S

Safari 197
security 116, 205, 218, 219, 237ff., 270
skills 216
Snapchat 43, 50, 64, 82, 174, 175, 179, 195, 196, 227, 230, 265, 277, 282, 285
software developer 221
subscription 57, 59, 60, 63, 90, 249

T

technology 16, 35, 87, 94ff., 191, 194, 200, 223, 224
testers 188ff.

Tinder 54, 60ff., 83, 84, 103, 140, 141, 150ff., 159, 230, 271
Tonsser 251ff.
Trello 128ff., 159, 211
TripAdvisor 86, 109
Twitter 43, 50, 83, 174, 265

U

user interface 215, 226
user segments 103, 104

V

validation 112
value proposition 102, 105, 257, 268, 271
venture capital 251
Venyo 92, 102, 103, 107, 108, 110, 169
viral 107
Vivino 54, 64

W

web app 195
WHAT 25, 112, 147, 165, 181ff., 277
WhatsApp 174, 205, 270
wireframes 22, 178, 185, 187, 191, 200, 211, 226, 235

Z

Zuckerberg, Mark 35, 92, 122, 199

REFERENCES

1. http://www.behaviormodel.org/
2. The Agency for Culture and Palaces, Media development in Denmark 2017, Internet usage and devices, p. 11
3. The Agency for Culture and Palaces, Media development in Denmark 2017, Internet usage and devices, p. 3
4. Mary Meeker, Internet Trends 2017 – Code Conference, May 2017, p. 9
5. Flurry, http://flurrymobile.tumblr.com/post/157921590345/us-consumers-time-spent-on-mobile-crosses-5
6. Phunware, https://go.phunware.com/mobile-future-survey-report, 2017
7. Google, 2017, p. 3: https://think.storage.googleapis.com/images/micromoments-guide-to-winning-shift-to-mobile-download.pdf
8. ComScore, Mobile's Hierarchy of Needs, January 2017, p. 7, comScore, The Global Mobile Report, June 2017, p. 33
9. https://www.emarketer.com/Article/eMarketer-Unveils-New-Estimates-Mobile-App-Usage/1015611
10. http://flurrymobile.tumblr.com/post/157921590345/us-consumers-time-spent-on-mobile-crosses-5
11. https://www.statista.com/statistics/276623/number-of-apps-available-in-leading-app-stores/
12. https://www.statista.com/statistics/266210/number-of-available-applications-in-the-google-play-store/
13. App Day, January 2016, the Association of Danish Media
14. Google, December 2017: https://www.thinkwithgoogle.com/marketing-resources/customer-lifetime-value-marketing-apps/
15. http://andrewchen.co/new-data-shows-why-losing-80-of-your-mobile-users-is-normal-and-that-the-best-apps-do-much-better/?utm_content=buffere4fa2&utm_medium=twitter.com&utm_source=social&utm_campaign=buffer
16. Google, November 2016, p. 9: https://www.thinkwithgoogle.com/advertising-channels/apps/app-marketing-trends-mobile-landscape/

17 Google, November 2016, p. 11: https://www.thinkwithgoogle.com/advertising-channels/apps/app-marketing-trends-mobile-landscape/
18 Barker 2017
19 iTunes Podcasts: Masters of Scale with Reid Hoffman #4 Facebook's Mark Zuckerburg in Imperfect is Perfect, 24 May 2017
20 https://www.statista.com/statistics/371889/smartphone-worldwide-installed-base/
21 App Annie Market Forecast 2016-2021, 2017, p. 4: http://go.appannie.com/report-app-annie-market-forecast-2017
22 https://www.statista.com/statistics/385001/smartphone-worldwide-installed-base-operating-systems/
23 DeviceAtlas: The Mobile Web Intelligence Report, August 2017, p. 17-18
24 comScore: The Global Mobile Report, September 2017, p. 32-33
25 Google, November 2016, p. 7: https://www.thinkwithgoogle.com/advertising-channels/apps/app-marketing-trends-mobile-landscape/
26 App Annie: App Economy Survey Part, 2017, p. 8
27 Statista: App Economy Survey Part 2, 2017, p. 8. https://www.statista.com/chart/1733/app-monetization-strategies/
28 We have chosen not to include Windows, because in October 2017, Microsoft officially announced that they wouldn't support the operating system in the future.
29 Steven Blank: The Four Steps to the Epiphany, p. 30
30 Everett Rogers: Diffusion of Innovations, p. 247
31 https://www.statista.com/statistics/434516/us-smartphone-app-reasons-download/
32 Sarasvathy: Effectuation, p. 12-18
33 http://www.annexcloud.com/blog/2016/03/03/39-referral-marketing-statistics-that-will-make-you-want-to-start-a-raf-program-tomorrow/
34 https://developer.apple.com/ios/human-interface-guidelines/overview/themes/
35 https://material.io/guidelines/
36 E.g. www.betatesters.io, mechanical turk
37 http://keystones.dk/analyse/
38 http://keystones.dk/wp-content/uploads/2018/02/Keystones-h%C3%B8ker-kalkule-2018.pdf
39 https://mortenresen.dk/podcast/
40 http://www.vf.dk/~/media/files/analyser/andre%20analyser/baanalyse%202017%20registerbaseret.pdf
41 Thomas Marschall: Angel Business, p. 75
42 http://techsavvy.media/historien-

tonsser-kaelder-millioninvestering/
43 http://finans.dk/live/erhverv/ECE8742919/dansk-fodboldkomet-lander-sin-stoerste-investering-til-dato/?ctxref=ext
44 Nicolaj H. Nielsen: The Startup Funding Book, p. 32-33
45 Nicolaj H. Nielsen: The Startup Funding Book, p. 32-33